The Person of Christ

FOUNDATIONS FOR FAITH

General editor: Peter Toon

FOUNDATIONS FOR FAITH

The Person of Christ

A Biblical and Historical Analysis of the Incarnation

David F. Wells

Crossway Books • Westchester, Illinois
A Division of Good News Publishers

To

John Stott,

My Dear Friend,

Who First Told Me of the "Lord of Glory" (1 Cor. 2:8)

Copyright © 1984 by David F. Wells
First published by Marshall Morgan & Scott and Crossway Books, 1984
All rights reserved
Printed in the United States of America for
Crossway Books, 9825 W. Roosevelt Rd., Westchester, Illinois 60153
ISBN 0-89107-315-9
and
Marshall Morgan & Scott, 1 Bath Street, London ECIV #9LB
ISBN 0 551 01167 X

Bible quotations from the New International Version,
copyright © 1978 by the New York
International Bible Society, are used
by permission of Zondervan Bible Publishers.

Contents

Preface

I marvel now at the ease with which I accepted the invitation to write this volume. I should have known better! I rapidly discovered myself sinking—at times I felt irretrievably so—in the quagmire of scholarly discussion. The completion date at which I was aiming turned out to be unattainable. I therefore wish to thank Peter Toon, the general editor, for his indulgence. He has not only allowed me to overshoot this mark but also to produce a book which is somewhat different from the others in the series. That, I know, is worrisome to an editor desirous of producing uniformity of format, style and approach in a series.

This manuscript was sent for review to Peter Toon, Jeffrey Steenson and to my two colleagues, Roger Nicole and Royce Gruenler. I am indebted to them for their knowledgeable comments and wise assistance. Naturally, I am alone responsible for the finished product.

Finally, I wish to express my appreciation to the trustees of Gordon-Conwell Theological Seminary who granted me a half sabbatical to work on this book.

INTRODUCTION

Theologians in recent times have seldom ever found themselves at the center of public attention. The Western world is becoming too blasé to care very much about the fate of the Christian tradition and is altogether too absorbed in its own business to think very much about the exponents of that mode of thought. In July 1977, however, the normally unruffled surface was broken, albeit only momentarily, by an event that did register in the secular press.

In that month a book entitled *The Myth of God Incarnate* appeared. It was a symposium of essays whose overall intent was to dispel the historical understanding of the person of Christ by casting doubt on the way the doctrine of Christ has been framed. Had the church been correct, it asked, in thinking that the New Testament authors expected their words about Jesus to be taken at face value? Is it not a mistake to substitute for their metaphors a metaphysical way of thinking of him as God? Is the traditional, Chalcedonian conception internally coherent, and is it credible any longer in the twentieth century?

The authors of the symposium achieved notoriety overnight. Indeed, the publicity and controversy which their book provoked was out of all proportion to the intrinsic merit of the essays. There was, in fact, nothing particularly novel about any of the questions raised; the editor of the volume, John Hick, went out of his way to disclaim any novelty.[1] But the general public chose to disbelieve him!

The furor which followed the publication of this volume probably did have something to do with the prominence of most of the authors. It also had something to do with the provocative title which was given to the volume. Some of the essayists have protested their innocence on this score, claiming that an untutored public missed the intended double *entendre*. For in theology, a myth is a story composed for the purpose of communicating a truth. The details of the story are to be taken seriously but not literally. In common parlance, by contrast, a myth is a fantasy or fabrication, to be taken neither seriously nor literally. Was Christ, then, being put in the same category as Snow White? The inconsistent way in which the essayists have used the word *myth,* without explanation or apology,[2] only mystified the public and heightened the sense of scandal.

Yet I doubt that these two factors alone can account for the sense of drama that soon enveloped the book and its authors. After all, are we really to believe that those who reported on it in the secular press had actually read and understood all the essays, replete as they are with the gnostic code words of a scholarly elite and all of the mysterious jargon of the academic process? That seems unlikely. What I believe most readily explains the interest was the fleeting glimpse that this book gave into the mindset of some of the theological *illuminati* of our time. The secular press stepped back, dumbfounded.

THE ALIENATED THEOLOGIAN
The volume under discussion, in fact, gives a graphic portrait of what Van A. Harvey has called the "alienated theologian." It is this phenomenon, rather than the book itself, which I believe has attracted all the attention. And it is this phenomenon which must be grasped if the contemporary discussions on Christology are to be understood. It is the mood in which most theological thinking is being done.

The alienated theologian can be defined quite readily. He, says Van Harvey, is "the professional who is concerned with the articulation of the faith of the Christian community but who is himself as much a doubter as a believer."[3] What is of interest in this statement is the changed role it assumes theologians are playing, as well as the implied reasons for this change. Both of these aspects need to be explored a little further.

It used to be that the role of the theologian was to clarify, expound, and defend Christian truth. No longer is this the case. What is much more common is the theologian in the role of questioning, doubting, and denying parts of what has been traditionally thought of as the substance of faith. Perhaps the new role has grown out of the old. In the course of defending Christian faith, the theologian perhaps made some unsettling discoveries. What had seemed totally defensible, then began to look riddled and vulnerable. A crisis point was possibly reached at which time the theologian had to decide whether it was any longer moral to conceal these inner doubts and mental agitations. Finally it was decided that the ethical thing to do was simply to make manifest these growing doubts in all of their intensity. In the modern period, however, revelations such as these have seldom led to defrocking or resignation. On the contrary, the doubter has often become a *cause célèbre* and has taken his or her place in that larger company which is now defining theology as being essentially a process of critical doubting. The stones of Christian tradition consequently are being turned over as a matter of professional duty to see what other unsightly bugs can be discovered blinking in the unexpected light!

It is, Van A. Harvey says, as if there were a group of Israelites[4] who had been part of the mighty Exodus from Egypt, and seen all of the extraordinary acts of God in providing manna and guidance in the wilderness, but who had slowly become disaffected. They disengaged from the larger throng. They felt uneasy with the unphilosophical talk about Yahweh and did not like the songs which the other Israelites sang. The manna, cloud, and fire, they began to feel, were purely "natural" phenomena which only superstition and cultural conditioning would interpret otherwise. As they tagged along, occasionally expressing their feelings, they came to feel that the people would make much more certain progress if they eliminated the literal belief that Yahweh had actually delivered them from the Egyptians. If Moses seemed to believe this, his ideas should not be taken at face value, for such a confidence was uncertain, unthinking, and unhelpful. True faith, they countered, is in the very questioning of faith, and true belief resides in the process of doubting. Something simply accepted cannot be deeply believed. The ancient press, I am confident, would have found an element of dubiety in that situation, even as the contemporary press did in *The Myth of God Incarnate!*

No such group, of course, is recorded as having given Pharaoh this comfort and consolation in his hour of distress, and I am certain that no such group even existed. The theologian as doubter is a modern phenomenon. He or she is the product, on the one hand, of a modern view of knowledge and, on the other hand, of a radically shifting cultural milieu.

KNOWLEDGE AND CULTURE

What is peculiar about this modern view of knowledge is its logic and method. There once was a time when the theologian's passion for belief was seen as a positive virtue, but today any precommitment of this nature is considered injurious to serious scholarship. The passion for belief has been replaced by a passion for "truth." The new objective, in turn, has acquired a new method, which is that of adapted scientific procedures, an adaptation that demands the scholar's disengagement from the matters under consideration rather than the former involvement with them. Only when this objectivity is clearly displayed can we be relatively sure that disquieting facts are not going to be brushed under the rug and arguments are not going to be arbitrarily tilted in one direction rather than another. The less stake a theologian has in the outcome of the investigation, the more credible are his or her findings.

This method, as Harvey has elsewhere argued,[5] has produced a kind of enveloping logic, a broad and accepted "common sense" among scholars, as to what it is appropriate to believe and not to believe. It therefore becomes immoral in the modern setting to give the appearance of advancing an opinion with more certainty than a consensus feels the evidence warrants or of sifting evidence with a predetermined interest in the outcome. By contrast, what is moral is the unrelenting skepticism which fuels this methodological engine.

On the surface this does not seem unreasonable. After all, there is no particular wisdom in holding opinions for which there is scant evidence, and it is only the charlatan who distorts findings or conceals evidence so that a particular view will not be challenged. But what is not so readily acknowledgd is that this modern procedure—which leaves the impression of the scholar's total detachment—actually always operates within an assumed cognitive structure. This has been argued so frequently by religious philosophers that it seems unnecessary to elaborate extensively upon it here. Suffice it to say that this engine of skepticism, in its supposedly objective way, has nevertheless succeeded in posing questions within certain presuppositions which, in the nature of the case, cannot be satisfactorily answered. There is, one has to admit, a decided advantage in being the questioner in such a situation!

For example, much of the current discussion about the significance of Jesus assumes the finality both of Lessing's dictum that historical facts can never yield eternal verities and of Troeltsch's argument, or at least one prong of it, which deals with analogy. This asserts that the past and present always bear a relationship to one another, so that what does not happen today could not have happened in other times. It is not commonly recorded today that fishes and loaves have mysteriously multiplied on the supermarket shelf, or that the dead have come back to life, or that fishermen defy the laws of gravity and walk on a surface where normally only a boat would suffice. It is therefore assumed that occurrences like these could not have happened in the New Testament period.

The degree of rejection, it is true, varies with the type of the miracle. Those miracles which are concerned with the interruption of the laws of nature seem least likely. The healing miracles, however, seem to assault our modern sensibilities a little less violently. After all, there is wide recognition today that there is a mysterious interrelation between the material and spiritual aspects of the person. Stress and anxiety, for example, often produce physical concomitants, and it is not beyond the bounds of possibility that Jesus could have perceived the underlying causes of a physical malady and, by addressing these, "healed" the person. But it is common practice today, in the name of scholarship, to assume that many of the miracles did not happen or, at least, that they did not happen in the way in which they are presently recorded.

With these assumptions and ground rules, seemingly unanswerable questions can be posed to the Christian tradition. How, for example, can we believe in the authenticity of Jesus' teaching if that teaching is validated by a resurrection whose factuality historians can never judge as being any more than merely probable? How can one declare with any confidence what Christianity is if the Gospel accounts we have of Jesus are simply collections of traditions which tell us more about the early faith community or the redactor than they do about Jesus? How can we believe in any of the recorded miracles when there are no comparable events in the modern period to establish as "control cases" by which the Gospel accounts can be judged?

It is this situation which explains why so many scholars in the twentieth century have sought to disengage Christian faith from its historical rooting.[6] Rudolf Bultmann was persuaded, for example, that no biographical information about Jesus, and especially about his self-conciousness, can be reliably discovered with the layers of tradition that have been joined together in the Synoptic Gospels. We can actually ascertain only the barest outline of his life. He was born, he apparently did view himself as some sort of a Jewish prophet, and he was executed under Pontius Pilate. But for Bultmann, Christianity needs to know nothing about the historical Jesus. Christianity is concerned with opening oneself up in existential decision; it is not concerned with relating mentally to historical facts. So decisive was this break for Bultmann that when he was asked what effect the discovery of Jesus' bones might have on his theology, he is reported to have roared with laughter at the absurdity of the question.[7]

Karl Barth, in a different and less radical way, also disengaged his theology from that kind of history *(Historie)* which can be ascertained by the canons of critical scholarship.[8] Indeed, his massive theology is so constructed that little, if any of it, could be changed by anything that modern critical scholarship argues about the nature of the New Testament or about what it says. These and many other solutions like them have sought to evade the outcome of modern biblical scholarship by so shaping Christian faith that it need not answer any of the questions that cannot be answered satisfactorily. There has, however, been a price to be paid for this development. Modern Christologies, Donald Dawe asserts,[9] have come to resemble the prodigal who bravely ventured forth into the world only to discover, some time later, that he was left with husks. The very safeguards to scholarly objectivity have, in many cases, formed a cognitive structure which is reductionistic.

It is this modern view of how knowledge is gained and tested that has created severe difficulties for scholars seeking to maintain a credible view of Christ. For to remain credible in our modern context has often necessitated the excision or radical recasting of large swatches of the traditional understanding. Protestant theology, from its liberalism to its new hermeneutic, appears, Harvey admits, "as a series of salvage operations." It "attempts to show how one can still believe in Jesus

Christ and not violate an ideal of intellectual integrity."[10] This is exactly what *The Myth of God Incarnate* was about, and for a few moments it provided a glimpse into the soul of part of the Christian scholarly world which simply amazed outsiders.

There is, of course, another angle of vision on this process which is provided through the work of Peter Berger. Berger has shaped, from a sociological point of view, our understanding of the structure of modern consciousness.[11] And it is his contention that approaches such as the ones which have been mentioned are really efforts to make the Christian tradition conform to the cognitive limits and expectations of our modern consciousness. These are sincere efforts at "translation," undertaken at a high intellectual level, and they are successful because their results resonate with something the man in the street senses. There is, he proposes, an affinity between the ideas proposed and the common experience of modern, secular people, but it is an affinity which is only possible because theology has been stripped down to anthropology, the external God being scaled down to and made identical with personal perception.[12]

While this "reinterpretation" of the transcendent is undertaken for seemingly theological reasons, Berger counters that it is really the intellectual echo of the breakdown of Western civilization and the fruit of an assumption that the cognitive expectations of the modern person are normative for today and superior to all that are past.

The monolithic world view that prevailed formerly has undoubtedly given way, in modern times, to a multiplicity of world views. These jostle and compete with each other in the marketplace of ideas. At the same time, the criteria by which one world view is judged as credible and another is not are the product of the culture itself. For our ideas are in reciprocal relationship with society, constantly giving to it and borrowing from it. The social norms, which modern theology frequently reflects, are those of an empirical, pluralistic consensus. They are not the norms which are friendly to historic Christian faith with its notion of a transcendent God who can act miraculously in this world. This has, therefore, forced much of the modern theological enterprise into a process of accommodation. The problem in this, however, is that much theology has convinced itself that it can know no more and say no more than modernity judges is appropriate. This capitulation to the *Geist* of the age resembles the drunk, Berger charges, who walks carefully in the gutter in order to make certain that he will not fall into it! In other words, the dilemma of the modern theologian is at least as much sociological in origin as it is theological. The earnest concern to maintain intellectual credibility of which Van Harvey speaks is, Berger counters, a failure of nerve to break ranks with what modernity has agreed to call "truth."

CHRISTOLOGY AND ITS SETTING

The difficulties implicit in developing a theological viewpoint today are not restricted to matters of Christology. They are difficulties that are felt throughout the whole structure of Christian thought; this, however, makes the situation more complex rather than less.

No Christology can be constructed which does not presuppose, as Baptista Mondin has stated, both a clear conception of God and a clear conception of human nature.[13] The younger sciences, specifically psychology, sociology, and anthropology, have made monumental strides in understanding human nature. It is simply no longer possible to speak of human nature as if it were a type of eternal essence which has been deposited in a waiting body, an essence which can be isolated, analyzed, and described with detachment as some of the older theologians seemed to imagine.

As a matter of fact, both the doctrines of God and that of the person have frequently been caught up in the same broad shifts that have taken place in our culture. In the twentieth century our philosophical style has increasingly stressed becoming over being, existence rather than essence, dynamic emergence within the world rather than abstract aloofness from the world. It is a shift to broadly accepted existential motifs. Subjectivity rather than objectivity; the individual against the mass; human nature as unformed and nonexistent until, by our decisions, we give ourselves shape and substance; involvement rather than intellectualizing; choices rather than bare information—these are the themes that run through much of our literature. Consequently, the idea of evolution—that unfolding of reality which itself exhibits something of the divine—is far more likely today to provide the immediate matrix for Christological thought than the older ideas of God and man which now seem unreal and abstract. Joseph Sittler has pointed out[14] how this shift has been registered in the deliberations of the World Council of Churches. The meeting at Lund in 1951 had as its theme "Jesus Christ and the Church"; the meeting in New Delhi in 1961 had enlarged its purview, setting as its topic that of "Christ, the Church, and the World." The context in which Christ is being interpreted has been enlarged beyond the pristine categories which Greek philosophy defined and which the Chalcedonian Definition used to include the whole of contemporary, cosmic experience. Karl Rahner, likewise, has asserted that the Second Vatican Council was really an attempt to find a world spirituality not limited by institutional confines like the church or the sharply defined patterns of older doctrinal thinking.[15]

The direction of this new thinking has placed the famed Chalcedonian Definition in jeopardy. Indeed, Christologies in the latter part of the twentieth century have been more or less unanimous that their starting-place must be the rejection of this definition.[16] The discomfort with the Chalcedonian formulation is, however, felt at two quite different levels. There are those who are uneasy with the conceptuality employed by the framers of this statement and revealed in words like "substance" and "nature." They generally argue that the employment of these philosophical terms could never take place in a neutral context; the terms presuppose a certain philosophical understanding. This philosophical understanding therefore becomes an alien ingredient in the theological statement of which it has become a part. It is true that there is no more reason to think that the philosophical outlook these terms represent is any more divinely mandated than was the Ptolemaic world view which Copernicus and Galileo rightly contested. By the same token, however, alternative terms which reflect our own modern, cognitive interests do not, of necessity, carry with them greater fidelity and plausibility.

The more serious challenge to Chalcedon, however, comes from those who reject not only its terms but the reality which those terms sought to protect. Most commonly this challenge arises, as I have suggested, from a restlessness over the proposition that the "human" and the "divine" are separate entities. This is particularly unappealing to the modern mind, for it seems to presuppose a divine which is antecedent to the human, a God who is not identical with the content of human perception and who transcends the horizons of human conceptuality. What is far more acceptable is the argument, which takes a variety of forms, that God is emerging within human consciousness. This is the thought that what is divine can in vague and shadowy ways be seen in all people; but in one, Jesus of Nazareth, it reaches a crescendo of affirmation.

At the time when the Protestant liberals espoused this view, they provoked the obvious question as to what, therefore, was unique about Christ. The question is, of course, even larger than that, for one must ask what is unique about Christianity, about its Word written and living, about the God who lies behind each and, in different ways, is met in each. The answer then, as now, is that this uniqueness consists more in degree than kind. The nineteenth century therefore embarked on a search for spiritual authenticity at lesser levels in other religions, and we are now talking about anonymous Christians, world spirituality, and Christ's presence in other religions. It is this drive to broaden the truth content of Christianity that actually collides head-on with the particularity and uniqueness of the Christ-event which Chalcedon seeks to protect.[17]

COHERENCE AND UNDERSTANDING

The nature of the unity within and between the two Testaments has always been an issue within the church. Modern biblical interpretation certainly has no monopoly on it, although this is not apparent from the way in which many contemporary exegetes write. Questions of unity and diversity are discoursed upon with all the enthusiasm which usually accompanies fresh discoveries. As a matter of fact the issue surfaced before the last apostle had died, and three generically different approaches to this issue have emerged with the passage of time. In the early church some sought the Bible's unity in the midst of all of its diversity through mystical experience. It was this to which the Bible pointed in allegorical manner, and it was this that made "sense" of it all. Later on, especially in the Middle Ages, the unity was sought in rational systems which, once grasped and applied, could bind together the whole of the Bible and explain it all. Today we have little faith in rationality and little interest in mysticism of this earlier sort. We most commonly join the search for a form of organization which will bring order out of confusion in new literary techniques. The presupposition of this is that if we uncover enough literary layers, the real, authentic, and final meaning of Christianity will at last be found. We will have hit the rock bottom beneath all the succeeding additions of diverse interpretation.

The literary search is an extremely complex story which more or less coincides with the whole development of modern biblical criticism and cannot be allowed to divert our attention away from Christology. But it plainly cannot be ignored either, since much Christology is being formulated in this vain hope of finally liberating from the grips of ancient, literary obscurity the largely misunderstood Jesus!

The famed and ill-fated "quest for the historical Jesus" began on this very foot in the nineteenth century.[18] There were three presuppositions with which all of the divergent and contradictory biographies of Jesus began. First, it was assumed that the Chalcedonian Christ, a single person in whom full humanity and full divinity subsisted, was a figment of pious imagination. If it was seen to find support in Paul, this only reinforced the liberal Protestant hypothesis that between the simple Jesus of the Gospels who had no Christology and the towering God-man of Paul there was a great gulf fixed. The movement sought to get behind the layers of piety and theology, which it was believed had obscured the personality and doings of Jesus rather than clarifying them. Second, each of the authors of these "lives" assumed that their sources were completely different from what had traditionally been used. It was not uncommon among traditional Christians, even in the nineteenth century, to see in the four Gospels pieces of a jigsaw puzzle which needed simply to be fitted together into a harmonious picture. With the advent of biblical criticism, the Gospel of John was first detached as not really belonging to the other Gospels if only because its idiom and thought-forms were so different. But then the Synoptics themselves were critically unraveled and pieced together in altogether radical and novel ways.

The objective of this search was to address the question which formed the third presuppostion behind all of these works. This was to solve the paradox presented in the Gospels of a figure who seems to think that he is Messiah but seldom if ever acts accordingly. As a matter of fact, it was this paradox which proved to be the undoing of this movement. For the self-consciousness of Jesus is either so concealed from the reader of the Gospels or is treated with such reserve by the Gospel writers that these nineteenth-century biographers simply had to fabricate its substance for Jesus and foist it upon him. Albert Schweitzer, who participated in this search while demolishing all the other searchers, candidly acknowledged that to make the figure of Jesus live, one has to invest it with one's own hates and loves. What this meant, though, was that the so-called historical Jesus began to look more and more like the nineteenth-century liberal Protestant scholars who were his biographers. In an apt phrase, Schweitzer observed that they had looked down the deep well of human history and had seen their own faces reflected at the bottom. So the Jesus who had been concealed in ancient, literary obscurity was rescued only to emerge in the guise of a German, rationalistic academic!

It is difficult now, a century later, to sense the elation which this quest generated in its earlier years or the sense of despair which accompanied its demise. At the beginning, it seemed, the enigmatic Jesus was about to be revealed and explained; at the end, both he and the faith which has grown from him seemed more uncertain than ever. As it happened, this demise also coincided with certain basic shifts in European culture and the onset of the First World War. This wrecked whatever remnants of liberal Protestantism were left in Europe, although it was to continue flourishing in North America until the Depression of the 1930s. Out of the theological rubble arose Barthianism, followed by a host of lesser viewpoints. Common to most of these was the sense that Christian faith cannot again be tied into a figure who remains uncertain and enigmatic even after prolonged historical reflection and the employment of the sharpest critical tools.[19] Perhaps the most radical of the theologies in this vein was Bultmann's, and in its exaggerated tendencies it showed more clearly than the others how profoundly unsatisfactory this solution was. It seemed as though Bultmann believed that the delicate beauty of the water-lily would live on forever despite the fact that its stem, by which it was bound to the earth, had been cut. Bultmann was wrong; the lily quickly became withered vegetation. His immediate disciples, the so-called post-Bultmannians, once again had to launch a new quest for the historical Jesus.[20]

This new quest, however, did not shed all of Bultmann's skepticism about the Gospels as sources. It was acknowledged again that these Gospels do not constitute the neat blocks of material which, fitted together, provide a consistent biography, that they do not offer a window into the inner workings of Jesus' mind, and that in their present form they are the creations of the early community, documents crystallized out of faith for those who have faith. This last proposition, however, was not quite as innocent as it seemed. For what it shared with Bultmann was the idea that the history of the Gospels is not objectively separate from the interpreter. Neither Bultmann nor his disciples (Ernst Käsemann, Günther Bornkamm, and Ernst Fuchs, for example) have been willing to allow this history to determine what twentieth-century scholars should think.

Instead, it is countered, we are necessarily involved in a hermeneutical circle in which the believer imparts to the history quite as much meaning as is derived from it. It was therefore not quite as significant as appeared at first sight that the "new-questers" were willing to see more "history" in the Gospel narratives than had Bultmann. Käsemann, for example, allows *contra* Bultmann that Jesus did associate the kingdom with his own presence. And Fuchs asserted, even more dramatically, that in his actions Jesus was acting in God's stead, welcoming on earth the outcasts as God does in heaven. Yet as Fuchs was to remark later, each person can accept "as true only that which he recognizes as valid for himself since he knows his own life to be determined by it."[21] So the existential narrowing of what is historically true in the Gospel record is occurring in the "new-questers" as it did in Bultmann; the only real difference is that their perception, arising out of their self-understanding, is not quite as narrow as Bultmann's in matters of historical nature.

There are, as a matter of fact, numerous scholars who are not part of the immediate Bultmannian circle and who do not share all of Bultmann's positions, but who nevertheless also accept the broad outlines of his approach. This acceptance can be seen in the consensus among many New Testament scholars that material from the Synoptics had three settings or contexts: first, there was the setting in the life of Jesus *(Sitz im Leben Jesu);* second, there was the setting in the life of the church, during which time the material changed shape *(Sitz im Leben Ecclesiae);* third, there is the setting in the theology of the evangelist as once again the material is reshaped to take its place in the perspective which the Gospel writer wished to present *(Sitz im Evangelium).*[22] It is these assumptions which have radically affected the way Christologies are formulated, because each biblical statement has to be examined to ascertain which of the *Sitze* it represents. Is it the unvarnished word of Jesus? Or does it reflect the reshaping which the community undertook? Or does its present form bear the marks of the last redactor? Perhaps a saying might carry the marks of all three settings but then to arrive at Jesus' own view of himself, the first setting has to be disentangled from the second and third, which is no mean undertaking. In fact as far as Bultmann was concerned, an effective disentangling must begin with the affirmation that Jesus' message is presupposed by the rest of the New Testament but is not a part of it.

How this works out in practice could be illustrated in many ways. Norman Perrin, however, provides two sharp illustrations of the impact which form and redaction criticism necessarily have had on the study of Christology. Take, for example, the statement in Matthew 12:32: "Anyone who speaks a word against the Son of Man will be forgiven, but anyone who speaks against the Holy Spirit will not be forgiven, either in this age or in the age to come." A traditional Christology would probably tend to key on the use of the title "Son of Man," and see in this an assertion of a Messiahship which is heavenly, patterned after the figure in Daniel 7:13, one that is in contradistinction to the earthly, political ideals associated with Messiahship in Judaism. Perrin, however, begins by noting the differences between the Matthaean passage and that in Luke 12:10. Luke has Jesus talking about "blaspheming" against the Holy Spirit rather than merely speaking against him, and Matthew has included the phrase "either in this age or in the age to come," which Luke omitted. Perrin's conclusions are as follows. First, the addition in Matthew of the eschatological theme reveals that the church was beginning to think of the future glory and of the Son of Man's role in this. And it was reflecting back on Jesus with this other perspective in mind. It was also thinking of itself as the community being prepared for the end time, the sign of which, in Jewish thought, was the coming of the Spirit. This community was to be rejected by the Jews as Jesus had been. In this saying, then, there is the seed of the church's own theology of mission. Finally, the words of condemnation reflect already the church's consciousness of failure in its mission to unbelieving Jews. The text, in other words, tells us about the consciousness and thinking of the early believers; it cannot be used as a statement about Jesus' identity.

Again, a comparison should be made of the statements in Acts 2:36 and Acts 3:21. In the first there is an assertion that "God has made this Jesus whom you crucified both Lord and Christ." The context provides the sense of these words. Following the resurrection and ascension of Jesus, he has begun to reign, actively subduing the enemies of God on earth. The second passage, however, is different. It presents Jesus as remaining "in heaven until the time comes for God to restore everything." Why, then, has this reign been taken out of the present and projected into the future? Reiterating the views of R. H. Fuller, Perrin suggests that the explanation lies in the church's internal reckoning with a delayed *parousia* which it had not previously anticipated, and its experience of the Spirit which in a sense had softened the necessity for an immediate end to the world by providing some elements of this divine rule in the present. In other words, it is the church's *experience* which is reflected in these two Acts passages, not so much Christological substance which can be utilized in a doctrine of Christ's person. It reflects the *Sitz im Leben Ecclesiae* primarily, although it is also part, obviously, of the broader Lukan theology, the *Sitz im Evangelium.*

What is of interest in these reflections both on the quest for the historical Jesus and on the new literary approaches to the Christological sections in the New Testament is the assumption that a meaning can be elicited from these passages which has eluded the church for the better part of twenty centuries.[23] As it turns out, however, this hidden meaning has been coming to light in direct proportion to the sense that the historical Jesus has been obscured by the Gospels. Redaction and form criticism are, in fact, the warning bells to ships in the area that nearby lies an historical skepticism upon which any vessel venturing too close may founder. These approaches, beginning with the assumption that the historical Jesus can only be known in the barest and most insubstantial outline, plainly have to find the meaning of Christianity elsewhere. They do it by piecing together what Christianity meant for the first believers or what it meant for the first writers. This literary detective work, however, requires the scholar to work behind the scenes, not with the text as itself providing the meaning, but with the text as a clue to the meaning which lies elsewhere. So once again a rational procedure has been adopted to get at the "real" meaning of the New Testament. Perhaps we testify to our own myopia when we denounce Anselm and medieval scholasticism for bringing to the Bible a whole skein of thought without which, it was assumed, the meaning of Christianity would be forever obscure, while failing to see that the procedure adopted in much form and redaction criticism is fundamentally the same. The literary history behind the text is "self-evident" to the form critic; the world of truths behind Anselm's concrete reality was "self-evident" to him and his generation. The problem with many "self-evident" truths, however, is that they are evident only to their believers.

DEVELOPING A CHRISTOLOGY

It is clear from these examples, which have been randomly selected but which could be multiplied many times over, that it is unwise to approach the New Testament with a "system" or a "key." The writings of the New Testament must be respected as having their own individuality, but they must also be accorded some integrity as pieces of writing; otherwise literary analysis will degenerate into futility. In this connection then, it seems to me that four basic assumptions need to be made about the Christology contained in the New Testament.

First, it does not seem to me plausible that if the Scriptures have been given to the church by God for its instruction, admonition, and discipline, the Christology taught in those Scriptures will be so entangled in the problem of literary origins that only a handful of scholars will be able to make sense out of it. This does not mean that a consideration of backgrounds or of comparable utterances in the Qumran texts might not throw new light on aspects of this Christology. Nor does it mean that there was not a history to the record of what Jesus said and did before the New Testament authors (but especially the Gospel writers) did their work. It means, simply, that the existing biblical record is itself a sufficiently faithful rendering of Jesus' deeds and words, so that we are not driven to seek a meaning to what he did in some higher, rational system or in some largely unknown history lying behind the text. There is neither a system nor a history which has the "real" meaning. To work as if there were is to reverse the facts. It is to assume that the biblical text is the shadow of which this other factor is the reality. It is the text which is the real thing, and the history behind it and the systems which accompany it are the shadows.

Second, it is consistent with the practice of historical research in other fields to assume that the New Testament record is innocent in respect to the accuracy of its portrayal of Jesus until proven guilty. It does not seem to be appropriate procedure to assume that the text is distorted and its authors mistaken until corroboration for what they say can be found in parallel and external sources. It is true that the Gospels were written in the context of faith, but that does not mean that they are thereby distorted. The fact that Solzhenitsyn was a *zek* in a Soviet prison camp does not *ipso facto* guarantee that his record of such camps in *The Gulag Archipelago* is mistaken. As a matter of fact, his firsthand suffering probably provided him with more incentive to faithfully reveal the truth of these repressive camps than any writer from *Tass* could have mustered. If the presence of faith in the early Christian writers was to tilt the scales in any direction, it would seem more likely that it would move them toward truthfulness than toward fabrication, given the high morality of that faith.

Third, it seems to me to be inaccurate and mistaken to argue, as many form and some redaction critics have, that the Gospel writers had no interest in producing biographies. It is true that their work does not follow the style in which biographies are customarily written today. It is also true that each Gospel writer, by a process of selectivity and paraphrastic condensation, has presented Jesus from a different angle of vision. But to conclude from this that they therefore had no interest in the human figure is mistaken and rests, it would seem, less on the discernible facts than it does on contemporary, existentialist assumptions.

To say, however, that there was an interest in the human Jesus which was taken by the Gospel writers does not give legitimacy to any attempt to intrude modern, psychological understanding into the narrative in order to "explain" it. The sheer folly of this procedure has been painfully demonstrated by the first "quest for the historic Jesus" movement, and only an ignorance of history would permit any kind of repetition of what happened then. The proponents of modern-day "psychohistory" often seem unaware of this disastrous chapter in the story of biblical criticism and perhaps assume that with our much larger understanding of psychological principles today we can succeed where others previously failed. Some think they can actually discover the inner workings of people long since dead. Such an outlook, in my judgment, is often more optimistic than the facts will allow.

Fourth, it is necessary to recognize both the diversity and the unity that we encounter in the New Testament portrayal of Jesus. The impetus of redaction criticism has sharpened the focus on differences within the Gospels, but of course there are other literary strands in the New Testament where divergence is also exhibited. Perhaps the most troubled aspect of this is the relationship of the Johannine literature, but especially of the Gospel, to the Synoptic accounts. Certainly it is the case that John writes in an idiom that is different from that of the Synoptic authors, however that idiom and its cultural locus is to be identified. The difficulties entailed in relation to the Synoptics, however, are greatly reduced if C. K. Barrett's argument is correct—namely, that John was familiar with those accounts. The differences could then be seen not so much as antithetical departures from the Synoptics, but as variations within a commonly understood theme. In addition to the Christological material in the Johannine literature, there is the Pauline corpus (which I am assuming includes all thirteen letters traditionally ascribed to him), the pre-Pauline material which exists in the hymnal fragments and miniature creeds which Paul used, as well as Acts 1-12 and perhaps James. There are additionally the differences in the Christologies presented in the Petrine corpus and in Hebrews.

The most pressing question at this point is whether this diversity actually obscures any unity to the New Testament Christology.[24] Is there any unity that remains or are we driven to speak of "Christologies," not as the variations on a common theme, but as themselves divergent and cacophonous themes? It seems to me to be a fundamental mistake either to deny the differences in the interests of preserving the New Testament's unity or to dissolve the unity in the interests of respecting each author's distinctive view of Christ. The New Testament's unity and diversity are not contradictory elements; they are complementary.

The legitimate gains of redaction criticism, however, must be recognized, and the effect which these have on the way the other New Testament materials are employed must be developed. With respect to redaction criticism itself, it seems to me that its focus on Synoptic differences has forced us to see the Gospel authors as being creative in their own right. Yet it is a creativity within certain bounds. In some instances, the Synoptic authors appear to be quoting Jesus verbatim, but in others they appear to be summarizing much larger discourses, and in their work of summation they select material in accordance with the particular view of Christ which they are presenting. In this sense, their creativity shows through; it is not, however, that kind of creativity which fabricates events or sayings and inserts them into the story in order to make a theological point. It is a creativity which selects material while preserving the continuity and integrity between the larger discourse and the shorter summary.

This recognition has some interesting consequences for the way in which our Christology is constructed. It used to be presumed that the Gospels give us the biographical outline of Jesus' life, and the epistles the theological reflection upon it. In liberal Protestantism so much was made of this distinction that Paul was charged with having distorted the historical Jesus by interpreting him in Hellenistic categories.

In actual fact, the picture is so different as almost to be the reverse of what was formerly believed. There are two changes in the older view that have occurred and need to be noted. First, if the Gospel writers are creative in the sense just defined, then their works are quite as much works of theology as are Paul's. There are not two categories of literature for the New Testament's Christology, the biographical of the Gospels and the theological of the epistles; there is only one. Not only is this the case, but if there is a continuity between the self-consciousness of Jesus and the structural Christology of Paul, upon which Jeremias and others have rightly insisted, then there are "biographical" elements implicit in Paul's theological treatment. The older categorization has simply broken down.

Second, our dating of the New Testament is more disputed but, I believe, more certain than it was previously. Obviously there are significant differences in these determinations, especially where some of the letters traditionally attributed to Paul are considered to have been authored by others. Nevertheless, there are good grounds for arguing that the Pauline literature predates that of the Synoptic Gospels. In Paul, we are chronologically closer to the historical Jesus than we are in the Synoptics. It is therefore not unreasonable to think, given this twofold shift in the older understanding, that the so-called biographical and theological categories are really just different angles of vision on the same reality, not competing accounts or divergent perceptions. Hence it is that in the pages which follow I treat the literature not in chronological sequence or even in single blocks, but as tributaries flowing into a single, thematic river, even if those tributaries retain their identity as currents within the whole.

The narrow focus of this study could be misleading to the reader, and it certainly has been frustrating to the author. The interconnectedness of Christian thought and, in the modern period, its confused entanglements with culture mean that a multitude of other issues form the constant backdrop to the particular subjects under consideration. Within the limits imposed by this study, I have sought to provide the broader context as much as possible, but my efforts have had to be circumscribed.

What follows is an analysis, in Part I, of the biblical testimony to Christ, in Part II, of the historical development of this understanding, and in Part III, of the modern affirmation or reinterpretation of this tradition. It is, in other words, the ongoing reply to Jesus' question, "Who do people say I am?" (Mark 8:27), and the answers across the ages have continued to reflect the same speculative diversity as they did in Peter's day.

Part 1: Biblical Foundations

1 THE FRAMEWORK

The shape which our Christology assumes is determined by the presuppositions and operating assumptions with which we start. Included in these are assumptions of a literary type, which determine how Scripture should be analyzed and employed, as well as those of an epistemological nature, which decide whether our twentieth-century cognitive horizons will be permitted to limit or change what can be accepted from the biblical writings, which have their own horizon. Almost as important as these, however, are the choices that we make with respect to the interpretive framework, the categories of understanding, which we employ in our analysis of the biblical material. It is this last issue which is the focus of this present chapter.

FORERUNNERS

The question of categories has emerged in an unexpected way. It has been brought to prominence by the failure of the "lives of Jesus" movement. This movement attempted to write Jesus' biography, as the titles of many of its works declared—titles such as Friedrich Schleiermacher's *Life of Jesus* or Shirley Jackson Case's *Jesus: A New Biography.* Given the presuppositions with which these authors began, however, the Jesus which resulted was one who was stripped of the supernatural dimension. The supernatural was "reinterpreted," the uniqueness of Jesus being concentrated under the thought of the mystery of his personality, the power of his morality, or the sublimity of his teaching.[1] Such a Jesus was, in fact, no different from any other great leader and teacher, and the faith he taught was generically no different from the other great religions of the world. But does this reinterpretation really do justice to the figure at the focus of the Gospel accounts? Do we not have here what Bultmann called disparagingly "a middle class conception of Christianity," and one which is quite out of touch with the "strangeness of the New Testament"?[2]

In modern theology, the first sharp warning along these lines was Johannes Weiss's *The Proclamation of the Kingdom of God,* published in 1892. Liberal theology had been in the habit of reducing everything Jesus said to what could be experienced and of looking at Jesus only through the narrow prism of that experience. In Europe, Jesus came to be seen as the prototype of the religious person, a Protestant liberal par excellence; in the United States, with its more activistic temper, he was seen as the social reformer par excellence, especially in the theology of Walter Rauschenbusch and the workers in the social gospel movement. What Weiss perceived was that in this liberalism, significant elements of Jesus' consciousness and teaching had simply been excised. This was especially true of the Kingdom of God. Under no circumstances could the Kingdom in Jesus' teaching be treated, as liberals insisted on doing, simply as an aspect of their own inward experience or as identical with social progress. Rather, in Jesus' thought it was an alien territory to be entered, a treasure to be received, which was still entirely in the future.[3] Weiss claimed,[4] as Schweitzer was to do,[5] that when the arrival of this Kingdom was delayed, Jesus then seized upon the audacious plan of speeding up the timetable by offering himself as a ransom. The Kingdom, in both Weiss's work and Schweitzer's, had been established as the category without which Jesus' work and words could not be adequately understood, and the problem of its delay was now firmly lodged on the theological agenda.

In the twentieth century, however, there have emerged some correctives to these radical views, but few people have been willing to discount Weiss and Schweitzer completely. The category of the Kingdom cannot be disregarded as the liberal Protestants in effect did, and by the same token the Kingdom cannot be dissolved into subjective, existential decision as Bultmann thinks. Just as unsatisfactory, however, is the Weiss-Schweitzer notion, currently being revitalized by Jürgen Moltmann,[6] that the Kingdom is purely and simply a future reality. The corrective lies in recognizing the centrality of this conception in Jesus' self-understanding, but in seeing it as having components that are both present and future, the Kingdom as partly realized and yet still to be consummated. This understanding has put the texts regarding the delay of the *parousia* (Matt. 10:23; Mark 9:1; 13:30) in much softer and less problematic light.

The stepping-stone toward this more balanced conception was probably the work of C. H. Dodd, although it should be noted that his celebrated *The Parables of the Kingdom* was anticipated by Geerhardus Vos' *The Teaching of Jesus Concerning the Kingdom of God and the Church* in 1903.[7] In his study, Dodd challenged Schweitzer's wholly futuristic understanding of the Kingdom, although he did start with Schweitzer's own question: could the early Christian hope of a return of Jesus be indefinitely delayed without destroying the whole basis of

Christian hope? His reply was that it is clear from the Gospels that only the final consummation is postponed, but that there is already a realization of the Kingdom taking place. He claimed that ἤγγικεν in Mark 1:15 and ἔφθασεν in Matthew 12:28 (Luke 11:20) echo a Semitic understanding which should lead us to translate them as saying that the Kingdom "has come."[8] But there were other specific sayings in which it seemed clear that the Kingdom had come, such as Luke 10:9, 11; 11:31, 32; Matthew 11:4-6; 11:12 (Luke 16:16). Likewise, many of the parables witness this same truth, such as Matthew 12:28, 29 (Luke 11:20, 21), and Matthew 13:16-23 (Luke 8:9-18; Mark 4:13-25). The insertion or intrusion into the historical of what is divine and supernatural through the life, death, and resurrection of Jesus is, said Dodd, "explicit" and "unequivocal."

Dodd's work, to be sure, did not pass uncriticized.[9] First, many scholars felt that if Schweitzer was wrong to discount the present aspect of the Kingdom, Dodd was wrong to dissolve the future aspect. Perhaps Dodd was not quite as guilty as he was charged, but it is certainly true that he bent over backwards to subsume those texts dealing with the future under the rubric of the Kingdom's present realization. Second, his argument that the teaching on Jesus' return did not originate with Jesus himself but was a creation of the early Christians who misunderstood him has had a mixed reception. Those enamored with *Formgeschichte* generally rejoice to find yet more evidence for what they argue was everywhere apparent, but there have been large numbers of scholars who have countered that the literary basis for so radical a conclusion is too slim. Yet, despite these weaknesses Dodd's work both reinforced the importance of the Kingdom as a means of understanding Jesus' life and brought a corrective to Schweitzer's radicalism. In consequence, it is clear that no view of Christ's person and work which is separated from the context of the Kingdom can claim to reflect a biblical mode of thought. In him the eschatological future is brought into the present, and the entire Jewish timetable of events connected with Messiah has been changed.[10]

THE KINGDOM AS A CATEGORY
Synoptic Gospels
The Messianic Kingdom had a long history in Jewish thought before Jesus made reference to it. In his teaching, however, its emphasis and content became unique. Jeremias has pointed out that the term βασιλεία (τοῦ θεοῦ/τῶν οὐρανῶν) was not widely used in the Old Testament Apocrypha and Pseudepigrapha, or in the Targums and Philo; in rabbinic literature there are only a few scattered references to it; in the Dead Sea scrolls there are only three usages. In the teaching of Jesus, however, God's Reign is mentioned directly thirteen times in Mark, nine times in sayings common to Matthew and Luke, twenty-

seven additional instances in Matthew, twelve additional instances in Luke, and twice in John's gospel.[11] What is as impressive as the high numerical incidence is the *content*, which is without parallel. In Jesus' teaching a transformation is effected in the traditional Jewish ideas, and what results is a completely fresh missionary message and mandate at the center of which is Jesus himself. Clearly the βασιλεία language was authentically and uniquely that of Jesus. The Gospel of John hardly uses it at all, and references to the Divine Reign are relatively rare in the epistles. Yet, as we shall see, it would be a mistake to imagine that this concept which more or less passes with Jesus ceased to be a point of Christian understanding. The language of Jesus and Paul is different, but at the core of their respective teachings is the same common assertion that the supernatural Rule of God has already begun in the historical process. Jesus talked about entering the Kingdom and Paul about believing the gospel, but at the center of each was Jesus, without whom there could neither be a Kingdom nor a gospel. In him, the "powers of the age to come" are experienced through the gospel; and in him the "powers of the age to come" are experienced in the Kingdom.

Jesus inaugurated his ministry with the announcement that the Rule of God[12] had come (Mark 1:15; cf. Luke 4:43; 8:1; Matt. 4:23; 9:35). But what are we to make of this? How are we to define it more precisely? Norman Perrin has argued that it is incorrect to think of the Kingdom as a concept or an idea, but it is what he calls a "symbol."[13] What he means by this, to put a positive construction on the idea, is that the Kingdom represents and evokes a whole range of ideas and cannot be reduced to any one concept or teaching. It is a complex reality, but the complexity lies less in what the Rule of God *is* and more in how, when, and where it is realized. The Kingdom, Herman Ridderbos, asserts "is preeminently the idea of the kingly self-assertion of God, of his coming to the world in order to reveal his royal majesty, power and right."[14] The primary thought is not so much the *locus*, the mode, the objects, the time, or even the consequences of the Rule, but the thought that God himself has begun to reign.

This is why, in Jesus' teaching, the accent so often falls upon the sovereign initiative which God takes in establishing the Kingdom. We can search for it, pray for it, and look for it, as Ladd but pointed out,[15] but only God can bring it about (Luke 23:51; Matt 6:10, 33; Luke 12:31). The Kingdom is God's to give and to take away; it is only ours to enter and accept (Matt. 21:43; Luke 12:32). We inherit it, possess it, or refuse to enter it, but it is not ours to build and we can never destroy it (Matt. 25:34; 5:3; Luke 10:11). We can work for the Kingdom, but we never act on it; we can preach it, but it is God's to establish (Matt. 10:7; Luke 10:9; 12:32).

Yet it is clear that this Rule had two distinct foci in Jesus' thought—namely, salvation and judgment. God's Rule is realized in both, albeit in quite different ways. Salvation is present, while judgment is future. The one is taking place more or less unnoticed, but the other will be public. The first is a slow process realized in time; the second will be a decisive event at the end of time. Common to both, however, is the conquest of sin, death, and the devil first in the personal domain and then ultimately on a cosmic scale.

It has been conjectured that the presence of this twin focus in Jesus' teaching is what confused John the Baptist. He apparently did not conceive of the Kingdom being realized slowly, silently, in the present, and projected this conquest wholly into the future. The note of judgment, symbolically portrayed by the austerity of his life, was always paramount. For Jesus, the judgment of the future was asserted, but always counterbalanced by the teaching that this Divine Rule is already bringing salvation and conquest with it. Neither Jesus' style of life nor his message had the unremitting quality of severity in it as did John's. Indeed, the tension between the partial realization of this Rule and its as yet unfulfilled completion is everywhere present in Jesus' teaching, and every effort to obscure the one emphasis by the other must be judged as mistaken.

This theme, then, provides the broad but proper context in which the Christ-event is to be interpreted, for it gives a single, integrated framework in which the Rule—inaugurated by incarnation, effected decisively by Jesus' cross-work, and concluded by the *parousia* and its concomitants of the final subduing of all evil and the return of the pacified cosmos to the Father—can be understood. It is a framework in which all of the aspects of Christology find themselves in comfortable and meaningful relationship to one another. Other categories are too narrow. They either exclude some essential part of Christology itself, or they create a disjuncture between this and God's revelation of himself on the one side and of ethics on the other. The result has been a grievous fragmentation of our understanding, for our Christology tends to become identified merely with a biographical study of the historical Jesus in which his divine self-consciousness is reduced and his miraculous works discounted, or his significance for today is completely severed from the Divine Rule which was initiated in and through him, or else Christology and ethics become entirely disengaged from one another. In the New Testament, the apostles are so insistent that Christians live ethically because they are so persuaded that the powers of darkness have been overthrown and that the conquest at the cross will be made public throughout the cosmos at the time of the *parousia*. To that extent, the coming of the King in human birth marked the beginning of the end of history. It ushered in the fall of Satan (Luke 10:18; cf. John 12:31; 14:30; 16:11) and the emergence of a people formed to manifest the forgiveness and victory of this Rule. All of these themes are bound together and made comprehensible by the biblical teaching on the Kingdom, and their intricate interelations can be satisfactorily sustained within it. It is, then, the *sine qua non* for a full and proper understanding of Christology.

That the saving and vindicating Rule of God has been born with Jesus and is made effective through his words and actions, and is made redemptively effective through the cross, is everywhere attested in the Gospels. Yet it is also plain that this is the Rule of *God*. Everything that occurs within this Kingdom reveals his character, power, and purposes. Consequently, as Ladd puts it, the "presence of the Kingdom is to be understood from the nature of God's present activity; and the future of the Kingdom is the redemptive manifestation of his kingly rule at the end of the age."[16] Yet insofar as both occur in and through Jesus, the second coming is but the outworking of the first, as judgment is the inevitable corollary of salvation. The two foci—salvation principally connected with the first coming and judgment with the second—are chronologically separated; but already in the first, the inauguration of this Rule, there is the anticipation of the second, its end.

Thus the arrival of this Rule begins to fulfill the prophetic vision of God's enemies being scattered (Mic. 4:11-13; Isa. 13:19; cf. Jer. 7:12-34; 26:6, 9; Joel 3:1-17; Zech. 12:1-9), for Satan's forces are put in disarray (Matt. 12:28, 29/Luke 11:20-22) and they recognize with fear who Jesus is (Mark 1:24/Luke 4:34; Mark 5:7/Matt. 8:9, 31). Jesus, the strong man, plunders the household of Satan (Mark 3:27/Matt. 12:29). Feebly, Satan offers Jesus the realms over which he has held sway (Matt. 4:8-10/Luke 4:5-8) and is rebuffed. That note of judgment pronounced on cities (Luke 21:20-24; 23:27-31; Matt. 11:20-24/Luke 10:13-15) falls decisively on the powers of darkness, who lie behind all human rebellion (cf. John 12:31; 14:30; 16:11; Col. 2:15; Heb. 2:14; 1 John. 3:8). Whether Jesus brings salvation or judgment depends entirely upon the reception given to his words and work (Matt. 10:32, 33, 39; 16:25/Mark 8:35/Luke 9:24; Matt. 22:1-14; 25:1-13, 32; Luke 17:33).

It may seem paradoxical that this Rule has to be announced and declared; indeed, in that type of theology developed by Gustav Aulén and Anders Nygren on the Lutheran side and by Barth and his conservative followers on the Reformed side, this has always been a kind of nagging riddle. The overwhelming emphasis they have given to the objectivity of this Kingdom and the sovereignty of its progress has had the effect of undercutting the urgency and activity of preaching. In the Gospels themselves, however, the preaching of the Kingdom—especially to sinners (Mark 2:15-17/Matt. 9:10-13/Luke 5:29, 32; note the parables following the question in Luke 15:1, 2) and the poor (Matt. 11:5/Luke 7:22)—was the means of effecting the presence of the Kingdom, and Jesus did not conceal what was occurring. Ultimately this

Rule will result in the overthrow of all the forces of evil and the regeneration of this cosmos (Matt. 19:28), but first it must take root in human life. It takes root when its proclamation is believed; through the act of repentance and faith the King himself is made known to the subjects now in his realm.

There is, however, a constant tension between this Kingdom which is entered through Jesus, this Rule under whose power and authority human experience can now fall, and that part of the Kingdom which is yet to be realized. This future dimension is most evident in the Olivet discourse (Matt. 24:4-36/Mark 13:5-37/Luke 21:8-36). This world has yet to see aspects of the Kingdom not now evident, but this same thread is woven through many other discourses as well. The Lord's prayer seeks the arrival of these other dimensions (Matt. 6:10/Luke 11:2). This prayer expresses a desire for justice, a desire which is finally realized in judgment (Matt. 24:14; 25:31-46). And the Rule of God will assert itself in the resurrection of those people of faith (Luke 20:36) who will join the faithful of other ages (Matt. 8:11), shine like the sun (Matt. 13:43), sit in his eschatological Kingdom (Matt. 20:21), eating bread and drinking wine in a joyous banquet (Matt. 8:11; 26:29/Mark 14:25; Luke 13:29, 30). Thus will his Rule, which is mysteriously at work and even now asserting itself, gradually (Luke 13:20, 21; Mark 4:26-29) become fully manifest. The final manifestation of God's glory and power, especially in the Son, will shatter nature, destroy all evil, and bring either salvation or judgment to all people. This βαδιλεία has already become "tangible and certain in Jesus," Schnackenburg says, and through him it now penetrates "into 'this aeon' and works upon men . . . and waits only its manifestation in glory."[17]

Undoubtedly, within this general consensus each of the Synoptic Gospels tends to emphasize different aspects of the coming of this Divine Rule in and through Jesus. Mark in particular underscores Jesus' humanity, stressing his limitations (6:5, 6; 13:32; 15:31) and the fact that his Messiahship was concealed from official Judaism. This latter aspect has caused scholars considerable difficulties. In 1901 Wrede published his book *The Messianic Secret in the Gospel,* claiming that Jesus never asserted that he was divine Messiah and the Christian community never realized he was until after the resurrection. In order to provide an alibi, the Gospel of Mark was altered to include both the knowledge of Jesus as Messiah and injunctions to secrecy as a way of explaining why no one knew about this (1:25, 34, 44; 3:12; 5:43; 7:36; 8:26, 30). Also inserted were the special interpretations of parables (4:10-20, 34; 7:17-23) and teaching on his death and *parousia* (8:27-38; 10:32-34; 13:3-37). At the time of its publication, Wrede's book was stiffly attacked by Schweitzer and also by more moderate scholars like William Sanday and A. E. J. Rawlinson. The theory, which then seemed to languish for supporters, was, however, revived in 1935 by

R. H. Lightfoot,[18] and it has been given fresh currency by Bultmann. Leaving aside some of the critical concerns that are involved, it can still be asserted that the theory lacks internal coherence. For Mark's Gospel allows that others did openly recognize Jesus as Messiah, even if the Jews often did not. This was true of demons, of the woman at Bethany, and the centurion at the cross (14:3-9; 15:39), and the universality of the Kingdom's reach was thereby underscored.

Naturally there is much in common between Matthew and Mark, but there are some notable differences. If Messianic claims are subdued in Mark, they are emphasized in Matthew (1:1, 20; 9:27; 12:23; 15:22; 20:30, 31; 21:9, 15) in a promise/fulfillment context.[19] There are also additional uses of the title "Son of God" which, as a title, carried Messianic expectations (14:33; 16:16; 27:40, 43; 28:19). The universal thrust of the Kingdom is asserted in Matthew, but in a different connection. The evangelist is concerned to underscore the continuing validity of the law (e.g., 5:17-20) against a nascent antinomianism, but also against the tendency to submerge Christ within a reinvigorated Judaism. So his selections stress the proper use of the law and its universal application.

It is difficult to discuss the distinctives of Luke's Gospel apart from a consideration of Acts,[20] and what is true of the Gospel is not contradicted by Acts. In recent years, what this distinctive might be has produced a profusion of studies, ably reviewed and digested by Howard Marshall.[21] There is merit to his proposal that what sets Luke apart is his focus upon salvation; or, if one might be allowed to broaden Marshall's thesis slightly, it is the focus of salvation which the King's Rule brings. The emphasis on this Rule is not significantly different from that of the other Synoptics except that its outworking is traced out particularly in the realm of salvation. This note is struck in 1:31 with the angelic instruction to Mary about the naming of the child, for Ιησους is a later form of Joshua, meaning "Yahweh saves." In the birth stories, which I am assuming are authentically a part of the Gospel, the actions of God in rescuing his people become clear. So Mary celebrates God as her Savior (1:47), and Zechariah develops this thought further (1:68-79). God is declared to have raised up a powerful Savior from the house of David. Thus do the angels celebrate his coming (2:11). This theme of salvation is then pursued *in extenso* in Jesus' ministry, his message and his work being organized around this motif.[22]

This variety within the Gospel authors, however, is not so great that it strains their unity;[23] indeed, it would be more accurate to say that their sense of the Divine Rule breaking in on the world was simply followed out in different directions as they selected the materials from which they worked. These distinctive elements are not in competition with each other so much as being the components of a larger whole. Certainly there is everywhere an accord that it is God alone who has the capacity to redeem his people, that that moment of redemption was begun with the coming of Jesus, that the focus of its assertion and its achievement was at the cross where the powers of darkness were overthrown, and that its termination and climactic conclusion will come at the end when Jesus returns and the earth is cleansed. It is this accord, of course, which worked havoc with the timetable of Jewish expectations.

At about the time that Christian faith was born, Judaism had begun to make clear that there was a distinction between "this age" and "the age to come." These two ages were related to one another in a chronological sequence. This αἰών ended with the coming to earth of Messiah, and with his arrival there began the heavenly αἰών. These ages were consecutive, and the conditions of the former did not persist into the latter. It was this conception that was radically reordered both by Jesus and the apostles.

In recent years the precise nature of this reordering has been the object of considerable scrutiny, especially in relation to the use of words for time in the Bible.[24] It is at least clear that for the biblical writers time was not simply a subjective category—a way of seeing things imposed on the world by the experiencing subject—as Kant proposed, nor yet was it for them simply an illusion as Hegel imagined. For them, time is objective, a part of the warp and woof of things. And modern physics has tended to confirm this, for even if time becomes bent and warped in an Einsteinian sense, it retains its relationship to the other dimensions of space, which are clearly objective. Space and time seem to be inextricably bound up together. Yet this in itself does not resolve all the problems, for it still has to be asked whether there is a qualitative difference between that kind of existence which is temporal and that which is eternal. Plato thought that there was; some scholars, following Cullmann, have opposed this, suggesting that eternity is simply the unending elongation to chronological time. This is not entirely convincing for the reasons suggested by James Barr,[25] and perhaps the difficulty we experience in affixing precise meanings to the time words is that the New Testament authors were often using these words as the servants of a larger and paradoxical reality which they sought to elucidate—namely, that penetration of the αἰών to come into this present αἰών. The appearance of what is eschatalogical within the historical has taken some of the precision off the meanings of these words as strict definers of chronological moments, periods, or progressions.

Certainly the New Testament is emphatic that that time-line of Jewish expectation has been disrupted; indeed, it is no longer the same time-line. That age which Judaism had despaired of ever seeing in this world has arrived; it is mentioned in a multitude of ways in the Synoptics but is explicit in passages such as Matthew 13:39, 40; 28:20; Mark 10:30/Luke 18:30; 20:34, 35. In John it emerges, for example, in his insistence that eternal life is a present possession and not merely that which begins at death, the termination of this earthly αἰών.[26] That ζωή αἰών of "the age to come," is something that had already been given (10:28; 17:2, 3), and is received by believing Jesus' word (5:24; cf. 6:68; 12:50) or simply believing in Jesus (3:36; 6:47, 54). (This last reference assumes, as I believe is the case, that eating the flesh of Jesus and drinking his blood is not the Johannine equivalent of the Last Supper, but simply a discourse in the meaning of faith.)

The Pauline corpus

The two-age terminology is echoed in Paul's letters as well (Rom. 8:18-23; 12:2; 1 Cor. 1:20; 2:6, 8; 3:18; 10:11; 2 Cor. 4:4; Gal. 1:4; Eph. 1:21; 1 Tim. 4:1; Tit. 2:12, 13), although more distinctly in some passages than in others. And it is also true that Paul is not always precise about where the exact parameters of these ages lie. He can speak of the age to come as still being in the future (Eph. 1:21; cf. 2:7), but of the present age as being the end-time (1 Cor. 10:11; 1 Tim. 4:1). Yet in the main it seems clear that this present age is that which is characterized by a sinful rebellion against God, and the age to come is that in which Messiah reigns, an age even now present because its Head is.

Perhaps what is fundamental in Paul's thought is not so much the two-age terminology itself as the eschatological reality which this terminology seeks to explain. For him, an in-breaking of another kind of reality has occurred through Christ, such an in-breaking that it is able to send its clarifying shafts of light deep into all human experience. He speaks of the "revelation" of Christ, the "revelation" of this mystery, and the "revelation" of faith (Rom. 16:25; Gal. 1:12; Eph. 3:3).

The disclosure of this divine reality is what has led Herman Ridderbos to speak of Paul's doctrine of justification as an outworking of his eschatology. Clearly this is so. Those who are "in" Christ experience not only a personal renewal but the entry into a new world, a new spiritual environment, a new habitat. The old has passed and the new has come (2 Cor. 5:17). The great turning-point in this eschatological moment was the coming of Christ (Gal. 4:4; 2 Tim. 1:9, 10), and our entry into it is through our identification with his death and resurrection. To say, as some have, that Jesus' resurrection was for Paul only a symbol or metaphor for interpreting Christian experience is to say too little; to say that in our dying and rising with him the age to come has intersected eschatologically with the line of our personal existence is alone the way to do justice to Paul's thought. For there is a clean breach between our existence outside of Christ and that which is "in" him, between our life in this αἰών and that which is already in the heavens (Eph. 1:3) where we hold citizenship (Phil. 3:20). Christians have their Christian existence "above" and are to pursue those values appropriate to this other dimension (Col. 3:1, 2).

In his doctrine of the Holy Spirit, Paul again reiterates these eschatological themes, for it is the Spirit's task to shed upon the church those
supernatural gifts and that empowering which bespeak another age.
Thus it is that the Spirit initiates this transition from one "age" to the
other by investing the gospel with such power that its impact surpasses
any effect produced by mere oratorical skill or eloquence (1 Thess. 1:5;
1 Cor. 2:4; Rom. 15:18, 19). This same Spirit, by whom the transition is
effected through re-creation, possesses and inhabits believers (1 Cor.
2:12; 3:16; 6:19), bestowing upon them gifts (1 Cor. 12:1-31), and
guarantees to their self-awareness the certainty of that fuller realization
of the age to come (2 Cor. 1:22; 5:5). That, perhaps, is why Paul in
every case save one (Rom. 8:24) speaks of salvation either in the present
or in the future (e.g., Rom. 5:9; 10:9; 1 Cor. 1:18; 5:5; 9:22). Salvation
means living by the reality of that age to come even now in the present,
through the work of the Spirit, by union with that Christ in whom the
new age has dawned.

CONCLUSIONS

It is abundantly clear from this overview that the New Testament has
provided its own categories for interpreting the figure of Jesus, and we
do violence to its thought if we supplant them with others more familiar and congenial to us. The Protestant liberals did this, choosing to
replace the Kingdom by the category of conventional biography; the
Bultmannians are doing it by discounting the human and historic
significance of Jesus and eliciting his contemporary meaning through
existential verities. In the one case the in-breaking of God with and in
Jesus was muted, and in the other the significance of this in-breaking is
seen to come, not so much through Jesus, but in each believer. Thus
these theologians have developed hermeneutical categories which are
reductionistic, and the result is that the real significance of God's
action is largely or completely lost.

The framework of interpretation which the New Testament offers
is close to what Willi Marxsen has called "kerygmatic biography." The
meaning of Jesus is not found outside of the parameters of his life; his
biography contains within it its own interpretation. What is elucidated
within his historical life, however, is unique to him, and thus this
biography cannot in any sense be described as conventional. It is un-
conventional because in Jesus' life has come, as it cannot in any other
life, the triumphant in-breaking of God into our world, the redemptive
conquest of sin, death, and the devil through his cross and resurrection.
This conquest is itself the Messianic Age, an age which comes with the
Messiah and remains as *incognito* as he was in the midst of the present
αἰών. This paradox of the future now lying concealed in the present, of
what is eschatological now piercing the historical, inevitably has
worked havoc with our language. But the reality which our language
seeks to describe is not diminished by our linguistic insufficiency.

This very paradox of the eschatological future intruding into human life is seen in Christ and is experienced in redemption. One enters the sphere of this Rule by believing on Christ, and one believes on Christ by obeying the gospel. Thus the gospel is itself a realization of eschatology, even as the Kingdom was. And just as the complete consummation of that Kingdom is yet to come, so is the complete realization of those truths which the gospel enunciates. It is therefore impossible to separate the two comings of Christ, the first in grace and the second in glory. The beginning of this Rule had within it the intimations of its end; the offer of grace in the gospel has within it the intimations of judgment. God's Rule first asserts itself within the crosswork of Jesus, destroying the penalty for sin, and then within the cosmos itself, destroying ultimately and completely every force of evil, every power contrary to God's.

The gospel and equally the Kingdom are thus placed in an eschatological framework, and so are they experienced. What is divine employs what is human in Jesus at the cross in conquering our guilt and the devil who lies behind it, and what is divine breaks through the human in our preaching of the biblical Word. That Word becomes rooted in human life by the Spirit as it is made to transcend and surpass all of the powers of mere human oratory in its effectiveness. And once lodged in our nature and consciousness, this gospel brings with it by the Holy Spirit that sense, that inner persuasion, that we belong to another age. If the Christian lives in this world as did Jesus, he can no more be part "of this world" than was Jesus, for by faith the Christian has been joined to Christ. Thus Christian experience finds within itself these same elements of another αἰών asserting itself within the fabric of this αἰών, of another reality the experience of which always leaves the Christian an alien in this world.

This is the matrix within which the New Testament focuses its attention upon Christ; these are the ideas which provide an interpretive framework within which his birth, death, and resurrection assume their proper meaning. Without this framework, they take on as many meanings as we care to assign to them, few of which might have been intrinsic to the events themselves. Theology was correct to put this matter of categories on its agenda, for what is decided here affects the kind of Christ we will find in the Gospels and proclaim in our age.

2   THE IDENTITY OF JESUS

In moving from the Synoptic Gospels to the epistles, it is difficult to escape the feeling that one has traveled from one world into another. In the Synoptics, the language of the Kingdom is dominant; in the epistles it is rare. In these Gospels we are everywhere in touch with the human Jesus as he teaches, forgives, denounces, weeps, and heals; in the epistles, references to his earthly life are scant. In the Gospels, the other-worldly dimension in Jesus, that which is transcendent and supernatural, is often concealed; in the epistles, it is the human figure which recedes and the other-worldly dimension which is magnified and explored.[1] Are these, in fact, two worlds? And are we looking at quite different Christologies?

A great deal hangs on how we resolve these questions, for if Jesus was not the towering figure portrayed by John and Paul in particular, then his relationship to the Kingdom becomes enigmatic. How could someone less than Paul's Christ inaugurate the Divine Rule? The answer, of course, is that he could not, and so those scholars who have seen the figure in the Synoptic Gospels as being something less than the Christ we meet in the epistles have had to forge a quite different relationship for him to the Rule of God. Frequently he has been pictured, then, as a prophet and seer, the One who pointed toward this Rule, but not the One who inaugurated it; he has emerged from these studies as a person of exalted morality, of great perception, but not as God incarnate. That being the case, it then becomes a matter of no small interest to see where Paul might have derived his ideas about the Christ-figure, since they evidently did not arise from the circumstances of Jesus' life and work. Once this question has been resolved, it then only remains to trace out the process of evolution that takes us from the Galilean prophet of the Synoptics to the cosmic Christ of the epistles. And many scholars have assumed that the discovery of this develop-

33

ment—what its ingredients and stages were—holds out our best hope of discovering the "real" meaning of Christianity without which the New Testament itself will remain blurry.

In the twentieth century, New Testament studies have tended to focus on selected aspects of this question: those studies with a more theological interest concentrate on the assumed disjuncture between the Christologies of Jesus and Paul; others with a more historical interest concentrate on the development and change in thought as we move from the Synoptics to the epistles. These two types of study tend to reinforce one another, because they are dealing with the same question and in most authors there is at least some recognition both of the theological and the historical dimensions.

It was W. Wrede's book *Paul,* published around the turn of the century, which posed the issue as sharply as anyone had done and set up the main lines of discussion which have continued to this day. According to Wrede, Paul enjoyed an advantage not shared by the other apostles in that he had never known Jesus. This emancipated his thought. Those who had lived with Jesus and had come to know him as an ordinary, historical person could never have seen him, as Paul did, as a supramundane being and the Creator of all. Paul's ignorance spared him this difficulty. It enabled him to cloak the figure of Jesus with ideas of an infinite Christ that had already formed in his mind; Jesus was merely "the wearer of all these mighty predicates which had already been established."[2] And thus constructed, this Christ became the center of Paul's thought.[3] But from where had he derived these ideas? Wrede was uncertain, but suggested that Paul was in contact with a Judaism quite different from that of Jesus, that he moved in Hellenistic circles whereas Jesus had not, that he was influenced by the evolving faith in the churches, and that these contacts were possible sources for such a Christ-figure.

Wrede's disjunction between Jesus' Christology and that of Paul was next picked up by Schweitzer. He injected a new element by insisting that both Christologies were framed by eschatological concerns and so, in this respect, Jesus and Paul stood on common ground. Their difference lay in that Jesus pointed to the Kingdom which was delayed in coming and, in his attempt to precipitate its arrival, futilely threw himself into martyrdom; for Paul the Kingdom did, in fact, come with Jesus. Jesus "has made an end of the natural and is bringing in the Messianic Kingdom."[4] This shift in interpretation is reflected in the different understandings of the Kingdom in Jesus and Paul. In Jesus, the Kingdom is a future reality in which there is complete peace and tranquility; in Paul, it is present and there is conflict between good and evil.[5] It is a temporary state which is but the stepping-stone to the final, eternal Kingdom.[6] For Schweitzer, Jesus turned out to be a failure, Paul was mistaken, and their respective Christologies were quite different.

And so the line of thought has come down to Bultmann. Like Schweitzer, he agrees that Jesus and Paul both thought within an eschatological framework; that much they had in common. The eschatologies, however, were different. Jesus did not see himself as Messiah, but he did speak so forcefully of the "age to come" that he precipitated in Paul's mind the idea that it had actually come with Jesus.[7] Like Wrede, however, Bultmann looked for the origins of Paul's Christ-figure not in the historical Jesus, but in current religious thought. Specifically he argued that the interpretive cloak which is draped over Jesus came, not from Judaism, but from gnosticism. Its redeemer myth became the Christ of Paul's preaching.[8]

Bultmann, of course, also provided an historical account of how the faith of Jesus became the Christianity of the early church. His work proved to be provocative and seminal, the result being a flood of studies, such as those by R. H. Fuller[9] and more recently James Dunn,[10] which have looked to the various prevailing cultures as providing the distinctive ingredients in the emerging Christological patterns.[11] The outcome has been to affirm that Jesus did not know himself to be preexistent and divine, but what he did not know and did not say about himself was left to others to see and say. His interpreters knew more about him than he did about himself, for they affirmed his divinity whereas he did not.

This radical kenoticism is built on two literary presuppositions. First, it is assumed that the Gospel of John, being a later theological creation, does not give us access into the self-consciousness of Jesus. Second, the narrative portions in the Synoptics, which would include the accounts of Jesus' baptism, miracles, transfiguration, and resurrection, arose within the community of faith and likewise cannot be used to elicit Jesus' self-consciousness.[12] This then leaves very scant material within the Synoptics from which the Christology or self-understanding of Jesus can be discerned, and what is discerned in this material suggests that in Jesus' own view he was only a prophet.

These views, sketched here very briefly, are nevertheless indicative of broad tendencies in New Testament scholarship and raise difficulties for the church. Why is it that only now, two thousand years after the event, we are at last beginning to understand what Christianity is all about? But, of course, by the word *we* what is in view is only an elite coterie of scholars. There are masses of Christians, all over the world, who have no ability to pick their way through the layers of literary tradition in Scripture and are quite incapable of digressing on the differences between *Historie* and *Geschichte*. Are we to suppose that the real interpretation of Jesus is alone accessible only to a tiny minority in the church—its learned scholars—and that the remainder of Christian believers is excluded from such knowledge? To suppose such a thing is to subject the meaning of Scripture to a far more restrictive "tradition" than anything proposed by Rome in the sixteenth century and to invest our new magisterium—the coterie of learned scholars—with an authority more stifling and far-reaching than the Roman Catholic magisterium ever exercised.

If God gave the Scriptures to the church for its nourishment, which he did, it will follow as an inevitable consequence that he did not intend those Scriptures to be co-opted by a magisterium either ecclesiastical or scholarly. On the contrary, his stated intention is that the believer might exercise his or her priestly obligation in reading and learning of him through his Word. The Scriptures must, therefore, be returned to the church. That being the case, how can we elicit from the Scriptures a Christology which will nourish and guide our faith?

MAKING DISTINCTIONS

To begin with, we need to make two distinctions. First, there is a distinction between self-consciousness and self-understanding. The former term is heavily psychological and has to do with our inner awareness. There are many constituents of this awareness. There are moral and religious impulses, as well as factors that simply belong to our humanness or arise out of our circumstances—such as fear, anxiety, love, joy, satisfaction, a sense of security or a lack of it. We could, of course, pursue this further by saying that the content of our inner awareness derives also from the accumulation of past experience, some of it going back to infancy. Much of this past experience is absorbed into and becomes a part of our subconscious self. And, insofar as the Spirit of God has re-creatively wrought his work within us, no doubt this too becomes a factor in our subterranean self.

The second term, self-understanding, overlaps the first in some ways but is not identical with it. This term is less psychological and more cognitive. It has to do with the value we place on ourselves and the meaning we draw from our lives. Our self-understanding answers the questions as to who we are and why we do what we do. There will be psychological components in our answers, but self-understanding differs from self-consciousness as interpretation does from fact. Our self-consciousness is the raw material upon which we work; what we make of it is our self-understanding.

In terms of the historical Jesus, we can say without equivocation that the Synoptic authors almost completely exclude from view his self-consciousness. Since they hardly discuss his self-consciousness at all, it is fallacious to declare, as Dunn does, that Jesus was not conscious of being divine. This is akin to arguing that the editors of the *Boston Globe* plainly have never heard of cheetahs nor know anything about them, because no mention of these animals can be found in any edition of the newspaper! Jesus' self-understanding, the interpretation he placed on his actions and the meaning he gave to his life, can be discerned without venturing down this slippery path of what exactly his self-consciousness was like.

That, however, leads to a second distinction. It is the distinction between an explicit and an implicit Christology in the case of Jesus himself. What is explicit is what Jesus said about himself by way of assertion, clarification, or interpretation. What is implicit are those gestures or actions which he performed in which he revealed his identity. These actions can be viewed as Christological even if they are not verbally interpreted, provided the action enshrines, proclaims, and reveals who he was. These actions, such as the miracles, presuppose a self-consciousness which is not revealed in the text and underscore the folly of stating unequivocally that Jesus had no divine self-consciousness.

Such a distinction, of course, requires that the "criteria of dissimilarity" be employed in ways that are quite different from those familiar in the writings of the Bultmannian school. Bultmann proposed that material from the Synoptics could be eliminated as inauthentic on two grounds. First, some material was incorporated in the Gospel accounts from rabbinic sources. If, therefore, a saying of Jesus can be paralleled in a rabbinic source, then that saying needs to be eliminated because of its similarity to this source. Second, some material, dated in the post-resurrection period, has found its way into the preresurrection phase of Jesus' life. Similarity with later Christianity, especially in its Palestinian phase, is the ground for its elimination. What remains after this twin procedure is material which is neither rabbinic nor churchly and late. What remains is what is quite unlike anything else.

In a recent development, however, Royce Gruenler's *New Approaches to Jesus and the Gospels* has met this challenge head-on. His reply is not primarily along the lines of the critical presuppositions of the Bultmannian school, although he thinks poorly of the approach as a literary tool, but in terms of the material which this school has identified as indubitably authentic. He argues that even this truncated core of sayings (Luke 11:20; Mark 2:19, 21, 22; 11:16-19; Matt. 13:44-46; Luke 15:11-32; Matt. 18:12, 13; Luke 15:8-10; Matt. 22:1-14; 20:1-6; Luke 18:9-14; 10:29-37; 11:5-8; 18:1-8; Matt. 18:23-33; Luke 9:62; Mark 10:23, 25; Luke 9:60; Matt. 7:13; Luke 14:11; Mark 10:15; Matt. 5:39-41, 44-48; Mark 7:15; Matt. 6:12; Mark 4:3-9, 26-29, 30-32; Luke 11:2; Matt. 8:11) actually yields far more than the Bultmannians have allowed. Using an analysis of the intentionality of the language, rather than being limited by a sterile view of these words from a lexicographical angle, Gruenler shows that they disclose a great deal about Jesus. What they, in fact, reveal is One who knows who he is, who has authority to forgive sin, and who sustains a relation to God the Father which cannot be explained merely in terms of personal confidence or trust.

IMPLICIT CHRISTOLOGY IN THE SYNOPTICS

Jesus interpreted the meaning of his life and revealed the identity of his being when he inaugurated the Kingdom of God. This revelation is, however, largely implicit, for it lies in what he did more than in what he said. But as soon as we have discovered that Jesus saw himself as bringing in the "age to come," that it had come with the Kingdom, that the Kingdom had come with and in himself (Matt. 11:2-6/Luke 7:18-22; Matt. 13:16, 17/Luke 10:23, 24; Matt. 12:41, 42), and when we have discovered the nature of this "age" and Kingdom from the teaching of Jesus himself, we can adduce much about the way he understood himself. This "age," we have seen, was supernatural, could only be established by God himself, would bring blessings and benefits which only God could give, would achieve the overthrow of sin, death, and the devil (which only God could accomplish), and was identified so closely with God himself that no human effort could bring it about and no human resistance turn it back.[13] If Jesus saw himself as the one in whom this kind of Kingdom was being inaugurated, then such a perception is a Christological claim which would be fraudulent and deceptive if Jesus was ignorant of his Godness. It is this self-interpretation within the general rubric of the Kingdom that needs to be pursued further.

First, we need to note the significance of Jesus' baptism. In all the accounts, the Spirit falls on Jesus, thus visibly inaugurating the Messianic age (Matt. 3:13—4:11/Mark 1:9-13/Luke 4:1-13; cf. John 1:32-34), for Jews knew that the coming of the Messianic age would be signaled by the Spirit's outpouring. And insofar as Jesus heard the words of affirmation, "You are my Son, whom I love; with you I am well pleased," the event's implicit Christology became explicit. The words appear to be a combination of Psalm 2:7 and Isaiah 42:1. This is obviously the case for Psalm 2:7, where the LXX rendering is virtually identical with Mark 1:11. The identification with Isaiah 42:1 is less clear. Morna Hooker has made the interesting suggestion[14] that since the appearance of Isaiah 42:1 in Matthew 12:18-21 is much closer to the LXX than it is in 3:17, Matthew was using a translation unknown to us. If this is indeed Isaiah 42:1, then we have in combination a passage from one of the Psalms presenting the conquering King and one from the group of passages in Isaiah picturing the Servant. In the temptation narratives which follow, each assault is aimed at severing these roles. Jesus is offered the Kingly crown by a path other than that which the Servant would have to tread.

The broader relationship of Jesus and the Spirit, visibly inaugurated at the baptism, unfortunately is not clarified a great deal in the Synoptics. Indeed, some scholars such as C. K. Barrett[15] have questioned the authenticity of these texts linking Jesus and the Spirit (Matt. 3:11, 12, 17/Mark 1:8-12/Luke 3:16, 21; Matt. 4:1/Mark 1:12/Luke 4:1;

Matt. 1:18, 20; 12:18-21; Luke 1:35; cf. Luke 2:25-27; 10:21). Such an association, it is argued, would have betrayed the "Messianic Secret." This assumes that Jesus under no circumstances would ever have allowed that he was Messiah; that is simply not the case. Cullmann has contended that Jesus was reticent to own the title Messiah publicly lest his role be understood in a nationalistic fashion. Privately, however, he did allow the use of the title and provided the proper meaning for it. Furthermore, the sparseness of the references to the Spirit in the Synoptics bespeak their authenticity. By the time these Gospels were written, Paul's letters were beginning to circulate, and they provide an enormous quarry in some one hundred and twenty references to the Spirit, from which pieces might have been taken to augment what is in the Synoptics. This did not happen.

What is present, however, is enough to declare the arrival of Messiah. In one passage in particular, Jesus interpreted the doing of his mighty works in the context of the Spirit's arrival. The "finger" of God by which these works were done (Luke 11:20) was synonomous with the Holy Spirit (Matt. 12:28).

That Jesus realized that he was bringing with him the age of Messiah was, from the time of the baptism at least, beyond question. It was visibly signaled and audibly declared. And the Synoptic authors plainly wanted their readers to understand this. Recent studies on Matthew, for example, have shown that there is a conceptual integrity that ties the birth narrative and the baptism together. The overriding truth Matthew wants understood by his readers from the story of Jesus' birth, says Jack Kingsbury, is "that Jesus, who is the royal Messiah, is uniquely the Son of God."[16] Repeatedly Matthew stresses the promise/fulfillment motif (1:22; 2:15, 17, 23). Some scholars, it is true, have argued that the Old Testament prophecies created the narrative, but it is much more likely that the narrative simply used those prophecies (Isa. 7:14; Mic. 5:2; Hos. 11:1; Jer. 31:15), for if these prophecies are removed, the narrative remains completely intact.[17]

The words at Jesus' baptism are, of course, reaffirmed at the Transfiguration (Matt. 17:1-8/Mark 9:2-8/Luke 9:28-36). In recent years this event has been the cause of considerable discussion, a significant body of opinion feeling that it was a later creation which was inserted into the narrative and bears the postresurrection understanding of Jesus' identity. This argument assumes, of course, that Jesus had no consciousness of divinity or preexistence and that in all likelihood he was simply a prophet; this is not an assumption that stands up to the evidence. Furthermore, the Transfiguration fits naturally and logically in the narrative. It follows Peter's confession of Jesus' Messiahship (Matt. 16:16/Mark 8:27-30/Luke 9:18-20), and the same elements emerge as we have noted were present at the baptism. Jesus' Kingly glory is this time visibly represented in his bodily transformation, but coupled with this the need to suffer is explicitly developed (Matt. 16:21-23/Mark 9:31, 32/Luke 9:22). What is new, of course, is the discussion with Moses and Elijah (representing the law and the prophets), whose importance Jesus transcended. He is presented as being superior to all the Old Testament forerunners because in his person he is uniquely different.

Second, this sense of Godness must have lain beneath Jesus' actions in confronting and overcoming Satan, for this is a work that only God can do. Jesus presents himself in this role in Mark 3:23-27 (Matt. 12:25-29), and what is of interest is the contrast between himself as the "stronger one" (ὁ ἰσχυρόῖερός) who bears the Spirit (cf. Mark 1:7, 8) and the "strong one" (ὁ ἰσχυρός) who is lord of evil and is conquered. The older view that the unclean spirits were seen in an animalistic sense by Jesus has been discredited; he views the unclean spirits as subject to Satan, and each exorcism is a victorious confrontation with Satan. (Cf.. Matt. 10:8; 17:14-20/Mark 9:14-29/Luke 9:37-43; Mark 6:12, 13/Matt. 10:1/Luke 9:1). Jesus' purposes could not be frustrated by evil (Matt. 16:28).

Third, the affirmation of this divinity is implicit in the miracles he performed. The healing miracles, which cause fewer difficulties in our contemporary culture than do the nature miracles, are regularly presented as part of that salvation of the whole person which Messiah would bring (Luke 7:22, 23). Indeed, the verb σωζω, "to save," is used of these healings (Matt. 9:21, 22/Mark 5:28-34/Luke 8:43-48; Matt. 14:36/Mark 6:56; Mark 10:52/Luke 18:42, 43; Luke 7:50; 8:36). These healings were the visible indications of the presence of the supernatural Rule of God coming in and through Jesus. Indeed, even nature itself felt the impact of its arrival. It is not possible to explore all the grounds on which the nature miracles have been disputed. The Gospel writers themselves seemed to be in no doubt, however, that miracles were the result of divine power and sometimes referred to them as "powers" (Matt. 11:20-23; Mark 5:30; 6:2). Jesus was the One in whom such power resided from birth (cf. Luke 1:35) and in whom such power was native. "Jesus accomplished mighty works, to which adequate parallels have not been found," concludes Vincent Taylor, "with an ease and certainty which bespeak a consciousness transcending the ordinary powers of human personality."[18]

Fourth, his relationship to the law, so sacred to the Jewish mind, bespeaks a role more than that which was merely prophetic. This is especially evident in the Sermon on the Mount. The questions as to whether Matthew utilized a variety of sources (such as Mark, Q, and M), and whether the utterances of this "sermon" were given in a variety of contexts and then gathered together, either by the church or Matthew, need not engage us, for it is simply Jesus' awareness of himself implicit in these sayings which is important. Particularly significant is the section referred to as the Antithesis (Matt. 5:21-48). There seems to be a consensus that while Jesus was criticizing oral tradition, which is especially evident in 5:43b, his intent was actually to deepen the application of the moral law. This becomes plain later when issues of the law are debated (Matt. 12:1-4; 15:1-20; 19:1-21). Indeed, the authority to so interpret the law may have led Matthew to present Jesus as the New Moses. This is what W. D. Davies has seen[19] in the parallel which is drawn between the births of Moses and Jesus (in danger and obscurity, and in contexts which are hostile—Pharaoh and Herod—which both result in flight, in the one case out of Egypt and in the other into it). Certainly Jesus was seen as having, and must have known that he had, amazing authority (Mark 1:22; 11:28), for it was that authority intrinsic to the Rule of the Kingdom, which he was establishing.

Finally, we need to note the sense of purpose with which he spoke of his death. In his own assessment, this death was not a mere martyrdom, but the vocation of the Servant through whose suffering and service the Reign of God would be decisively established. The critical problems associated with this title and others related to it will be addressed in the following chapter, but there seems little doubt that he went to the cross believing, as Taylor puts it, that it was "an inalienable part of his Messianic vocation." The Synoptics report his declaration that he "must" suffer (δεῖ as used in Mark 8:31; Matt. 16:21; Luke 9:22; cf. Luke 24:26). This could, of course, be seen as a shrewd estimate on Jesus' part as to what the outcome of Jewish hostility would be; indeed, some scholars have proposed this. It should be noted, however, that it runs contrary to what Jesus elsewhere declares regarding the voluntary nature of his sufferings (e.g., Mark 10:45; cf. John 10:17, 18), and it makes him the victim of his circumstances, which is precisely the opposite conclusion from the one the Gospel writers want us to draw.[21] He went to the cross freely, in fulfillment of his Messianic vocation, and it was with this purpose in mind that he offered forgiveness to fallen sinners even before he had gone to the cross. His actions, in this regard, had an implied Christological significance, for who can forgive sin but God alone? (Mark 2:7/Luke 5:21).

The question of whether Jesus was human or not is not frequently addressed directly either by Jesus himself or the Synoptic authors. Both he and they assumed that he was. Only later did this become a matter requiring specific affirmation.

Jesus' humanity was implicit in his actions, and it was affirmed in what he said in conjunction with other matters. It is most vividly evident in Mark and least in Matthew. Jesus speaks of his body, head, hands, feet, blood, and bones (Matt. 26:12; Mark 14:8; Luke 24:39; 7:44-46; Matt. 26:28/Mark 14:24/Luke 22:20). Luke in particular emphasizes the reality of his body. One notes the insistence in Acts on the corporeality of the Ascension, for it is visible and seen with human eyes

(Acts 1:9). This same insistence lies in Luke's Gospel. Luke 23:55 modifies Mark 15:47 to indicate that they saw a *body*. The statement in Luke 24:22, 23, found only in this Gospel, makes the same point about a *body*. In Luke 24:36-43, also found only in this Gospel, Jesus denies that he is a phantom and points to *flesh and bones*. And there is no doubt from the structure of the Gospel that Luke is insisting on the unbroken continuity of the human Jesus who turned toward Jerusalem in Luke 9:51 with the one who was crucified, rose from the dead, and ascended.[22] It is throughout the same Jesus.

Jesus is additionally portrayed as exhibiting all of the human emotions and characteristics. In Mark he is moved by pity (1:41) and compassion (8:2), he is distressed (7:34; 8:12), angry (3:5), annoyed (10:14), surprised (6:6), disappointed (8:17; 9:19), hungry (11:12), and asks questions (6:38; 8:29; 9:21; 10:18). In Luke we see him subject to his parents (2:51), regularly going to synagogue (4:16), praying (6:12), being tempted (4:2, 13; 22:28), joyful (10:21), distressed (22:15), and compassionate (7:36-50).

The sinlessness of Jesus' humanity[23] is likewise implied throughout the narratives but nowhere explicitly asserted or defended. The reason for this initially appears to have been the secrecy with which the matter of Jesus' conception was treated. There is no indication that anyone outside the immediate family circle was knowledgeable about it (cf. Matt. 13:55), and perhaps even the brothers of Jesus were ignorant. When Matthew and Luke came to record this event, they treated it with the utmost delicacy, for it was susceptible of misunderstanding. It is still misunderstood. W. Pannenberg and Emil Brunner, for example, reject it, as do many others, because of its similarity to the pagan myths of gods coming to earth and mating with beautiful women.

It would be a mistake, however, to see the accounts of Jesus' conception as the biological explanation of the Incarnation. Luke asserts that the Holy Spirit "overshadowed" Mary (Luke 1:35; cf. Matt. 1:20); επισκιάζω, used here, is again used in his account of the Transfiguration (Luke 9:34). To Jewish minds, this almost certainly pointed back to the divine cloud which covered the Israelites' camp in the desert. This cloud was the mysterious presence of God visually presented. Perhaps we also have a parallel here to the creation account. In both, the Spirit is active; in both, he imparts life. What emerges from the Spirit's creative work in the beginning was called "good"; what emerges from this work in Mary is called "holy."

What this affirms, then, is that Jesus was born without the involvement of a human father and that his humanity was created through Mary. Such a conception did not itself guarantee Jesus' divinity, although it was certainly compatible with it; what it affirmed was that Jesus' humanity had a supernatural origin. The reason that Jesus was not sinful had less to do with the mode of his conception than it did with the uniqueness of his being. It was because he was divine that he did not sin, and his taking of flesh through Mary in this fashion was a taking of that kind of flesh in which he, as God, could be in union. There was, therefore, no reason to explore the circumstances of his conception in order to explain his sinlessness if, implicitly and explicitly, he had made it clear who he was.

EXPLICIT CHRISTOLOGY IN THE SYNOPTICS

Some of the strongest explicit statements which reveal Jesus' identity are the titles which he used of himself or allowed to be used of him. These titles, to be examined presently, put in a formal way the unique relationship that pertained between the Father and the Son; but this relationship was also expressed in other ways which were often less formal and probably are more important.

This relationship is powerfully exhibited in Jesus' use of *Abba* in prayer. In each of the Synoptics, Jesus addresses God by this Aramaic term (Mark 14:36/Matt. 26:39/Luke 22:42; Matt. 6:9/Luke 11:2; Matt. 11:25, 26/Luke 10:21; Luke 23:34, 46; Matt. 26:42;/cf. John 11:41; 12:27, 28; 17:1, 5, 11, 21, 24, 25). This is so striking that even Gentile churches, despite their Greek culture, retained its use (Gal. 4:6; Rom. 8:15), although the employment of this word is carefully circumscribed and no human may be so addressed (Matt. 23:9). Having surveyed contemporary Jewish literature, Jeremias concluded that "there is *no analogy at all* in the whole of Jewish prayer for God being addressed as Abba."[24] The reason for this was the fear of and aversion to improper familiarity with Yahweh, whose power and holiness is revealed throughout the Old Testament. Yet Jesus, with utmost regularity, addresses God by this term of intimacy and familiarity. And what is probably as important, he distinguishes his use of *Abba* from that of the disciples and does not associate himself with the disciples in saying commonly, "our Father." The disciples can use this term, Paul explains, because they have entered into a relationship with God the Father, through the work of Jesus, by the ministry of the Spirit. It is, then, a term which strikingly affirms the uniqueness of Jesus, although it does not further explain that uniqueness.

The same point, however, emerges in his cry of exultation in Matthew 11:25-27 (Luke 10:21, 22). The form critical view is that this general section in Matthew arose from the needs of the early church, 11:25-30 contrasting the freedom of Christian faith with the bondage of Judaism, the lightness of the yoke in the one with the intolerable burden of it in the other. These contrasts might indeed have occurred to Matthew, for the setting of 11:25-27 is different in Luke where the call to those who are burdened and weary is omitted. The supposition that it is ecclesiastical creation, however, is flimsy and unfounded.

Jeremias has contended that this was parabolic language reflecting the uniquely intimate knowledge of Father and Son.[25] Through it, Jesus exults that all things have been delivered to him. The use of the verb, παρεδόθη, may suggest, although it does not absolutely require, a pretemporal act.[26] The consequences of this deliverance have already been made plain by Matthew. Jesus has demonstrated his authority over Satan (4:1-11), nature (8:23-27), disease (9:1-8, 20-22), life and death (9:18, 19, 23-26). Yet here Jesus advances even beyond this to claim that the truth about himself as Son is known by his Father, and that he alone knows the truth of his Father's redeeming love. Implied at least is the thought that as the Son has revealed to others what he knows of the Father, so the Father has revealed to the Son what he knows of him.

This remarkable utterance—which is not, as some have contended, a bolt out of the Johannine blue—links naturally with what Jesus said elsewhere of the *parousia*. No one knew the time of its occurrence, he said, "not even the angels in heaven, nor the Son, but only the Father" (Matt. 24:36/Mark 13:32). During the period of Arianism, this text caused serious problems for the upholders of Jesus' divinity. Surely, it was said, if Jesus were God he would have known the time of his *parousia*. What we have here, however, is Jesus' view of himself presented in embryonic form, and his ignorance regarding the judgment does not negate his divine claim. This is the only instance in Mark of the use of "Son," the only other one in Matthew being 11:27. Jesus' standing is said to be above the angels. To a Jewish mind this carried an unmistakable divine claim. And this is consistent with what he says everywhere else. The angels are his, his to serve him in the Kingdom and his to serve as agents in the judgment (Matt. 24:31; 22:30; Mark 8:38). The muting of that knowledge which was God's by its union with that which was human is also preserved in the text. Jesus plainly is the central figure in the judgment. This itself is a divine claim (cf. Luke 21:36; 2 Thess. 1:9, 10; 2 Tim. 1:12; 4:8), but the knowledge of its exact time is muted.

It is necessary, finally to look briefly at the parable of the wicked husbandmen (Matt. 21:33-44/Mark 12:1-11/Luke 20:9-18), which has also become the object of considerable scholarly scrutiny in recent years. First, it has been argued by some, such as D. Nineham,[27] that the references to the Son were added later because it is improbable that Jesus would have known in advance about his death and the fall of Jerusalem (supposedly alluded to in Mark 12:9 and parallels); it is also felt improbable that he would have made Messianic claims in the light of Mark 1:44; 5:43; 7:36; and 9:9, 10. If regard is paid, however, to Mark 8:31; 10:45; 14:25-31, it will be seen that Jesus was well aware of his imminent death, and the appeal to the supposed need to be completely secretive about his Messianic status is hardly an element we encounter in Matthew or Luke. Second, it is argued that this parable was an allegory through which the early Christian community composed an attack on Judaism.[28] But it would be odd, if this were so, that there would be no mention of the Son's resurrection which, in terms of the polemic, would have been the ultimate vindication of Christian faith.[29]

The wiser course is to see this parable as one given by Jesus in which some of the improbable details of the story are inserted to heighten the teaching on the astounding patience of God. There are, to be sure, allegorical elements in the story. The vineyard stands for Israel (cf. Isa. 5:1-7), the owner for God, the assorted servants for the prophets, the husbandmen for the Jewish authorities, and the son for Jesus who is heir of all (cf. Heb. 1:1-14). The unique relationship of the son is, however, evident. He comes to the Jewish nation in the same way as had the prophets, and they treat him as poorly or worse than they had the prophets; but they are now dealing with a son and not a servant. The son, in fact, is Messiah. In Rabbinic literature the stone of Psalm 118:22, 23 sometimes had this connotation, and it is difficult to avoid that inference in this setting. So memorable was this self-interpretation by Jesus that the stone image recurred repeatedly in early Christian thought, both biblical (Acts 4:11, 12; 1 Pet. 2:6-8; Rom. 9:33) and patristic.

The reason Jesus' self-interpretation, be it implicit or explicit, has proved problematic for some has often been the assumption that the meanings he assigned to his actions and words could be no different from those which his religious milieu would impose upon them. This is not an assumption which can be justified. We have to allow, C. F. D. Moule has said, "for the sheer originality of Jesus," and this includes not only "the originality of what Jesus may have said, but also of what he was."[30]

What he was, however, has to be deduced in large measure from what he did; the ontological is hidden in the functional, but it is by no means obscured. He can *act* as Messiah in the Synoptics because he *is* Messiah; his actions disclose his identity. With him comes that Reign which is God's alone to inaugurate, whose arrival is signaled by the presence of the Spirit, the retreat of Satan, the overthrow of sin, sickness, and death. He carries with him authority to teach, power to judge, a capacity to love supremely, and the right to forgive. "That Jesus understood his ministry in terms of Messiahship," concludes Richard Longenecker, "is the underlying presupposition in the narratives concerning the baptism, the temptation in the wilderness, the transfiguration, and the 'triumphant entry'; and it is implicit in his controversy with the Pharisees regarding the nature of Messiahship (Matt. 22:41-46; Mark 12:35-37; Luke 20:41-44)."[31]

Jesus' self-interpretation as divine and the demonstration of his humanity, however, stand side by side in the Synoptics without further exploration. He reveals himself as all that God is, and he reveals himself within a humanity that is all that we are, barring our sinfulness; yet the interconnections between the divine and human are not examined. Indeed, they do not appear to have been matters of great curiosity to the Synoptic writers, either at a theological level or in terms of the psychology and self-consciousness of such a person.

THE JOHANNINE LITERATURE

The critical problems associated with John's Gospel in particular have produced a large and diverse literature, a survey of which would take us far beyond the parameters of this brief study.[32] Nevertheless, some of the assumptions beneath the present treatment of John's thought need to be declared even if they cannot be defended.

There can be no doubt that Jesus is presented differently in John as compared with the Synoptics. Important incidents recorded in the Synoptics are omitted in John's Gospel, and his Gospel contains long discourses completely omitted in the Synoptics. The Synoptics picture Jesus in his public ministry, but John largely omits the public teaching. Apart from Jesus' disputations with the Jews regarding his identity, the teaching is mostly given privately to individuals or when he is with his disciples and away from the crowds.[33] These differences were noted early in the life of the church. According to Eusebius, Clement of Alexandria declared that John, "conscious that the outward facts had been set forth in the [Synoptic] Gospels, was urged on by his disciples, and, divinely moved by the Spirit, composed a spiritual Gospel."[34] It is in the contrast Clement made between "the bodily facts" (τα βωματικὰ) of the Synoptics and the "spiritual" interpretation (πυευματικὸν) of John that the problem lies.

In recent years this perception has led to the assumption that John's Gospel is a free-floating creation which is out of relation with the Synoptics both from a literary and a theological point of view. This assumption was in part challenged by C. H. Dodd's seminal volume *Historical Tradition and the Fourth Gospel,* for he argued that behind John is an old and historically reliable tradition which has given to the Gospel substantial historical authenticity. Dodd nevertheless still felt that the Gospel had been composed independently of the Synoptics.

Taken in balance, the position argued by C. K. Barrett—that John's Gospel in its order and its language does indeed show a knowledge of Mark[35]—has plausibility. It also makes the argument that John's Gospel is a tendentious creation much more difficult to sustain.

The differences in style and idiom between the Synoptics and John, assuming that there is this connection with Mark, might possibly be explained by the different methods of their composition. In a radical, but not implausible, new departure, some scholars have argued that rabbis taught their disciples to learn by verbatim memorization.[36] They have suggested that Jesus himself appears to have utilized this method, which would account for the literary similarities in the Synoptics. At some later date, it is postulated, the apostles themselves then composed the narrative sections, and the whole was memorized and passed on by methodical oral delivery. This formalized account would appear to have been in John's mind, or even before him in some written form, and to this he added his own reflections and recollections in a separate Gospel.

But this still leaves open the question as to how much license or liberty he allowed himself in composing his work. Did he read back into Jesus' early life an understanding that had only come to him subsequent to the resurrection? And did he ascribe a consciousness to Jesus which was only proper in a postresurrection state? There are three observations which are in order with respect to this issue.

First, the overall historical reliability of John is now widely recognized, and his reporting of minute topographical and factual matters has been vindicated. It would betray an improbable inconsistency if John did not work with the same degree of accuracy in his writing about Jesus.

Second, in the Gospel itself John shows that he is concerned to distinguish between events which happened and the significance which may or may not have been drawn from them. There was often a large difference between what Jesus said and what the disciples understood his saying or teaching to mean (e.g., John 2:18-22; 7:37-39; 12:16; 21:18-23). The argument that John allowed later faith to create or influence earlier "history" seems, in consequence, most unlikely.

Third, the presentation of Jesus in John's Gospel is compatible with that in the Synoptics. The compatibility lies in the fact that Jesus' self-interpretation, his identity, is unchanged as we move from the Synoptics into John. What is added in John are elements of Jesus' self-consciousness which are not explicit in the Synoptics. It is not unreasonable to think, however, that they are implicit in his self-understanding. The supposition that we move from a "low" Christology in the Synoptics to a "high" one in John, from adoptionism to an incarnational model, would only be viable if the implicit Christology of the Synoptics could be disallowed. But that aspect of the Gospel record cannot be disallowed. What we are looking at, therefore, is the process whereby John explicates what had been assumed but not stated in the Synoptics. We might speak of it, not as a process of evolution, but as one of development. We are left with a fuller picture of Jesus, but not with a different Christology.

Since it was John's stated purpose to present Jesus in such a way that outsiders to the Christian faith might have grounds for believing in his divinity (John 20:30, 31), the study of the Gospel's Christology cannot be pursued apart from a knowledge of the Gospel's structure. It would border on the irresponsible to attempt, as Dunn does, to elicit its Christology from texts which are isolated from the whole.

In this regard, it has become clear in recent years that the main body of Christological material runs from 2:1—12:50.[37] The prologue (1:1-18) serves as an introduction to it, and chapters 13—21 are a compressed account of Jesus' farewell, crucifixion, and resurrection. The main section is arranged around seven miraculous "signs" (2:1-11; 4:46-54; 5:2-9; 6:1-14; 6:16-21; 9:1-7; 11:1-44),[38] before or after each of which are seven discourses which draw out the spiritual significance of these "signs" (3:1-36; 4:1-42; 5:19-47; 6:22-65; 7:1-52; 8:12-59; 10:1-42). Interspersed within these discourses are the seven resounding "I am" sayings (15:1; 14:6; 10:7; 6:35; 8:12; 10:11; 11:25). "John's center," writes Stephen Smalley, "is to be found in seven signs, bound together with discourses and text-like sayings which expound various aspects of the theme of eternal life as that is to be found in and through Jesus Christ."[39] Thus his deeds and his words, the "signs" and their discourses, function and person are again presented, as they were in the Synoptics, as belonging intrinsically to one another.

And, as we have already noted, this Gospel shares with the Synoptics the conviction that Jesus must be interpreted within an eschatological framework.[40] The form in which the Jewish two-age formulation enters John's Gospel and epistles is in the words, "eternal life." Not only is this "life" to be found in and through Jesus (John 1:4; 5:26; 1 John 5:11, 12), but he himself is "life" (John 11:25; 14:6; cf. John 5:26; 1 John 5:20). This "life," eternally with the Father, historically manifested in Jesus (1 John 1:1-3), entered into by those who receive his "word" about himself, is none other than that supernatural "age to come" which cannot be entered except through him in whom it arrives. Thus are Jesus' words the very words of God (John 3:34; 8:14; 14:10), and that is why they bring "life" (John 5:24; 6:68; 8:51).[41] What kind of a person is it, then, who brings with him that "life" which is "eternal"?

In Johannine studies, at least two quite distinct lines of interpretation have emerged in answer to this question, each believing that it holds the key to John's Christology. On the one hand, some scholars have focused their attention on the flesh/glory paradox and examined the mutual relations of these components. On the other hand, a newer line of thought has approached the person of Christ through the role or function he performs in the Gospel. These lines of thought have often followed their interests independently of one another, but in fact neither is complete or satisfactory without the other.

The magnetic pole to which much of John's Christological thought is attracted is undoubtedly that of δοξα. Jesus said he was from above (John 6:33), but left God's presence (John 6:62; 8:38; 10:36), and his love (John 17:24). As such he had eternally preexisted (John 8:42, 58; 17:8). It was from this realm that he descended (John 3:13; 6:33, 38; 10:36), and it was from this realm that he had been "sent." This thought occurs forty-two times in the Gospel[42] and has led some to think of John's Christology as one of mission. He was "sent" into the world (John 3:17; 9:39; 10:36; 12:46; 16:28; 18:37), and he had come into the world from God (John 3:31; 8:42; 13:3; 16:27, 28; 17:8).[43] He is, in short, the unique Son. The new terminology we find, both in the Gospel and first epistle, is μονογενής (John 1:14, 18; 3:16, 18; 1 John 4:9). It should be rendered "unique" (cf. Luke 7:12; 8:42; 9:38; Heb. 11:17).[44] This word does not itself require a metaphysical framework, although it was not incompatible with a metaphysical understanding, especially that provided by Jesus himself when he claimed that "before Abraham was born, I am!" (John 8:58).

There is, however, another magnetic pole to which John's thought is drawn, and that is the entry of this unique Son into "flesh" (John 1:14; cf. 19:17, 34, 37). But the question that his portrait presents is what kind of σάρξ this is. On the surface, this is not a question that arises naturally from the narrative. After all, John speaks of him as ἄνθρωπος more frequently even than do the Synoptics (e.g., John 7:46; 9:11, 16; 10:33; 11:47, 50, 51; 18:14; 19:5). And he pictures Jesus as displaying the full range of human emotions and needs, such as weariness and thirst (John 4:6; 19:28), affection (John 11:5), anger (John 11:33, 38), joy (John 15:11), and love (John 13:34; 15:9-13). Jesus speaks of his own body (John 6:53-56), albeit in a context which is not decisive in this matter, and of his soul (John 12:27). His sinlessness may be in view in John 14:30.

In the epistles, John insists that this enfleshing is a permanent condition, a point upon which Luke had also insisted. This is the implication of the perfect participle, ἐληλυθότα in 1 John 4:2. This union of divine and human should lead us to the affirmation that Jesus is the Christ (1 John 2:22; 5:1) and that he is the Son (1 John 2:23; 5:5).

This overall insistence, however, has not answered the question for some as to what kind of σάρξ this is. Käsemann, in fact, has recently revived the older idea that here we have a Christology which draws from the Hellenistic beliefs of "divine men." John nowhere speaks of a Θεος ἀυηρ, but it is unmistakable, says Käsemann, that his portrait is one of "a god striding over the earth."

The problem is that John is supremely interested in the way the divine δοξα shines through the veil of σάρξ and resides in it.[45] The thing which interests John is not the processes of growth, nor is it the way in which Jesus slowly revealed his identity, but rather it is the *truth* about Jesus. Everything is of secondary importance in comparison to this. The Synoptics reveal the process and are seen as minimizing Jesus' knowledge of his divinity; John reveals his divine glory and is seen to be minimizing his humanity. In fact, the supposed adoptionist Christology of the Synoptics is but a concealed "epiphany" Christology whose concealment is stripped away by John. But we still need to inquire whether John clarifies for us any further how that heavenly and divine δοξα shines through the earthly and human 6αρξ. Is there a masking of the divine by the human? Does incarnation require a reduction either of the divine nature or of the divine prerogatives?

The answer to these questions is both incomplete and paradoxical. On the one hand, John is insistent that that Godness which was the Son's is not diminished in any important or essential way by the union with flesh. To see the Son is to see the Father (John 14:9; cf. 8:19; 12:45), for the Father is "in" the Son and the Son is "in" the Father (10:38; 14:10). He has the authority to judge (5:22), to give life which is eternal (5:24, 40; 6:27; 10:10, 28), to give commandments (13:34; cf. 14:21; 15:17), to answer prayer (14:14; 15:7). He personally meets the deepest human need (4:13, 14; 6:27, 35; 7:37, 38; 8:36), so that faith in him is the same as faith in God (12:44; 14:1). He and the Father are one (10:30), which the Jews interpreted as blasphemy. Affirmations such as these leave no doubt, says Taylor, that for John "Christ is the divine Son of God in a relationship which is fully ethical and spiritual, but also one of being and nature."[46]

On the other hand, there is a note of subordination in some of Jesus' utterances. The Father "sent" and "sanctified" him (John 3:17; 17:18); he says he is able to do nothing by himself and that the Father is greater than he is (5:30; 14:28). There appear to be two ideas, never quite separated, which are part of this relationship. On the one hand, the idea that he "descended" and came from "above" suggests something close to Paul's teaching on the humiliation and self-emptying of the Son (Phil. 2:5-11). This aspect of his subordination would therefore be of limited duration and would cease when he resumed his former glory. On the other hand, it is implied that there is an eternal priority of Father to Son in which the Father appears to initiate action. This relational priority will remain unchanged, presumably, even after the Son has resumed his glory (cf. 1 Cor. 15:24-28). A functional subordination does not, however, require an ontological subordination, for in the fellowship of love, unity of being and subordination of role are entirely compatible.

Perhaps, then, John has brought us to the brink of mystery in his searching for the divine δοξα which is seen through the veil of 6αρξ. We can go no further than to say that for him, the overiding Christian conviction was that in Jesus the divine and the human coincide.[47] Because this was so, Jesus functions in the Gospel as God. He judges, forgives, calls people to himself, works miracles, and gives commands. But because his function was to save, he gave his exegesis of God within a humanity whose connections with the sinners he came to save were necessary.

The relation between Jesus and the Holy Spirit is presented from a viewpoint that is somewhat different from that in the Synoptics. The intertwined relations of Son and Spirit are, if anything, heightened. Nothing is made of the baptism (John 1:32) as the occasion when the eschatological and Messianic age began, witnessed by the arrival of the Spirit. And little is made of the Spirit until the farewell discourse (cf. 3:5, 34; 7:39). In that discourse, in the Paraclete sayings (14:15-17, 26; 15:26; 16:5-15), the situation changes, and without these passages Christian thought could well have developed along binitarian rather than Trinitarian lines. The blessings of the Messianic age are brought by the παράκλητος, who is not so much an advocate or intercessor on behalf of the accused (cf. 1 John 2:1)—the common understanding of this word in rabbinic literature—but a helper and sustainer. His function is almost as the *alter ego* of Jesus, unveiling the meaning of Jesus and his words to the disciples, and unveiling the reality of sin and judgment in the world.

There are in John significant new perceptions of Jesus. The prologue, probably written last as an essential summary of John's Christology and therefore capable of serving as an introduction to the whole Gospel, takes the place of the birth stories in the Synoptics. The unique relationship of the Son and Father, of which only glimpses were seen in the Synoptics, is a constant factor in John's account and is explored much more deeply; the miracles in the Synoptics are seen as indicative of the arrival of the "end-time," whereas in John they testify to Jesus' divine Messiahship and are propaedeutic to faith. Yet in John, as in the Synoptics, Jesus is reticent to accept the title of Messiah (John 10:24; cf. 1:41, 45). He uses or accepts it only twice (17:3; 4:26), and John only uses it twice (1:17; 20:31). It is a reticence born, not out of self-ignorance on Jesus' part, but out of fear of misunderstanding. Also, the role of the Holy Spirit as witness to the arrival of the Messianic age is passed over in John, but the intertwined relationship of Jesus and the Spirit is deepened.

These differences, however, are those which result from different authorial purposes, different reading constituencies, and different conceptual tools. As to the identity of Jesus himself, in John there is neither departure from nor advance beyond what is found in the Synoptics. In Jesus, we meet that man in whom the divine resides, coheres, and inheres in permanent union, that channel through whom the "age to come" has already penetrated the fabric of our earthly existence.

THE EPISTLES

In addition to the distinctive approach of John, there are two other angles of vision within our epistolary literature which stand apart. They are provided by the Epistle to the Hebrews and by Paul as he worked through the variety of situations in which he was called to address matters of a Christological nature. Although the rest of the epistles are important in their own right, they do not offer substantially different perspectives on the person of Christ and therefore, due to limitations of space, cannot be considered here.

It is not uncommon in contemporary scholarship, as has been noted, to encounter the supposition that in the New Testament we have a series of Christologies which can be graduated according to their profundity or lack of it. The lowest point is usually identified as being in the Synoptic authors, and the highest point of elevation is seen to be in John. The Pauline epistles and that to the Hebrews are then seen as rungs lifting us from the less profound to the more profound. In the process, it is usually claimed, we move from that kind of Christology in which the flesh became Word to one in which the Word became flesh.

The groundwork which is laid for this developmental conception in the Synoptics has already been demonstrated to be false, and it would not be difficult to show that the supposed steps in the evolution, as elaborated for example in R. H. Fuller, owe more to twentieth-century assumptions of both an epistemological and literary nature than to first-century facts. It is therefore wiser to proceed on the understanding, as C. F. Moule has put it, that the New Testament authors stand on the same platform although they argue from different corners of it. It is two of these "corners" which we must now examine.

The Epistle to the Hebrews

"The common pattern of New Testament eschatology," writes C. K. Barrett, "is in Hebrews made uncommonly clear. God has begun to fulfill his ancient promises; the dawn of the new age has broken, though the full day has not yet come."[48] The fulfillment of promise and the coming of the new age occur in and with the exalted Son when he assumed lowly flesh at Bethlehem and then died on the cross at Calvary. This is the common motif that binds together the Synoptics, the Johannine corpus, Hebrews and, as we shall see, the Pauline epistles. If the language of the Kingdom is predominantly that of Jesus, the reality which it describes—the arrival of "the age to come"—is central to the thought of all of the apostolic interpreters of Jesus. It is, in fact, the common category by which he is understood.

For the writer of Hebrews, the "age to come" is already being tasted and experienced (6:4, 5) by believers, for the "world to come" (2:5) is one in which God's Son is ruling, and that Rule has now begun in the lives of believers. As in the Synoptics, so in Hebrews it is assumed that the beginning of the Rule carries with it the certainty of its conclusion, and therefore it is even possible to say that this "age" has reached its consummation (9:26). It is true that not all of the opposition to God's Rule has yet been quelled (2:8, 9; 10:13, 14); but, the author argues, the promised deliverance of God has begun. As a consequence, believers can now approach "the heavenly Jerusalem" (12:22-24) and have entered into that eschatological "rest" of which the weekly sabbath is a type (4:9). These are images of a salvation which is eternal (5:9), a redemption which is eternal (9:12), an inheritance which is eternal (9:15); and all of these benefits are secured through the covenant which is itself eternal (13:20), spiritual realities which are present already in the historical process.

Who, then, could bring into time this saving Rule of God by which the enemies sin, death, and the devil would be overthrown (cf. 2:14; 10:27; 12:18-24)? Hebrews unabashedly declares, in terms which are strikingly vivid, that this could only be achieved by the coming of the Son from "above" into our world and specifically into that kind of "flesh" which is also ours, within and through which he worked his conquest. "The conception of the two ages on which the primitive gospel rested," concludes E. F. Scott, "is fundamental also to the Epistle."[49]

The epistle opens, as Bornkamm has demonstrated, with a hymnal fragment in which Christ's preexistence, incarnation, atonement, and exaltation are recounted[50] (cf. 1 Tim. 3:16; Phil. 2:11). Indeed, the language of 1:3 so strongly attests Christ's divinity that on this ground alone the Arians refused to recognize the authenticity of Hebrews. Certainly the coming of the Son, it is declared, makes visible in the historical process, in space and time, what was otherwise completely invisible, and in this sense he is spoken of as the "representation" of God. What becomes visible, however, is the reality of the heavenly existence. In language strongly reminiscent of John's "above"/"below" contrasts (e.g., John 3:13; 6:62) or even the development of this in Paul's descent/ascent motif of Philippians 2:5-11 (cf. also 1 Pet. 3:18-22), Hebrews drives home the distinction between "heavenly"[51] and earthly existence (9:11, 23; 12:18, 22) and insists that by nature and by right the Son belongs in heaven and at God's "right hand" (1:3; 8:1; 10:12; 12:2).

Indeed, in straining to sharpen the distinction between the earthly and the heavenly, the epistle's author appears to employ Platonic or, at the least, Philonic language in 10:1. There he contrasts the law as "shadow" with salvation as the real thing and argues that the functioning of this law, in its prescription of gifts, occurs in a sanctuary which is but the "copy" of that which is real, which is in heaven, where Jesus' saving work is effectual (8:5, 6; cf. 9:23-28). At the very least, he must have been aware of the way his language would be understood, but he was unconcerned about readers mistaking the line of his thought provided they grasped how large was the distinction, how infinite was the qualitative distinction, between that which is earthly and that which is heavenly. But his thought was probably less Philonic than apocalyptic, and the "shadows" of which he speaks are not so much Platonic "copies" as prophetic foreshadows.[52] They point to the coming of the Messianic "age" in and through the Messiah.

The opening argument of the epistle suggests the author had

knowledge of a distinctive angelology held by the recipients of the letter,[53] although Jewish Christians commonly used this type of vocabulary up to the fourth century.[54] The comparison clearly sought to establish not only the Son's priority but also his divinity. For he is described as being Creator, sustainer, and heir of all things (1:2, 3). This appointment (ἔθηκεν in 1:2) is of a pretemporal nature (cf. Matt. 5:17; 10:40) and belongs in the divine order; its exercise can only be accomplished by one who is divine. Indeed, the author goes on to describe the son as the "effulgence" of God's glory (also a Johannine theme), the very impress of God's essence, and the firstborn (1:3-6). These epithets make an unmistakable assertion of divinity.[55] The use of Psalm 46:6 in 1:8—"But about the Son he says, Your throne, O God, will last for ever"—is therefore less problematic than some have claimed. The use of ὁ θεος here[56] as a title for the Son appears to be deliberate, for it can hardly be supposed that the author was unaware of how his readers might have understood this quotation. It is true that the quotation then speaks of "your God" as anointing the Son, but this reference is consistent both with Trinitarian considerations and the subordination theme common to many of the letters of the New Testament. For example, the Son is also said in Hebrews to be "appointed" (1:2), to have been "made" high priest (5:5, KJV), to have been raised from the dead (13:20), and now to have been seated at the Father's "right hand" (1:3). It is, however, a subordination of role and mission, not of being, and the utilization of Psalm 46:6 brings together the Son's Godness with his submission.

If the epistle provides an unqualified assertion of the Son's divinity, it provides an equally unqualified assertion of his humanity. He was a man from the tribe of Judah (7:14) who was as vulnerable to temptation (but not sin) as we are (4:15), who learned obedience as we do (5:8), and had to be perfected as we do (2:10). In 2:10 the objective of such perfection is said to be the bringing of sons to glory; in 5:8, 9, the author describes the process of such perfection in his reference to what Jesus suffered, to the crying and tears which accompanied his prayer; 7:28 describes the final result when the process had run its course (τετελειωμενον=having been perfected) and Jesus could act as high priest. "The most important confirmation of Hebrews' conception of Jesus' full humanity, however, is the statement that he *learned* obedience (5:8)." Oscar Cullmann goes on to say that "this expression, which has never been successfully explained away, presupposed an inner human development."[57] It might be true to say, then, that Hebrews is less interested in how the Son became human as in the fact that Jesus was fully human. He had to grow through obedience to the point where he could stand fully possessed of a sinless but mature nature before God (9:24) and act as high priest, the mediator of a better covenant (8:6; 9:15; 12:24). For the author, Jesus' sinlessness was not an incidental matter (4:15; 7:26); it was the sine qua non for the Son's sacrificial mission. His pure humanity was as much necessitated by his pretemporal appointment as was his full divinity, for each was indispensable to his saving work.

The author offers no theory as to how the divine became enfleshed. The process of incarnation is referred to (2:9; 10:5), but not explored. Yet it remains clear that for the author this process did not involve diminution of or modification in that Godness which had been the Son's. In the midst of describing Jesus' very human cries and tears, the author insists that it was the same divine Son who was experiencing this pain (5:8; ὤν is a participle having the force of declaring that though Jesus was and remained the Son, he nevertheless was suffering). Though he was from the tribe of Judah, he nevertheless was possessed of an "indissoluble" life (7:16).

The uniqueness of Hebrews' Christology, however, lies in the fact that the integrative motif in which both human and divine find their place is that of priesthood (4:16—6:20; cf. Christ's relationship to Melchizedek, discussed in 7:1-28). So, for example, the author seeks to show that although the high priesthood was restricted to those in specific lineage, Christ's right to such a position occurs by divine appointment (10:5), and those qualities which the high priest was required to display—a feeling for sinners and a special relationship to God (5:1, 2)—are displayed par excellence by the Son. Indeed, he has borne these responsibilities and done this work with a degree of completeness unknown under the older system. Thus his humanness is not of interest to the writer as a thing in itself, which cannot be said of later formulations, including Chalcedon, but for its significance in discharging the priestly sacrifice (cf. 12:3; 13:12). By the same token, the author advances no metaphysical framework for understanding Jesus' divinity save to add one enigmatic phrase, that it was "through the eternal Spirit" (9:14) that he offered himself in sacrifice. If this is a reference to the Holy Spirit, it is one of the curious omissions from the epistle that no corresponding mention is made of the Spirit raising Jesus from the dead (cf. Rom. 1:4). Perhaps the reason for such an omission was the author's overwhelming interest in showing the distinction of the heavenly and the earthly and of their unbroken union in him who was God and man. So the divinity of Jesus, too, is seen simply in light of that sacrifice by which the saving Rule of God enters our world.

If Christian faith rests upon what Jesus did through the cross on that order which is eternal, then it cannot affirm less or other than what Hebrews does with respect to Jesus' identity. For his sacrifice to be efficacious, he could not have been less than divine or other than human. But the argument in Hebrews rests entirely upon an assertion of Jesus' absolute worth as the final sacrifice rather than upon a reasoned doctrine of his person. Indeed, some have even supposed that

Hebrews has several doctrines of Christ, but it would be more accurate to say that the author makes use of numerous images and lines of thought which are not self-consciously woven into a consistent whole, but which nevertheless are useful in affirming the grounds on which Jesus must be reckoned as Savior and Lord. The very looseness of this combination of images in later years was to provide the quarrying ground for many a speculative theory about Christ's person, not all of which succeeded in affirming his absolute worth as does Hebrews.

The Pauline Epistles

Paul's reputation as a daring innovator who pushed the frontiers of Christian thought far into Hellenistic territory, in the process losing his connections with primitive Christian faith,[58] is not a reputation that is deserved. It is, in fact, quite unfounded. Given Paul's dazzling brilliance, his imaginative and creative genius, it is a temptation to see him in the mold of most of our own post-Enlightenment thinkers whose brilliance has usually been expressed in forms of individualism which deliberately defy all accepted forms of tradition. The temptation is especially great because the situational context in which Paul's epistolatory correspondence arose gave his formidable mind opportunities for new formulations and even for new theologies, which is not quite duplicated in the lives of any of the other apostles. But as these situations called forth from him his fresh formulations of Christian truth, it is his *conservatism* which is their most striking characteristic.

Even Bultmann has argued that Paul's reputation for innovation is overblown, proposing that much which seems new was actually adopted from Hellenistic Christianity; but the argument needs to be pushed still further. Paul was not merely conserving the Hellenistic understanding of Jesus but the most primitive understanding as well. This primitive, uniform understanding was one which was provided by Jesus himself. It came to expression in a common approach to the use of Old Testament passages in interpreting Jesus,[59] in hymns and creeds on which Paul draws, and in the ascription of names and titles to Jesus which recur in Paul's writings.[60] This consensus focused upon the historical facts of Jesus' birth, life, death, and resurrection, together with the theological meaning of those facts and the ethical consequences which flowed from them. It was this apostolic "tradition" which was conserved and explicated by Paul.

It is curious to observe, however, that Paul never defended this "tradition." He simply assumed it. Gresham Machen noted[61] that in his earlier epistles Paul gave little concerted reflection to Christology, presuming that the identity of Jesus was common knowledge among Christians. And it was. Paul did feel obliged to communicate his teaching early on to the Jerusalem leaders (Gal. 2:2), but they found no fault with his views. When he did defend himself, it was not against conservatives complaining that he had departed from the primitive and authentic "tradition." On the contrary, in every case he defended not himself but the "tradition" from which gnostics and others were departing through speculation or legalism. The "Christ he preaches," A. M. Hunter summed up, "is the same Christ as his precursors preached. He simply expanded and interpreted what was implicit in the affirmations of pre-Pauline Christians about Christ."[62]

Paul's precursors, we have already noted, interpreted Jesus in an eschatological framework, and Paul himself followed suit, utilizing the "two-age" terminology. This proposition, however, needs some further refinement, for Paul's eschatology contained a multitude of ideas, some of which have little or no early precedent.

This is especially true of those elements clustered around the end of time when the incursion of the Messianic "age" into time and history reaches its grand finale. With relatively little modification, Paul has, in these matters, carried over the traditonal structure of Jewish apocalyptic into his teaching. To what extent and in what ways he modified this teaching as the years went by and as his own faith deepened is a moot point, but it is not difficult to identify the cluster of ideas that are entailed. They include the imminent day of the Lord and judgment (Rom. 2:16; 14:10; 1 Cor. 4:4, 5; 2 Cor. 5:10; Gal. 6:7; 1 Thess. 1:10; 5:9; 2 Thess. 2:12), the apostasy and tribulation which will precede it (2 Thess. 2:3-12), the Antichrist (2 Thess. 2:3-12), the *parousia* (Rom. 13:11, 12; 1 Thess. 2:19; 3:13; 4:13-18; 5:23; 2 Thess. 2:1-8; 1 Cor. 4:5; 11:26; 15:51; 16:22; Phil. 4:5), the resurrection (1 Cor. 15:22, 51, 52; 2 Cor. 5:1-8) and, of course, heaven and hell (1 Cor. 13:10-12; 2 Cor. 5:1; Rom. 2:8; 2 Thess 1:9). Taken by itself and abstracted from the overarching understanding of the two "ages," this material, said C. K. Barrett, "can give only a one-sided and perverted picture of Paul's thought. His epistles are almost as different from the apocalypses in content as they are in form."[63] This difference in content arises from the new connections which Paul forged for these apocalyptic elements. The future, with its catastrophic elements of rampant wickedness and triumphant judgment, was integrally related to the present union with Christ, by whom the triumphant Rule of God is now individually experienced, and with the past where in Christ it was inaugurated. Past, present, and future were merged into a single conception in which the Messianic "age" entered into this world, now coexists with it, and then will finally destroy it. Thus we have in Paul's teaching on salvation, as Vos put it, "a central world-process, around the core of which all happenings in the course of time group themselves."[64] It is this panoramic and cosmic view which alone can do justice to the full range and richness of Paul's Christology.

Paul was certainly familiar with Jesus' biography, although the supposition that he had seen or heard Jesus in Jerusalem, while not impossible, has not been established beyond doubt. Paul knew that Jesus was the descendant of Abraham (Gal. 3:16) and David (Rom. 1:3; 2 Tim. 2:8), born of a woman (Gal. 4:4; cf. Rom. 1:3), lived under the law (Gal. 4:4), was betrayed on the night on which he instituted the Lord's Supper (1 Cor. 11:23-25), appeared before Pilate (1 Tim. 6:13), was crucified (Gal. 3:1), was buried and raised on the third day (1 Cor. 15:4; 2 Tim. 2:8), and ascended to heaven (Eph. 4:8; 1 Tim. 3:16). Paul was apparently conversant with Jesus' teaching, or at least parts of it, as reflected, for example, in his discussion of divorce (1 Cor. 7:10; cf. Matt. 5:31, 32), riches (Matt. 6:19, 20; cf. 1 Tim. 6:17, 18), as well as the other aspects of the Sermon on the Mount (cf. Rom. 12:9-21; Acts 20:35), and Jesus' teaching on support of missionaries (1 Cor. 9:14; cf. Luke 10:7). Of Jesus' character, Paul mentions the aspects of meekness and gentleness (2 Cor. 10:1), self-denial (Rom. 15:3), humility (Phil. 2:5-7), graciousness (2 Cor. 8:9), patience (1 Tim. 1:16), kindness and love (Tit. 3:4-7).

In two passages in particular Paul pushed beyond this general biographical outline into a firm theological affirmation of Jesus' full humanity. In Galatians 4:4 he spoke of Jesus being born out of (ἐκ) a woman rather than through her (διά), the consequence being that he lived as every other Jewish man lived, "under law." The words "born of a woman" were idiomatic for what was fully human (cf. Job 14:1, 2; 15:14, 15; 25:4, 5; Matt. 11:11). Whether this passage implies knowledge on Paul's part of the virginal conception is debated,[65] but the reason for the affirmation is clear. To redeem, the Son had to be fully human; so there is no reason to doubt Vos's conclusion that the "woman was not only the means or organ of his coming into flesh but from her he took everything which is proper to mankind"[66] to achieve that salvation. What Paul says in this text is reinforced by his statement in Romans 1:3 that "as to his human nature," the Son was "a descendant of David." That Jesus is said to have come out of (ἐκ) David's seed appears to be a deliberate affirmation of human solidarity with David and, beyond him, with all other people. This perception is strengthened by Paul's careful comparison elsewhere of the "one man" Adam and the "one man" Christ (Rom. 5:14-16; cf. 1 Cor. 15:21), and by his statement that there is only one "man" who is our mediator with God (1 Tim. 2:5) and that that "man" will return to judge the world (Acts 17:31).

These affirmations appear to rule out any possibility that Paul's view of Jesus was that he was in any way less than fully human; yet in recent years the charges have mounted that Paul's teaching flirts with mild docetism. The charges arise from two considerations. First, there is the problem of the qualifiers which Paul inserts in three statements concerning Jesus' humanity: "made in human likeness" (Phil. 2:7); "being found in appearance as man" (Phil. 2:8); "in the likeness of sinful man" (Rom. 8:3). Was Paul here wavering between affirming merely an outward human shell as opposed to a full human nature within that outward body? The answer appears to be that Paul was seeking to affirm Jesus' identity with our humanity while preserving his humanity from our sinfulness. What leaves a docetic impression from afar yields, on closer inspection, a reaffirmation of that part of the "tradition" which carried to Paul the twin truths of full humanity and complete sinlessness. Second, Paul displays what seems like an astonishing lack of interest in the historical Jesus, despite his knowledge of the major factors in Jesus' life and teaching. His later statement that he would not regard Jesus from a "worldly point of view" (2 Cor. 5:16) has been seen by Bultmann[67] as a further disparagement of the importance of the historical Jesus. Such a disparagement is necessary if the existentialists' mode of functioning is to be preserved, but it is an inexact understanding of Paul's view.

The reason for Paul's lack of interest in the human Jesus has nothing to do with docetism, but is the result of the deliberately selective treatment he gives to his Christology. His own conversion (Acts 9:1-16) provided so deep and powerful an impetus to his thought that his years as an apostle were to be spent exploring from every conceivable angle the meaning of the Christ whom he had encountered. His thought fashioned itself in the presence of that Christ whose Damascus light never faded from his mind, but this absorption in the meaning of the divine Son can hardly be read as a disparagement of his human life or as a denial of his full humanity.

The assumption of the Synoptic authors that the One in whom the Rule of God had come had to be divine, and that of John that the One who was from "above" revealed in his humanity the divine glory, and that of Hebrews that he who was to be mediator had to share both in our nature and in God's all find their reaffirmation in Paul. Yet this affirmation has not always been heard with the degree of certainty that one suspects was intended by Paul.

Bultmann has argued that the flat statement that Jesus was God cannot be found in the New Testament. The closest to this, he claims, is in John 1:1, 1:18, 20:28, 1 John 5:20, Titus 2:13, and Romans 9:5. All of these texts Bultmann believes to be of dubious authenticity.[68]

Cullmann, however, has rightly countered that the restraint in the language used about Jesus has little theological significance when it is seen that Jesus' divinity is affirmed both in the titles which are ascribed to him as well as in the roles which he fulfills. This is particularly clear in Paul's case when we consider Jesus' relationship to those whom he saves, to the created universe, and finally to God the Father.

The interplay between Christology and soteriology exhibits itself in at least five major areas of interest: first, Jesus as representative man; second, Jesus' substitutionary death; third, the meaning of being "in Christ"; fourth, the relationship between Jesus and the Spirit, who signals the arrival of the Messianic age; finally, the relationship between Jesus and the church. The fact that Paul develops his Christology as so much a part of other themes makes brief summaries of his thought almost impossible; to consider Paul's Christology is to be engaged with his whole theology. That may be more difficult than having to treat only an aspect of it, but at least it becomes abundantly clear that any accounting of his Christology which vitiates either the human or the divine elements in Jesus, vitiates the entire Pauline teaching. Our choice is to have his whole Christology or to have nothing from him at all.

The fact that Paul tells us Jesus was representative man (Rom. 5:12-21; 1 Cor. 15:21, 22) does not, in and of itself, mean that he must have been divine; Adam, after all, was also representative. But it is in the contrast of effects from these representatives that Jesus' divinity emerges. From Adam came sin, condemnation, and death; from Jesus came grace, righteousness, and justification. Paul sums up the contrast accordingly: The first man was of the dust of the earth, the second from heaven. As was the earthly man, so are those who are of the earth; and as is the man from heaven, so also are those who are of heaven (1 Cor. 15:47, 48, cf. Eph. 4:9, 10). The "man from heaven," which is probably Paul's equivalent of "Son of Man," which he does not use, presupposes the Johannine above/below distinction (cf. John 3:13). It presupposes, further, a supernatural origin and power for him, inasmuch as he is able to undo and reverse all that the first Adam has set in motion in human life.[69]

This, of course, poses the question as to how it was that he was able to bring to us grace, righteousness, and justification. The answer, deoped from many different angles in Paul, is that he was our sacrifice (Eph. 5:2; 1 Cor. 5:7; 11:25), pouring out his blood for us (Rom. 5:6, 9; Col. 1:20), dying in our place and in our stead (Gal. 3:13; 2 Cor. 5:14, 21; Rom. 3:25; 1 Tim. 2:6), not merely for sin in the abstract, but for sinners in particular (1 Thess. 5:10; Rom. 4:25; 8:32; 2 Cor. 5:14-21) as their propitiation (Rom. 3:24, 25; 5:9, 10). With respect to propitiation, Leon Morris has argued decisively that ἱλαστήριον cannot properly be translated as "expiation," and that its meaning is that of the turning away of divine wrath from the sinner through the interposition of a substitute.[70] Since it is God himself, in Paul's teaching, who provides the propitiation, rather than the sinner, there can be no confusion with the pagan notions of sinners pacifying their gods by various offerings and penitential acts. Christ is God's provision, the provision God himself makes, to pay the price for our violation of the law (Col. 1:14; Eph. 1:7; 1 Cor. 6:20). Because of his gracious gift we can, through our acceptance of it by faith, speak of ourselves as already justified (Rom. 3:24; 5:9, 16, 17; 8:33; Gal. 3:8-14), reconciled (Rom. 5:9, 10; 2 Cor. 5:18-20; Eph. 2:16; Col. 1:20-22), and redeemed (Gal. 3:13; Eph. 1:14).

What Jesus rectified on the cross was not some irrational whim in the mind of the Father, but the objective guilt under which we had fallen as sinners, as well as the control exercised over us through our sinfulness by the malignant forces of evil. At the cross Jesus openly embarrassed the powers of darkness, shattering their hold over us (Col. 1:13; Gal. 1:4; 1 Cor. 15:54, 57), restoring a right relationship to God. Such a conquest, which necessitated a substitution of this nature, is the work of God alone. "The apostle cannot think of [the divine] Christ and not think also of the cross he bore," declares H. R. Mackintosh. "The exalted Lord, known from the first as such, would not *be* Lord unless He had died 'for our offences' (Rom. 4:25ff)."[71] It was the inherent importance of Jesus as divine which gives to the cross its centrality, and it is the cross which reveals Jesus as divine.

Paul's creativity, exercised within the received tradition of apostolic thought, is perhaps nowhere more evident than in his treatment of the Holy Spirit. In some one hundred and twenty references, he pushed the frontiers of Christian thought far beyond what we have in John 14—16, in the process forging an identity between the risen Jesus and the Spirit which is so close that the believer is seen to be identified with the death and conquest of the Son through the Spirit (cf. Gal. 4:4-6; Rom. 5:5-8; 1 Cor. 12:3; Eph. 1:13; 2:18; 4:3-5). With this conquest was established, finally and irrevocably, the promised Messianic "age to come."

It is this identity of purpose and work, binding the Son and the Spirit, that also explains the paucity of references to the historical Jesus. To speak of the Spirit is to speak indirectly of the historical Jesus, for without Jesus and his work on the cross there could be no Spirit shed on the church (cf. John 14:16-18; 15:26). At the same time, this interconnection almost certainly is what led Paul increasingly to speak of the Spirit as the *Holy* Spirit, transferring to him what Paul had known of the historical Jesus.[72]

It is the work of the Spirit to illumine our eyes to see the truth of the gospel and to open our hearts to believe it (cf. Acts 16:14). Not only are we enabled to give credence to certain truths, but it is the Spirit who effects our organic union with Christ. Paul speaks two hundred and forty times of being "in Christ,"[73] of being made one with his crucifixion, death, and resurrection, which is the precondition of knowing God (cf. 1 Cor. 2:11-16; 2 Cor. 1:22; 5:5; 13:14). To speak of being "in" a teacher, and of participating at an ontological and ethical level in that teacher's capacities, would be preposterous if that teacher were not divine and if the Holy Spirit were not able to bridge time and space to fashion such a union.

Just as preposterous would be the supposition that Jesus is the "head" of his disciples, the "body" (Eph. 1:22, 23; 4:15; Col. 1:18), that there is an organic union between them such that his life is theirs and their gifts are his (1 Cor. 12:4-6; Eph. 4:8). Yet that is what Paul claims.

In the process, he collapses the former teaching of the Kingdom of God into his Christology so that to speak of Christ, to believe on Christ, is to enter the Kingdom. The Kingdom terminology largely falls away in Paul and is replaced by that of the gospel, the church, and the ethical life. Whether this transition was forced upon Paul by the demands of his missionary work—the "Kingdom of God" being a peculiarly Jewish idiom—or whether it was the result of a deepening understanding of the meaning of Jesus and his work is difficult to say. What is important is that the "two-ages" teaching was transformed through a deepened and expanded Christology.

The horizons of Paul's thought, then, reach far beyond the personal and ecclesiastical to include the universal and cosmic. If Christ is the Lord whom each believer serves, the Head to whom the whole body is responsive, he is also the Creator from which everything derives its existence, the center without which there is no reality. Whether one gazes into the firmament above with its billions of circling stars or into human consciousness below, Jesus has "supremacy" in everything. So Paul reasons in one of the most exalted Christological passages, Colossians 1:15-20.

In this passage Paul almost certainly was creatively adopting the words of a Christian hymn to reassert Christological truth in a context of Judaistic gnosticism.[74] It is an extraordinary passage in which Paul makes two main points. First, reality has been created "by him and for him" (1:16). Christ is its origin and ultimate goal (cf. Rom. 11:36; 1 Cor. 8:6; 15:28; Eph. 1:10), its principle of cohesion and its center. He is the πρωτότοκος over all creation (Col. 1:15). Had Paul meant that Christ was himself a creation, as the Arians supposed, he would undoubtedly have said that Christ was πρωτόκτιστος. What we have here instead is a Messianic title (cf. Ps. 89:27, LXX) ascribing to Christ preeminence over everything in creation. This relationship to created reality, both visible and invisible, tells us who Christ *is*. Second, as incarnate Son, making the invisible visible and tangible, he gives to us the perfect exegesis of the nature, character, and purpose of God. He is God's "image" (1:15; cf. 2 Cor. 4:4). As such, twice Paul says the whole divine fullness, or πκήρωμα, subsists in him (1:19; 2:9). The Godness of the Father is the Godness of the Son but, again, there is a subordination of role as well as a parity of being. All things are *of* or *from* the Father (1 Cor. 8:6), but they are *through* the Son. Yet to a Jewish mind, imbued with the sense that there was only one God who was Creator of all, this identification was an unmistakable assertion of Jesus' ontological unity with the Father.

This leads us finally to inquire about Jesus relationship to the Father. If the divine Son was preexistent (2 Cor. 8:9), shared in the Father's Godness (Phil. 2:6), and was sent forth to be incarnate (Gal. 4:4), does he retain his status as divine during his union with a human nature? There can be no question that for Paul, as for many of the New Testament authors, there is within the Godhead a hierarchy in terms of initiative; the Father does *send* the Son. And this subordination is intensified by the conditions of incarnation, the final outworking of which will be the submission of the Son to the Father when redemption has run its full course (1 Cor. 15:28; cf. 1 Cor. 3:23; 11:3). How far, then, do the exigencies of this submission, the conditions of this subordination, affect the *nature* of the divine Jesus?

The fact that we are asking this question owes little to our acquaintance with Paul and much to the heightened sensitivity produced by later theological speculation. This was not a problem for Paul, and if he addressed it at all it was only obliquely; it has become a problem for us, and we feel the need to address it directly. The nineteenth-century kenotic theologies raised this question with unusual force, and it has continued to trouble most twentieth-century theologians in various ways. Those theologians who are willing to speak of Jesus' divinity oftentimes will only do so in the most subdued tones because frequently they are beginning not with a pretemporal divine being who was enfleshed, but with the human Jesus in whom great mystery is manifested. The question, then, is whether this mystery is great enough to warrant the appellation of divine.

How far removed we are from the temper of Paul's thought is apparent when we examine the one passage where he seems to address the issue. Philippians 2:5-11, one of the most controversial sections in the New Testament, has excited an enormous literature which deals with the questions as to whether it was a pre-Pauline hymn, what its background is (Aramaic, Hellenistic, or Jewish), and what its Christology is.[75] But what is often missed is that Paul's concern is more ethical than metaphysical. His Christological statement of verses 5-11 is only adduced to reinforce his opening injunction to forsake selfishness (vv. 1-5). This should prepare us for some disappointments, for Paul is simply not on our modern wavelength.

There are at least three important options as to what he meant by saying that Christ Jesus was in the "nature" or "form" of God. First, it has been proposed that this is to be identified with the "image of God" in Genesis 1:26, 27, for εἰκων, which translated *selem* in Genesis 1:26, 27, is used interchangeably with μορφη in the LXX.[76] The thought would then be that what Adam lost by grasping, Jesus as a mere man has won by serving, in recognition of which he has been adopted into the Godhead. The problem with this view is that μορφή never does service for the Hebrew děmût, and only once for *selem* in the LXX. The identification of "form" with the "image of God" simply cannot be made. Second, μορφη has been proposed as a synonym for δοξα, in which case we would have a Pauline duplication of the Johannine flesh/glory Christology. This identification is not feasible linguistically. The connection, in fact, is quite different. The "form" of

God is itself full of δοξα. Third, it would appear inescapable that by "form" we are to understand that Paul meant the essence or essential characteristics of a thing.[77] He who was in essence a servant and showed the essential characteristics of serving was in essence divine and had those characteristics essential to being divine. [78]

What, then, does Paul mean when he goes on to say that Christ "emptied" himself to become enfleshed? The older kenotic Christologies interpreted this phrase metaphysically in terms of what preceded this statement in Philippians 2:6; in some way, he emptied himself of his Godness for the needs and duration of the Incarnation. But it is contextually more sound to say that the phrase must be defined by what follows it: his role as a servant limited and muted the ways in which his Godness could show. It is a metaphorical understanding of *kenosis,* and the context is ethical rather than metaphysical.[79] Far from qualifying or reducing the Godness of Christ Jesus, Paul has here invested it with profounder significance. It is not merely that Jesus was a divine being in human flesh; that divine being was itself love, self-effacing and self-sacrificing love. We are here as far removed from abstract notions of the divine as we can be. And we are barred by the fact of the Incarnation from gratuitously declaring what Godness must be like. The human Jesus provided the unique exegesis of Godness, of that God who is in essence holy love, and he did so within the limitations of being human. As this divine light passes through the darkened glass of his humanity, it is obscured but not refracted. In Jesus, God became *incognito,* but he did not disappear; he is hidden, but not lost.

The hiddenness of God in Jesus pertains, however, to our perception. God did not become less than God during the Incarnation; it merely seemed that way. The humbleness of his love has always caught us off balance. We expect something different. But we will never have anything different. Once and for all, that Son by whom all of reality was made and in whom all things subsist stripped away the insignia of his majesty and muted his δοξα by our flesh. He bore not only our flesh but our sins and turned his moment of greatest vulnerability on the cross into the moment of greatest conquest over evil. In him has come the triumphant Messianic age, that "age to come," in which we participate when by faith's union we are made a part of his family. None but God could overcome the chaos of evil, and none but he could bring in the new age; but by the same token only he who was human and shared with us in our human nature and ways could stand in our stead as substitute and propitiation. Human and divine, he was by Paul's judgment the inaugurator of the Kingdom and the Head of the church, the Lord of the simplest believer and the center of the entire cosmos.

Consequently, Paul moves easily into a complete linguistic identification of Christ with Yahweh.[80] If Yahweh is our sanctifier (Ex. 31:13), is omnipresent (Ps. 139:7-10), is our peace (Judg. 6:24), is our righteousness (Jer. 23:6), is our victory (Ex. 17:8-16), and is our healer (Ex.

15:26), then so is Christ all of these things (1 Cor. 1:30; Col. 1:27; Eph. 2:14). If the gospel is God's (1 Thess. 2:2, 6-9; Gal. 3:8), then that same gospel is also Christ's (1 Thess. 3:2; Gal. 1:7). If the church is God's (Gal. 1:13; 1 Cor. 15:9), then that same church is also Christ's (Rom. 16:16). God's Kingdom (1 Thess. 2:12) is Christ's (Eph. 5:5); God's love (Eph. 1:3-5) is Christ's (Rom. 8:35); God's Word (Col. 1:25; 1 Thess. 2:13) is Christ's (1 Thess. 1:8; 4:15); God's Spirit (1 Thess. 4:8) is Christ's (Phil. 1:19); God's peace (Gal. 5:22; Phil. 4:9) is Christ's (Col. 3:15; cf. Col. 1:2; Phil. 1:2; 4:7); God's "Day" of judgment (Isa. 13:6) is Christ's "Day" of judgment (Phil. 1:6, 10; 2:16; 1 Cor. 1:8); God's grace (Eph. 2:8, 9; Col. 1:6; Gal. 1:15) is Christ's grace (1 Thess. 5:28; Gal. 1:6; 6:18); God's salvation (Col. 1:13) is Christ's salvation (1 Thess. 1:10); and God's will (Eph. 1:11; 1 Thess. 4:3; Gal. 1:4) is Christ's will (Eph. 5:17; cf. 1 Thess. 5:18). So it is no surprise to hear Paul say that he is both God's slave (Rom. 1:9) and Christ's (Rom. 1:1; Gal. 1:10), that he lives for that glory which is both God's (Rom. 5:2; Gal. 1:24) and Christ's (2 Cor. 8:19, 23; cf. 2 Cor. 4:6), that his faith is in God (1 Thess. 1:8, 9; Rom. 4:1-5) and in Christ Jesus (Gal. 3:22), and that to know God, which is salvation (Gal. 4:8; 1 Thess. 4:5), is to know Christ (2 Cor. 4:6).

CONCLUSION

Indubitably there is a development in the way that Jesus, as human and divine, is treated in the New Testament. It is a development, however, from what is less explicit in the Synoptics to what is more explicit in the epistles; it is not a development from one kind of Christology to another, more exalted kind. There is one Christology for which different terms and conceptualities are employed. There is a terminological and theological diversity within a doctrinal unity.

The importance of seeing the continuity between Jesus' preaching on the Kingdom and Paul's on the gospel cannot be overemphasized. It is the clarity and definition which the epistles in general, but Paul's in particular, give to the meaning of Christian faith which must be allowed to cohere with that developed under the language of the Kingdom. If this is not done, if the Kingdom is disconnected from the gospel of the epistles, it usually becomes subject to the control of later, extrabiblical ideology and cultural norms. The Kingdom is an elastic concept and perhaps for that reason was employed by Jesus during the period of his self-disclosure, a period requiring delicacy and allusion more than confrontation and denotation. The elements of suggestion, connotation, and indirect disclosure were intended to find their culmination in the more direct, denotative period of the apostolic teachers. Where this is not allowed to occur, where the Kingdom is attached hermeneutically, it begins to carry freight which Jesus never intended for it.

There is no question that this occurred in Protestant liberalism.

The argument which was advanced was that the apostles, but Paul in particular, had fallen for the seductions of Greek philosophy and had turned Jesus' simple faith into a complex theology. It was with scarcely disguised self-righteousness that the liberals purported to be the followers of Jesus and the rescuers of Christianity from the perversions of Paul. This mode of thought, which at the time seemed so brilliant, has, of course, been relegated to the scrap pile of ideas which, however interesting, were also entirely fallacious. Thus it is no small marvel to note the rekindling of this old notion among some evangelical writers. The older justification is no longer advanced. It is now blithely assumed that Christianity is about the Kingdom, what Paul wrote was about the Kingdom, and what the Kingdom means, in most cases, is left-wing, political ideology! Discussion about Christianity is replaced by discussion about the Kingdom; biblical ethics is now Kingdom ethics; social responsibility is now Kingdom transformation. What is passed off as evangelical faith is really only a fresh outbreak of liberalism at some key points.

Although Jesus' own self-understanding is often expressed obliquely and indirectly when compared, for example, with Paul's teaching about him, it would seem that this single New Testament Christology could be expressed in four propositions.

First, in and with the person of the incarnate Son has come the promised Messianic age, and this identification is so close that the age or Kingdom can only be entered by believing in Jesus. Second, Christ was a premundane being from "above" who not only enjoyed preexistence but also parity of being with Yahweh. Third, there was a reduction in the manifestation, but not the nature, of this divinity for the purposes of incarnation. Fourth, Jesus shared not only our human ways, but our human nature. The later speculations as to whether he had two consciousnesses, two minds, or two wills are not really dealt with directly in the New Testament period.[81] These questions have to be answered inferentially from what is said, but these inferences need to correlate with the assumption, in the Gospels and epistles, that in Jesus we are dealing with a psychologically integrated person. How that integration is achieved is obscure to us because the question of Jesus' self-consciousness, as opposed to his self-interpretation, is obscure.

That these four propositions contain elements which would appear to be inconsistent with one another or at least that can be included in one coherent picture of the makeup of this person, Jesus of Nazareth, only with difficulty is undeniable. The New Testament, then, gives us the raw material on which sober reflection can build, but also the raw material off which irresponsible heresy can feed. The subsequent history of the church has shown how close reflection and heresy have always been to one another.

3 TITLES OF OUR LORD

The isolation of Christological titles as a discrete body of information is a recent development in scholarship. Concentrated study on these titles has yielded some fresh lines of thought, but the result has sometimes also been a fragmented understanding of the New Testament teaching. And where the underlying rationale for treating Jesus' titles in this way is an unwillingness to come to terms with the theological and ontological realities which are so central to any satisfactory Christology, the development should also be seen as deleterious. The titular evidence should be considered within the context of the New Testament as a whole; otherwise it ends up concealing as much as it reveals of Jesus. The titles are a part of the overall affirmation and should not be considered apart from it.

Cullmann has proposed that the titles used by or of Jesus fall into four main categories. First, there are the titles which are applicable to his earthly work (prophet, Suffering Servant, High Priest). Second, there are those relating to his future work (Messiah, Son of Man). Third, there are those relating to his present work (Lord, Savior). Finally, there are those which speak of his pretemporal existence (Word, Son of God).[1] The order in which the titles are discussed lacks logical merit, but the categories themselves, though a little artificial, are still useful.

WORD
The titles "Word" and "Son of God"[2] are, in some respects, rather different from one another. The λόγος language is sparse (principally John 1:1-18 and 1 John 1:1-4 and possibly Hebrews 1:1-3, Colossians, 1:15-20); that on the Son (by itself or in combinations such as "Son of God," "his Son," "beloved Son," "only begotten Son") is extensive. It appears in all the Gospels and many of the epistles. The one is a Johannine idiom which appears to have enjoyed little use in the Chris-

tian church; the other was widely used and employed quite commonly in the epistles. In their different ways, however, they affirm the divine status of Christ and, as a necessary part of that, his pretemporal existence in eternity.

A more precise denotation of what John had in mind by λογος appears, at first sight, to be difficult because the paucity of biblical references gives little contextual control for the term. It is this fact which has led scholars to search for a fuller meaning in one of the religious contexts from which, it is proposed, John must have borrowed the term. The source from which it is derived is then seen to provide the key to its meaning as a Christological title. There are two main sources which are seen as the most likely quarries for this term: Stoicism and Judaism (either in its Philonic variation or in the Memra of the Targums).

The Stoics believed that all matter was generated out of a fiery vapor. It was by this πνευμα that material was patterned and by which this world would be ultimately consumed. Between the time of its formation and that of its destruction, all matter and life bore the impress of the creative force. Everything in the universe reflects it. This force, the λογος, was therefore creative and providential, but it was never, in Stoic thought, personal or self-conscious. It determined life, but that determinism made the acceptance of fate an ethical principle. These points of antithesis, when compared with John's understanding of λογος, make it unlikely that Stoicism was the source of his teaching.

In Judaism, the most likely of the sources of John's thought appears to be Philo. Philo, in fact, united a Platonic conception of God with a Jewish one. From his Platonism, Phil derived the notion of God's utter, unbroken transcendence, of his discontinuity from the world. God is beyond the range of human experience and knowledge, unlike the highest human conceptions of beauty and virtue. His transcendence has created a chasm over which only a mediator can pass. From Jewish theology, Philo drew the beliefs that God is both Creator of and providential Ruler within the world. It was the λογος in whom these two streams of thought united.

The λογος existed as thought in God's mind. It was then expressed, much like human thought, in words, and in its new form was responsible for creation and providence. The λογος therefore separated God from the world—for it was the λογος who was Creator and sustainer—but also united him to the world indirectly because the λογος was his intermediary.

Philo's conception may bear some surface similarities to John's, but there were at least three important points of difference. First, Philo's λογος was neither fully divine nor preexistent, in contrast to John's teaching. It was for this reason that Philo argued "no mortal thing could have been formed as the similitude of the supreme father of the universe but only after the pattern of the second deity, who is the Word of the Supreme Being."[3] Second, it is doubtful that this Word was personal as it is in John. It seems to have sustained the same relationship to Supreme Being as words do to any human speaker. Words are expressive of the speaker's mind and intention, but they do not themselves have a separate personal existence. Third, in Philo this Word is a synonym for rational order in the cosmos or for patterns immanent in matter. It is never made identical with the self-disclosure of the "Supreme Being." In John, this Word was God and is never used as a synonym for rational order. In Philo, the Word separates God from the world; in John it relates them. John's λογος does what Philo's could never do—he forms a personal and incarnate union with Jesus.

The relationship between John's conception and this Philonic background appears, then, to be one of antagonism rather than dependence. "The evangelist," H. R. Mackintosh said, "uses Philo's term to deny Philo's thought."[4] At the same time, the prevalence of this discussion on the Word in John's culture may well have influenced him in deciding which of the Old Testament conceptions he should develop.

The Old Testament has a doctrine of the Word in which three ideas are gradually combined. First, the Word was associated with creation. The speech of God and the acts of creation are closely associated throughout Genesis 1, and the psalmist specifically states that the heavens were created by the Word of the Lord (Ps. 33:6; cf. Ps. 147:15-18; 148:5). Second, the Word was associated with revelation. The association is present in the early chapters of Genesis (3:8; 12:1; 15:1; 22:11) and is formalized by the time the psalter was composed. The Word not only sheds God's light upon our path, giving us a permanent disclosure of his will (cf. Ps. 119:9, 25, 28, 41, 58, 65, 76, 107, 116, 140, 160, 169, 170), but it is also personalized. "The word of the Lord is flawless. He is a shield for all who take refuge in him" (Ps. 18:30; cf. Ps. 107:20; 147:15). As such, the Word is closely paralleled by the personification of Wisdom and the ascription to it of divine functions. Third, this Word, so identified with God, is also said to be eternal (Ps. 119:89).

In the Prologue to John's Gospel, the speculative cast of ideas regularly encountered elsewhere, even in the Memra (doctrine of the Word) in the Targums (Chaldee paraphrases), is entirely absent. What we have is the realization of these three lines of thought in the person of Christ in a context that is ethical and soteriological. First, the λογος is the Creator (1:3) of all, even of those who rejected him (1:10). Second, he is the disclosure of God, this revelation being described in terms of light and darkness (1:4, 5, 7-9). Christ does not merely point toward God, but he is God (1:1). Third, because he is God, he is eternal. In 1:1, three times the imperfect ἦν is employed, signifying the Word's "continuous timeless existence."[5]

In the Word, then, we are met by the personal and eternal God who has joined himself to our flesh. In Jesus, the permanent and final unveiling of God has taken place, and the center of this truth is coincidental with the life of this man.[6] Jesus is the means through which and in conjunction with whom God has made known his character, his will, and his ways (cf. John 14:6).

SON OF GOD

What John intended to convey by his doctrine of the Word coincides with, although it is not completely identical with, the use of the title υἱὸς τον Θεοῦ in the rest of the New Testament. This title describes the unique relationship of Christ to God. Christ comes from the depths of God himself; he is God. But he is God in human form, a form which hides his Godness and which requires of him obedience to the Father whose being he shares.

It is true, of course, that there is a general usage of the title "sons(s) of God" in the Old Testament. It is used of heavenly beings (Gen. 6:2; Job. 1:6; 38:7; Ps. 29:1; 89:7), and it is used of God's people (Ex. 4:22, 23; Jer. 31:9; Hos. 11:1; Deut. 14:1; 32:5; Isa. 43:6). Finally, it is used of the Davidic King, the king's relation to God being described in terms of a son-to-father relationship (2 Sam. 7:12-14; 1 Chron. 17:13). In the New Testament, however, this title is used in a specialized sense when applied to Christ, but its use nevertheless bears more relationship to this Old Testament background than to any other. It is certainly the case that there is no convincing evidence that the belief in "divine-men" in the Greek world, men who appropriated the title "Son of God" and declaimed upon supernatural matters, provided the basis for the New Testament's use of this title.[7]

In the New Testament itself, the connections which are established for the "Son of God" prescribe for it much of its meaning.[8] It is connected with the "Son of Man," Daniel's apocalyptic figure, with the coming of the Spirit (Luke 24:49; Acts 2:33; John 20:21, 22),[9] and with baptism. In some texts where this title is employed, there is the use of "Abba," connotating an intimacy of relation with the Father (cf. Luke 10:22/Matt. 11:27; Matt. 15:13; 16:17; 18:10, 14, 19; 25:34; 26:53; Luke 22:29; 23:34; 24:49). The thought of vindication beyond death is also associated with the title, giving to it a significance beyond that which it had in its more general usage in the Old Testament.

Attempts have been made to see this title as one that was generated later in the communities of Christian faith.[10] The evidence suggests, however, that the title originated with Jesus himself (Matt. 11:27/Luke 10:22; cf. Mark 12:6; 13:32), although his use of it was sparing. It was certainly used of him at his baptism (Mark 1:11/Luke 3:22), temptation (Luke 4:9/Matt. 4:3, 6), and transfiguration (Mark 9:7/Matt. 17:5/Luke 9:35). It was used in address by the centurion (Mark 15:39), the high priest (Mark 14:61), and by the demons (Mark 3:11; 5:7). It recurs frequently in the Johannine writings because, of course, it was John's intention, in the Gospel at least, to show that Jesus was indeed the Son of God (John 20:31). Consequently, it appears frequently in the Gospel's teaching (e.g., 3:16, 17, 35, 36; 5:19-26; 8:36; 14:13; 16:10). The Son of God is the one who dwelt "above" and who came "below," who shared in the *shekinah* glory of God because it was also his glory as God, and who has veiled this in human flesh.

In the epistles it is within Paul that the title predominates and here, as in Hebrews, the interest is consistently and insistently doctrinal.[11] God calls us into fellowship with his Son (1 Cor. 1:9), who was sent into the world (Gal. 4:4-6) to be delivered to death by God himself (Rom. 8:32), in order to bear our sins, to effect our reconciliation, to bring new life (Rom. 5:10; Gal. 2:20), and to be raised from the dead (Rom. 1:4). It is this Son and his work which is the subject of the gospel and the means of salvation (Rom. 1:9; 2 Cor. 1:19; Gal. 1:16). He is now the goal for Christians in their life of spiritual growth (Rom. 8:29; cf. Eph. 4:13). He will return in glory (1 Thess. 1:10) and will yield up to his Father a cleansed universe (1 Cor. 15:24, 28). The preexistence of the Son was as fundamental to Paul's thought (Gal. 4:4-6; Rom. 8:3) as it was to John's (John 3:17; 1 John 4:9, 10, 14).

More than any other title in the New Testament, Hengel declares, "Son of God connects the figure of Jesus with God." For John and Paul in particular, the Son comes from the depths of God where he preexisted. He is God, and while on earth he holds intimate communion with the Father, a fellowship without human parallel. He does what only God can do in overcoming sin, death, and the devil, and through his conquest he raises those who trust in him to newness of life.

The work of Christ in the New Testament is described in the past, present, and future tense. To Paul, as for us today, Jesus' work on the cross occurred in the past, his relationship to us by the Spirit is in the present, and his return in glory to redeem in full those for whom he died is yet to occur in the future. The distinctions between the tenses are, however, more absolute in appearance than in fact. The work of Christ, though accomplished in the past, is nevertheless made contemporary to us by the Spirit as no other historical event can be. By the same token, the future, while it is yet to occur, is anticipated and even experienced obliquely in the present, for the "age to come" is already intruding into the present. This future began with the arrival of Christ, and his death anticipates the judgment which is yet to come. The timeline becomes distorted in the presence of the One who is eternal, who comprehends past, present, and future. The significance of Jesus' titles, therefore, always bursts through any temporal classification even though there may be, for a particular title, a concentrated significance and applicability within a time period. Out of the many titles used by or of Jesus for his work, three are selected for special examination: the Suffering Servant (past); Lord (present); and Son of Man (future).

THE SUFFERING SERVANT

Some of the other titles used in connection with Jesus' person or work could conceivably have been borrowed and adapted from surrounding cultures, but the Servant is indubitably biblical in origin. It arises from those songs which B. Duhm first isolated in Isaiah 42:1-4; 49:1-7; 50:4-11; 52:13—53:12. In connection with these passages, the most critical question, Morna Hooker writes, "is to discover at what point the identification of Jesus with the Servant came into Christian thought, whether it was inherent in the teaching of Jesus, or whether it was introduced by the Church to explain his death; and, if the latter, at what stage this was done."[12]

The basic argument against Jesus' use of this title as a self-designation was early delineated by F. C. Burkitt. He contended that the only textually unambiguous use of this title by Jesus himelf is in Luke 22:37, and that the context of this passage "suggests that He hardly regarded the passage as 'Messianic.' "[13] Furthermore, Burkitt noticed that the concentration of New Testament references occurred in writers using a Greek Bible (Matthew, 1 Peter, Hebrews, Luke, Acts) rather than the Hebrew (Mark, John, Paul). This led him to postulate that the identification of Jesus with this Servant was one that was forged in the Hellenistic church and that it was therefore a development which took place subsequent to Jesus' own life. Jesus did not use the title of himself. This line of thought has, of course, picked up some notable adherents along the way and is advocated, with minor changes, by Hooker and Bultmann among others.[14]

There are, in fact, three separate issues which need to be resolved. First, who is the Servant in the Isaianic songs, judged by the immediate context? Second, did Jesus identify himself as the Servant or was this a later development? Third, what should be understood by this title when it is used in its New Testament context? This third question, of course, may be answered in rather different ways, depending on how the second question is resolved.

First, then, who is Isaiah's Servant? There is no single or simple answer to this, because the title undergoes change between its first appearance in the song in Chapter 42 and its final appearance in Chapter 53. Initially it is a designation for Israel. This identification is then narrowed to the godly remnant through whom God will accomplish the purposes he has for the nation. Finally, the Servant is an individual in whom the nation's destiny is realized and through whom God works to save his people.

In its initial usage, that of the nation (44:1), the idea of divine ownership is underscored. The title is here used, not of an individual who trusts in God, as it was, for example, of the prophets who were described as Yahweh's "servants," but of the nation in whom Yahweh is carrying forth his purposes. It is the recipient of his grace (44:2). It is the object of election (48:20) and the instrument by which God will be glorified (49:3). Israel is spoken of throughout in the passive, as the object of God's grace, election, calling, and redemption. When Isaiah is led later to speak of these purposes coming to fulfillment in a single person, the mood changes. The Servant is not redeemed but is himself the Redeemer. He is active, not passive.

Within these songs, then, Isaiah begins to move from the nation as the designated Servant to a godly remnant within it (cf. Rom. 9:6). In Isaiah 42:6, 7 God enters into a special covenant with this remnant. Although the nation as a whole is afflicted with blindness and deafness, there are still some within it who see and hear (42:18, 19; cf. 53:9, 10). This remnant becomes the visible pledge of God's gracious favor (cf. 65:8). By the time we reach Isaiah 50:4-9, however, the prophet has come to see that Israel's mission and its destiny are to be realized ultimately only in one person. This person is one who will fulfill the prophetic role by interpreting God's will, the kingly role by releasing captives (49:2, 9), and the priestly by bearing sins (52:7, 8, 10, 12).

The Servant understood as the nation has much in common with the Servant understood as a single person, but there are also significant differences.[15] Israel despairs (40:27; 41:8-10), but this individual does not (50:5-7). Israel is rebellious (48:4; cf. 43:27); this person is not (50:5; 53:4-6, 12). Israel is blind and deaf (42:18-25), but this person listens attentively (50:4, 5). Israel suffers unwillingly (51:21-23) for its own sins (42:24, 25; 43:22-28; 47:6), while this person suffers willingly (50:6; 53:4-9) for the sins of others (53:4, 5). Israel is redeemed (43:1-7); this person redeems (49:5; 53:11, 12).

The second major question concerns Jesus' own use of the title. Assuming that he understood this Servant to epitomize what Israel should have been and yet, at the same time, to be distinct from Israel in his roles as prophet, priest, and king, did Jesus then understand himself as being this Servant? The explicit, direct use of this title, or words closely associated with it, is infrequent (Matt. 8:17; 12:18; Luke 22:37; John 12:38; cf. Acts 3:13, 26; 4:25-30, 8:32; Rom. 15:21), but allusions to the Servant Songs are numerous. Even Morna Hooker, who is disinclined to think that the Servant motif is important in New Testament Christology, has drawn up substantial lists of these references.[16] In the Gospels, however, it is difficult to escape the fact that the controlling idea is that of Isaiah's Suffering Servant in passages such as Mark 2:18-20; 8:31; 9:31; 10:33, 34, 45; 12:1-12; Luke 13:31; John 1:29; 12:38. As a result, Cullmann's conclusion, which appears to be consistent with the textual evidence, is that from the time of the baptism, Jesus was conscious of being the Servant of God. He often linked this with the

Son of Man and saw himself as both the inaugurator of a new age and the One who must die in order to inaugurate it. It was not the early church but Jesus himself who first made the identification between himself and the Suffering Servant.[17]

By the time we come to the epistles, Jesus is unambiguously declared to be central to the gospel and the Kingdom. God's Kingly rule, it is now explicitly asserted, can only be begun by and can only be entered through the Servant who suffered on the cross. This title, especially in Pauline theology, proved to be seminal, producing new linguistic idioms and theological constructs. It is the Servant theme that becomes central to Paul's Christology ("taking the form of a servant," Phil. 2:7), to his soteriology (1 Cor. 15:3, 4; 2 Cor. 5:21; Rom. 4:25; 5:12-19; 8:3, 4), and to his understanding of the new people of God (2 Cor. 4:5; Col. 1:24, 25).[18]

What, then, does this title contribute to our understanding of the person and work of Christ? The Old Testament material celebrates the Servant in terms of his earthly accomplishment. The accent is on the past. The future, however, is not absent, for this Servant, though humiliated and suffering for a time, is seen by Isaiah as exalted and rejoicing over the results of his work (Isa. 53:11, 12).[19] As we move into the New Testament, past and future are brought into balance with one another. Christ's work on the cross, in which he was pierced for our transgressions (Isa. 53:5), is seen to be decisive for the future. His atoning death was the purpose of his incarnation, and it is the foundation on which and by which God relates to us. At the cross the Servant bore our sins. We are "healed" by his wounds (Isa. 53:5) because in his death he stood in our place, accepting responsibility for our sins and exhausting in himself the punishment due to us.

The purpose of Israel was culminated in and consummated by Jesus. Israel had borne God's revelation in the world and had been the recipient of God's covenants. It had instituted the temple and, on divine instruction, had learned of its need to approach God through sacrifice because of its guilt and sinfulness. And Israel had owned that Yahweh's kingship made the nation his possession. In the Servant, God shows himself, offers himself in sacrifice, and establishes a Kingdom which is universal. Israel had been a vine (Ps. 80:8; Hos. 10:1; Isa. 5:1, 2; Jer. 2:21). As prophet, priest, and King, Jesus, who is Isaiah's Suffering Servant, is now the "true vine" (John 15:1ff.).

LORD

What it meant in the New Testament period to call Christ "Lord" is today clouded by at least three considerations. First, κυριος is used in different ways in the New Testament; second, there is debate over the Greek translation of certain Hebrew and Aramaic terms; third, there is some question about the exact relationship between the use of κυριος in the New Testament and how it was used in the religious and political context of the time. These matters need to be considered briefly before the significance of this title can be developed.

First, we need to eliminate from further consideration the vocative use of κυριος. There are a number of instances where it is used simply as a polite form of address or, perhaps, as the recognition of Jesus' religious leadership (e.g., Matt. 8:8, 21; 15:27; 17:15; 18:21). Bultmann is correct in arguing that passages such as these do not necessarily accord Jesus divine status and may ascribe to him only the honor which it was conventional for rabbis to receive from disciples.

Second, the attempt to dissociate κυριος, as used of Christ in instances other than the vocative, from Yahweh seems to be an impossibility. In over 6,000 cases in the LXX, κυριος is a linguistic substitute for YHWH, the device which afforded the Jews the opportunity of referring to God without mentioning his name. Second-century manuscripts of the LXX show this, leading Marshall to conclude that κυριος was used by Greek-speaking Jews "as a translation of *adon,* 'Lord,' and as the equivalent of Yahweh."[20] This translation was not the imposition on the LXX of later Christian interests.

There has, likewise, been a debate over the merits of translating the Aramaic *mārê´* as "Lord," Hahn believing, for example, that a better translation would be "rabbi." The argument has been that *mārê´* was never used absolutely of God. The Qumran scrolls, however, have provided instances of such an absolute usage, and Moule has observed that Palestinian communities "already had a word *mārê´* which was capable of being used in a sense uncommonly near to that of κυριος as a divine designation."[21] That being the case, the expression *marana tha* (1 Cor. 16:22) should not be seen merely as invocation with respect to the future coming of Christ, but also as the acclamation of his present status as sovereign.[22]

Third, the connections between the use of κυριος in the New Testament and its use in society are not always clear, it is argued. In the classical Greek period, κυριος was not a divine title, but by the first century this had begun to change. Initially the title was used simply of those rulers to whom subjects gave their allegiance, but with the growing belief in the apotheosis of the Roman emperors, the title began to take on added significance. Thus Nero was described in an ascription as "Lord of the World," and Domitian was referred to in letters as "our Lord and God."[23] Whether this affected New Testament Christian use seems most unlikely, however, since the ascription of Lordship to Jesus is so sharply contrasted with these other forms of Lordship (1 Cor. 8:5, 6; 12:3).

The religious context provided by the mystery religions suggested to W. Bousset[24] a different connection with the Christian usage of this title. Based on a new approach to the New Testament documents, he

suggested that at first Christians had ascribed Lordship to Christ merely in terms of the future, but through the influence of the mystery
religions came to think of it also as necessitating a present experience.
This theory, however, rests largely on "guess-work" according to
Moule, and it certainly goes against known facts. At the most, the
mystery religions and the caesero-worship provided a context in which
the Christian use of κυριος developed. Its content, however, was
uniquely and distinctively Christian.

The κυριος simply designates one who has the right, the authority,
and the power to rule over others. This rule could be exercised with
benign or malignant effects. Some "lords" were, in the political arena,
despotic; and in the commercial sphere where the word was applied to
merchants, it often carried with it the connotation of high-handed and
avaricious dealing. In the New Testament, however, the meaning of
κυριος is determined by the character of the One of whom it is used,
and its association with the sovereign, saving Rule of God gives to it an
unparalleled elevation of meaning.

That a linguistic bridge was built early between Christ as κυριος
and Yahweh seems beyond dispute, and this bridge led naturally to a
doctrinal identity between them. What could be said of Yahweh in the
Old Testament could equally be said in many instances of Christ in the
New Testament, and it was. Thus the words, "before me every knee will
bow, by me every tongue will swear" (Isa. 45:23), spoken of Yahweh,
were seen to apply to Christ (Phil. 2:10, 11). The writer of Hebrews,
likewise, used the words of Psalm 102:25-27, which celebrated Yahweh
as Creator, equally of Christ[25] (Heb. 1:10-12). These usages are, as we
have already seen, but a small part of an extraordinary development
which was characteristic of virtually the whole of the episolatory section of the New Testament. What could be said of Yahweh, could be
said of Christ. If the gospel was God's, then it was also Christ's. If the
Kingdom was God's, then it was also Christ's. To have faith is, indis-
criminately, to have faith either in God or in Christ, and God and
Christ were alike to be praised, thanked, and worshiped. That being the
case, the use of κυριος became indistinguishable from the use of Θεος
in its content.

The Lordship of Christ was therefore placed in an eternal perspective. As Lord, Christ was preexistent and the Creator of all things (John
1:1-3; 1 Cor. 8:6; Heb. 1:2, 3); and as Lord he will yield up to his
Father a redeemed cosmos (1 Cor. 15:23-28)[26] and institute the new
creation. And everywhere the conviction is expressed that because he is
the Sovereign Lord, all enemies who oppose God's will, truth, and
reign will be conquered (Acts 2:34, 35; 5:31; 7:55; Rom. 8:34; Col. 3:1;
Eph. 1:20; 1 Pet. 3:22; Rev. 3:21). This conquest is, of course, still to be
realized in its fullness, but it has already been experienced in part in the
church. The "last times" are being inaugurated (Acts 2:14-18),[27] the

"powers of the coming age" (Heb. 6:5) are being experienced, and he who is Head of the church now (Col. 1:18) will be acknowledged as head of all of creation[28] at that time when "every knee [shall] bow, in heaven and on earth and under the earth, and every tongue confess that Jesus Christ is Lord" (Phil. 2:10, 11).[29]

It is in Paul's theology, however, that the title really catches fire. H. Weinel early on noticed an elevation of style in many of the passages where Christ's Lordship is the central concern, and the fact that Paul referred to Jesus as "Lord" in some two hundred and fifty passages is itself indicative of the importance this title held for him. To believe, is to believe in Christ as Lord (Rom. 10:9; 1 Cor. 12:3), who is identified with God and also personally distinguished from the Father (Rom. 1:8; 1 Cor. 1:4, 9; 2 Cor. 1:3, Eph. 1:3; Rom. 15:6). Yet his is a name above every name. The essence of his being, with its power and functions, is unmatched and unparalleled in heaven or on earth. It was this being, glorious and radiant, who confronted Paul on the Damascus road and in whose presence Paul continued to fashion his thought.[30] And no term conveyed the sense of awe, of adoration and wonder better than "Lord."

To speak of Christ as Lord, then, is to identify him ontologically with Yahweh, to ascribe to him the worship which rightly belongs only to God, to acknowledge him as sovereign in his church and in his creation, and to see him as the vindicator of God's character in the world. This vindication, wrought on the cross, is only partially recognized, but the vindication is fully accomplished. This recognition is a part of and necessarily accompanies the progressive realization of God's Kingdom whose climax and culmination will occur at the return of Christ. Then will occur the unveiling to all of the world of what, in fact, has been true from the very beginning—that the second person of the Godhead is Lord.

SON OF MAN
There are few places in the New Testament which exhibit more plainly the mental and spiritual distance which sometimes exists between ourselves as interpreters and the biblical writings we are interpreting than in the Son of Man sayings. This is a title which appears in all the Gospels (some fifty times). It is a title richly attested but used in every instance by Jesus, and never by others of him. Only once is there any suggestion that the audience might have been uncertain about its meaning (John 12:34). Today, however, scholarship is in disarray over what Jesus meant by this title, and those who are certain about its meaning appear to be as numerically insignificant as those who in Jesus' day were uncertain about its meaning!

Justice cannot be done here to the immense and complicated discussion which has been generated by this title.[31] We can, however, take our bearings on this wider discourse in the following ways. First, the fact that the use of this title disappears completely from the New Testament after Jesus' death, save for one exception (Acts 7:56), suggests that this was *his* term and not a formulation placed on his lips by the early church as Bultmann and N. Perrin propose.[32] If this title was the creation of the church, we would also expect to encounter it in the epistles. The solution which most adequately fits the facts is that the Gospel writers were recording Jesus' own language, even with what may now appear to be this oddity of expression. We need, however, to raise the question, second, as to whether this term "Son of Man" really was so odd. If it was an oddity, then why did Jesus' many audiences apparently feel that they were sufficiently familiar with the notion to be compelled to ask about its meaning only on one occasion?

This consideration is not in and of itself decisive for thinking that the origin of the term must have been common knowledge, but it is certainly suggestive of this fact. And if this is the case, it would appear more likely that it is the Old Testament which is its source rather than some of the more exotic apocalyptic writings in which "Son of Man" also appears,[33] some of which may be dated later than the Gospels themselves.

These suppositions have recently been confirmed by an argument from a slightly different angle which has been advanced by Moule.[34] He has pointed out that in the Gospels, the phrase which is used is not simply "Son of Man," but rather "*the* Son of Man." Moule then postulates that behind the Greek, ὁ υἱὸς τοῦ ἄνθρωπου, lies an Aramaic phrase which also had the article. It is interesting to observe, however, that the Aramaic of Daniel 7:13 lacks this article. It simply reads k^e $\underline{bar}$ 'ᵉ $n\bar{a}\check{s}$, "like a son of man." Inasmuch as this is in a poetic construct, the presense or absence of the article has little significance. The presence of this definite article in the New Testament, however, would seem to signify, not so much the Danielic text itself, but the common consensus regarding this figure in Daniel. Jesus therefore refers to *that* Son of Man about whom his audiences apparently had knowledge. Of the multitude of literary and historical reconstructions which have been advanced, this appears to be a fruitful one. The question as to what Jesus may have meant by this title is not, however, settled even if this solution is accepted. Still unresolved are the questions, first, as to what "Son of Man" means in the Old Testament; second, as to how Jesus himself employed it; and, third, whether he used it as a synonym for himself in place of a pronoun.

First, then, what might we understand by the use of this term in the Old Testament? The term is used both generally and specifically. Generally, it is used as a synonym for mankind, but mankind usually understood within the framework of creation and of the moral and spiritual accountability which that creation implies. It is thus that the term appears in Psalm 8:4. In Psalm 80:17 it is used even more particularly of God's own people, and in the Targums, at least, it is given Messianic overtones (cf. Num. 23:19; Job 25:6, 35:8; Ps. 144:3; Isa. 51:12). More specifically, it is the term by which Ezekiel and others are addressed (Ezek. 2:3-6; 3:1, 17, 25; 4:16; 5:1; 6:2), perhaps as a synonym for "seer" and certainly to accentuate the glory of God in his relations to the prophet. In Daniel, it is given its most particular contextual significance. The appearance of this superhuman figure in Daniel 7:13, 14 has also occasioned voluminus literature. At the very least, this figure is one in human form who functions alongside the "Ancient of Days," who is clearly God, in judgment. In Daniel's vision God gives to the Son of Man an eternal Kingdom. This figure is quite different from the four beasts. They arise from the sea (7:3) and belong to this world; he comes on the clouds (7:13), and his realm is supernatural and eternal (7:14). Their kingdoms falter and fade; his does not. Whether this Son of Man is a person or merely the personification of saintliness is debated. What appears most likely is that this Son of Man is both an individual person and the representative of those who are spiritually chaste and faithful to God, with whom he has a corporate identity. The presence of these "saints" is acknowledged (7:18-22, 27). They share in the Kingdom of the "Son of Man," but the "Son of Man" stands in the presence of God alone, in a way that is not accorded to the "saints" (7:9, 10, 13), suggesting both identity and differentiation.

The second question, then, is in what sense Jesus used this expression. And, as a part of that, the third question needs to be considered, which is whether he used the term of himself. At first sight, certain answers to these questions appear to be hard to find. One notes immediately that Jesus did not use the term merely of the present, as one might expect if Daniel 7 was the principal source of the term, but also of the past and future. The easiest solution, which is to eliminate some of these sayings either on the grounds of mistranslation or of redactional reconstruction as Bultmann does, is also the least satisfying. The different tenses must be allowed to stand. Furthermore, the sayings related to the Son of Man appear to have a tension built into them between those that relate to the cross and those which relate to the *parousia*. In this connection, Vincent Taylor has proposed that the *parousia*-sayings came before the cross-sayings.[35] It is his argument that Jesus initially believed the establishment of the Danielic Kingdom to be imminent, and only when his vision faltered did he begin to insist that he now "must" die. In the Gospels, however, this kind of sequence and chronology is not at all represented, and to sustain this argument it becomes necessary to insist that the order within all of the Gospels is arbitrary. That, however, seems to be a high price to pay for sustaining a literary reconstruction whose merits, even if the theory is correct, are rather minimal.

There are, in fact, three main categories in which these "Son of Man" sayings are now commonly placed. These are 1) sayings having to do with Jesus' ministry (e.g., Mark 2:10, 28; Luke 7:34; 9:58; 19:10); 2) sayings referring to his suffering and resurrection (e.g., Mark 10:45; Luke 17:24, 25; 22:48; 24:7; John 3:14; 6:53; 8:28; 12:23; 13:31); 3) sayings referring to his future coming (e.g., Mark 8:38; 13:26; 14:62; Luke 12:8-10, 40; 17:22-30; 18:8; Matt. 10:23; 19:28; 24:30; 25:31). Given these three contexts, are we considering the work of an individual and, if so, is it Jesus?

The school of thought in which T. W. Manson was a prominent spokesman proposed that many of the Son of Man sayings applied, not so much to an individual, but to a community. It was Manson's contention that Jesus came to create the "Son of Man," a community of faith whose ideals, as it turned out, were embodied and exemplified perfectly by himself. The favor in which this argument was held earlier seems largely to have passed, with a few noticeable exceptions like Morna Hooker,[36] because a number of the sayings simply are not susceptible of an exclusive community interpretation (e.g., Mark 2:10; 9:9, 31; 10:45; 14:21, 41; Luke 7:34; 9:58). And those proposals which suggest that the "Son of Man" was an individual, rather than a community, but someone other than Jesus himself, seem even more strained and problematic.

We seem, then, to be left with the following conclusions. First, this term was used by Jesus of himself and his work, and the reason its use provoked little questioning is that his various audiences had a working knowledge of its Old Testament derivations. Second, Jesus employed a term which has specific content in the Old Testament, but in applying it to himself and his work it came to have a meaning both larger and more complex than it does in the Old Testament. It is nothing less than remarkable how unwilling some scholars appear to be to accord to Jesus that kind of responsible creativity of which their own writings are considered purveyors. In applying this title to himself, Jesus broadened and deepened its meaning. Third, there is a consequent range of meanings which attach to Jesus' own use.

In some instances the term appears to be little more than a synonym for himself. Jesus was apparently intent on making allusions to himself and his work which would be suggestive of a status and role of which his hearers were at that time oblivious and which would lay the foundation for later clarification and self-disclosure. In other cases, however, the substance was more directly conveyed, and veiled suggestion gave way to explicit assertion.

In these assertions, numerous threads in his teaching, threads which elsewhere were often little more than mere hints, were united in a single role and title. As "Son of Man" he affirmed his essential solidarity with mankind. He was, in particular, all that Adam was intended to be, but failed to become. Jesus was man. In him, we see what human nature and human life were to be like. Though Paul may not have been consciously reflecting on this aspect of Jesus' teaching, the parallels drawn between Adam and Christ (Rom. 5:12-21; 1 Cor. 15:45-49) and the proposition that Christ was the "last Adam" appear to lie seminally in this title. Not only so, but there are corporate overtones in the title, especially in its setting in Daniel, which lead to the supposition that in Jesus' mind he identified himself in particular with God's "saints." This, of course, was fashioned throughout his teaching under the rubric of the Kingdom and was, of course, to find many interesting developments in Paul's thought, such as his images of the church as Christ's "body" and "bride."

This identity, however, was explicitly related by Jesus to his own work on the cross. He was to become the bearer of God's Rule, the agent through whom sin and evil were to be overcome. And when he predicted his triumphant return in glory, it was not so much the vindication of his own life of which he spoke as the divine cause in which his role was so central and in which his teaching and acts stood as a compelling summons. Thus the title comprehended his life of humiliation, when he often did not know where to lay his head (Matt. 8:20), his mission to save the lost (Mark 10:45), his authority to forgive sin (Mark 2:10), his work of securing the basis for that forgiveness (Mark 8:31), and his resurrection (Matt. 17:9). It also included his glorious assumption into heaven, his return and role in divine judgment (Matt. 19:28; 24:30) and his place in the regeneration of the cosmos (Matt. 19:28). That this "Son of Man" is divine becomes an inescapable conclusion from these utterances, and the title "Son of Man" therefore becomes a synonym for the preexistent Messiah (John 3:13), in whom the character of God is perfectly revealed and by whom the will of God is perfectly executed.

The titular material in the New Testament does not stand by itself. It assumes the identity of Jesus and, in many instances, is a confession of that identity. Though these titles are tantamount to theological shorthand, the ideas which come to focus in each title are often complex. The titular material grows out of both the words and acts of Jesus and needs always to be placed in the full context of our New Testament writings.

Part 2: Historical Development

4 TRANSITION

During the days of Jesus' ministry, people speculated about his identity (Matt. 16:13, 14). Once the New Testament was completed, however, speculation shifted from who he was to *what* he was. What does it mean to say that Jesus was divine? Can it be held that this divinity was actually a "power" that came upon him? Are there gradations in the divine being which might allow people to say that while Jesus was divine, his Godness was not the same as the Godness of the Father? And what is meant by saying that Jesus was human? Is it possible that his nature, while being human, was in some respects different from ours? Are people obliged to think that he had two wills and two minds? Did both his humanity and his divinity have their respective personalities? If so, what were the relations between the twin centers of self-consciousness? If not, was he fully human and fully divine if either lacked personality? Is it appropriate to think that some experiences should be predicated of the divinity while others can be related to the humanity?

The answers to these questions only came with the passage of time and often under the provocation of heresy. The formulation of a theological response, both to the questions raised and to the heretical aberrations which had raised them, was a slow, protracted business. The problem lay as much in the process of doing theology as in the questions the church was seeking to address.

In the early centuries the theological process was complicated by a series of factors, three of which deserve some consideration here. First, it was necessary for the church to establish how orthodoxy was going to be defined, for unless this was done any heretic could masquerade as having the truth. This task, however, was greatly complicated by a second factor—namely, what role philosophy could legitimately play in this defining process. In time, this led to quite different attitudes and strategies when one compares the approach of the Latin West and the

Greek East to heresy. Third, the doing of theology during the fourth and fifth centuries, which were critical for Christology, was greatly affected by a series of emperors who sought to dictate what the theological outcome would be, and their reasons for so doing were often less than laudable. Although this chapter is concerned with these issues as they surfaced in the patristic period, what it presents is a case study with applicability in most ages subsequent to the patristic.

WHAT IS ORTHODOXY?

The first problem with which we are concerned in the postapostolic church's theological work was its definition of orthodoxy. How was orthodoxy to be defined, and what were the criteria by which heresy could be identified?

If by orthodoxy we mean the correct *(orthos)* view *(doxa)* on Christ or any other matter of importance to our faith, then some theologians have said we may think of it in two entirely different ways. On the one hand, what is orthodox is what the apostles taught. Used to describe the apostolic teaching or tradition,[1] orthodoxy is a fixed, static, enduring, unchanging body of truth which is to be believed and obeyed. The inability or refusal to live within the cognitive boundaries of this teaching is what constitutes heresy. On the other hand, the word *orthodoxy* later on became identified, not merely with what the Scriptures taught, but also with what the church taught. As such, orthodoxy was the church's clarification as to what was involved in believing the teaching of Scripture. The church's work of defining and protecting the apostolic teaching has been, from that time onwards, a continuing responsibility, since each age and culture has had its own questions and its own peculiar temptations in the light of which the meaning of Scripture has had to be reaffirmed. Orthodoxy, when used of the church's interpretive work, is therefore fluid and open to revision. Every such system of orthodoxy must be probed for deficiency by the biblical Word, and every generation must develop its own interpretive orthodoxy relative to its own particular challenges.

This distinction between these two orthodoxies[2] appeared early in the life of the church, but in a relatively short period of time it also began to disappear as the one orthodoxy was merged into the other. The reason for this was the increased pressure that was brought to bear on the church both by schismatics and by heretics. In such circumstances, the most effective protection against doctrinal perversion, it seemed, was to insist that the church alone had the authority and the means of interpreting the biblical Word aright. Tertullian even argued,[3] on the grounds of a legal technicality, that the church alone had the "right" of access to the Scripture; heretics had no "right" to read and interpret these documents. Biblical orthodoxy therefore became identified with and merged into ecclesiastical orthodoxy. Christianity, therefore, was what the church said it was; it was what was "handed down by pen and mouth from age to age, generation to generation, mother to child, teachers to taught, pulpit to pew."[4] So complete did the identification become that Bossuet, the reigning Catholic apologete in the seventeenth century, could declare that any variation in or departure from ecclesiastical teaching was heretical. Orthodoxy, in other words, had now been completely identified with its second form, that of church teaching, and heresy was defined solely in relation to what the church defined as being "the faith."

The Protestant Reformation therefore appeared thoroughly scandalous to informed Roman Catholics. When the Reformers attacked the substance of ecclesiastical orthodoxy they were, in the eyes of Roman Catholics, attacking biblical orthodoxy, for these two orthodoxies could not be distinguished from one another. The Reformers insisted, however, that they had to be distinguished because the ecclesiastical orthodoxy was destroying aspects of the biblical orthodoxy.[5]

The question which was at stake in the patristic period, which flared up again in the Protestant Reformation and which, with today's emergence of third-world Christianity, is again demanding special theological attention, is obviously that of continuity and change. In what does the unchanging Christian faith consist, and how do we recognize and preserve it amidst the changing of culture and the challenges of heresy? The answer to this question, of course, has profound implications for the way in which any Christology is constructed, as well as how past formulations of faith are viewed. Three quite different solutions to this problem have emerged.

First, there are those who have insisted that the continuity of the faith is preserved insofar as the language and thought of the biblical Word is believed. The religious language which emerges to express this faith, as well as the conceptuality in which it is framed, are in many ways cultural phenomena. Language and conceptuality therefore may change. Neither is inviolable. Neither is wedded to the biblical Word. Indeed, both are constantly to be judged by that Word. It alone does not change.

This view, which obviously makes biblical orthodoxy primary to and dominant over any ecclesiastical or theological orthodoxy, must make two assumptions. First, it must assume that the inspiration of Scripture secures for us an identity between the mind of God and the teaching of Scripture, for only the thought of God could have the necessary quality of infallibility and changelessness. Second, it must assume that this thought can be found with confidence in and through the biblical writings. It is the difficulty of making this second assumption that has drawn many people who hold the first presupposition into the Church of Rome. Protestants undoubtedly have at time been proponents of individualistic hermeneutics, "each man claiming the right to set aside the past," as James Orr said, "and put his fresh-coined fancy in its place."[6] The problem of continuity and change, of preserving what is infallible truth within the mind of the fallible interpreter affected by his or her own culture, is not, however, resolved simply by appealing to councils or Popes. They, too, are fallible and culture-bound despite any dogma to the contrary.[7] And if refuge is sought in the collective leading of the Holy Spirit in the church as an antidote to an individual's infallibility, it may be replied that majorities, not only in politics but also in matters of faith, have frequently been wrong. In the end there is no escape from human fallibility in interpretation, not for those within nor for those without the Roman Catholic magisterium. It is this fact that underscores the need to have the objective, functioning authority of the biblical Word which is above the interpreter and which provides the necessary means for the ongoing testing of the validity of every interpretation.

A second solution, then, is that advanced by Roman Catholicism. In the modern period, the problem of continuity and change has been sharply focused by John Henry Newman.[8] In what does Christian faith consist, and what is changeless amidst the changing of cultures? The answer which he provided and which the Second Vatican Council reaffirmed[9] was that the changeless core lay in the germinal doctrine of Scripture; what could legitimately change was not merely its expression but also its implicit substance. For there can be, he affirmed, a legitimate growth in the Church's understanding of what was intended in any text or passage of Scripture, even though this meaning is not explicitly affirmed in and in some cases cannot possibly be extracted from Scripture.[10] This view also requires one to make two assumptions. First, the inspiration of Scripture must be affirmed in such a way that infallible truth is secured by the written Word. Second, it must be assumed that the interpreter—in this case the Roman magisterium—can discern the additional but hidden meanings of Scripture.

This second assumption troubled Newman himself. As a result, he devised two safeguards against a promiscuous use of Scripture. The first was internal and concerned the nature of truth;[11] the second was external and required the assumption of an infallible church.[12] When the church begins to "see" a meaning in Scripture which it had not fully understood before, this truth may be regarded as a valid extension of biblical truth, if it meets the criteria of seven tests which Newman enumerated. The first three tests appear to be sound. First, this truth must have universal appeal, for God is the God of all. Second, it must preserve continuity of principle because there are not different Christian faiths. Third, it must be logically consistent with what is already established as biblical teaching. Newman's fifth and sixth principles, however, beg the question. He argued that a new "truth" must be shown to be potentially in Scripture and that it must conserve the original, biblical teaching. The problem is that these two tests provide no real criteria for discerning whether one is reading a "truth" into Scripture or reading a "truth" out of it. Mariology is a case in point. Traditional Roman Catholics argue that the main ideas in Marian thought—immaculate conception, sinlessness, and bodily assumption—are all implied in the angelic greeting (Luke 1:28). This teaching about Mary, it is claimed, is potentially in Scripture and, in fact, conserves the real intent of Scripture. It has nevertheless been rightly countered that Roman Catholics in so arguing are inserting a meaning into Scripture which is not only alien to the biblical teaching, but also perverts what is elsewhere plainly taught about Mary.

Newman's remaining two tests are even more vulnerable to criticism. He argued that Christian doctrine, if authentic, has power to assimilate other ideas into its substance and that a further test of the validity of any idea is whether it endures through time. Both tests take insufficient account of the reality of sin in our fallen world. Obviously religions other than Christianity are not true simply because of their record of survival, nor can Christian doctrine be judged authentic because some of its proponents are able to forge a synthesis with other teachings. In the end, Newman's tests have to be applied by an infallible church; otherwise they always yield uncertain and fallible answers. His internal safeguard, the nature of truth, dissolves in practice into his external safeguard, the functioning of a traditional magisterium.

The magisterium, however, must also make some assumptions. After all, many people capable of erring cannot arrogate to themselves a dominant authority which they deny to other individuals or groups unless that quality of sure interpretation is thought to be secured for themselves by the Holy Spirit. The Roman Catholic magisterium has traditionally made this claim, but it has to be said that the only way in which this argument can find biblical warrant is if it is claimed that it lies concealed within the biblical teaching. The magisterium therefore has to assume the presence of this concealed truth in Scripture before it can function authoritatively, and it justifies its authoritative functioning on the basis of what it is forced to assume. This is a case of circular reasoning.

Third, others have argued that Christian faith is preserved across the centuries neither through the biblical words nor the interpretation of the church, but in Christian experience. Christian identity is preserved through experiencing the same Christ, however differently this experience is described doctrinally and conceptually.

This was the proposal advanced by liberal Protestantism[13] in the last century, for example—the assumption being that there is in all people a God-consciousness. This consciousness comes to birth in different forms and is nurtured with different degrees of success by different people. The intellectual understanding of the experience almost inevitably borrows its conceptual tools from its own culture. These are both insufficient and fallible. They are neither durable nor final. In its contemporary form, this understanding has been given special currency by existentialist Rudolf Bultmann. The New Testament authors, he argues, employed conceptual and narrative forms which were peculiar to the first century. Included in these would be their understanding of the supernatural, miracles, heaven, and hell. No twentieth-century person, Bultmann avers, can believe such things. What we need to do today is to discover the experience which was communicated through these "myths" and, by replacing the ancient world view by a modern one, reaffirm in ways vernacular to our modern world the meaning of Christian faith.[14]

The question, then, is how to relate the absolute and unchanging truth of God's revelation to a relative and shifting culture. Conservative Protestants have made the truth of God's Word primary, sometimes failing in the process to mesh what is says with the age in which they live. Traditional Roman Catholics and liberal Protestants have paid far more attention to what changes in this relationship than to what does not. Catholics have simply written later changes back into Scripture on the supposition that what the church comes to "see" later must have lain concealed beneath the surface of the text in the beginning. There is, nevertheless, a serious attempt to deal with the issue of continuity, however flawed that attempt ends up being. In liberal Protestantism the attempt is abandoned more or less completely. Christianity merges into the changing culture and becomes identified with its finer aspects.[15] Each approach, correspondingly, sees heresy in a different way. Conservative Protestants define it as a departure from the teaching of Scripture. Since traditional Roman Catholics equate the teaching of Scripture with that of the church, heresy for them is a departure from the church's teaching. In liberal Protestantism, truth is such a relative and privatized matter that it becomes impossible and undesirable to define heresy with any degree of precision. It is these different attitudes toward both heresy and orthodoxy which frequently explain the widely divergent accounts that we now have of the emergence of Christological thought in the early church.

In the early church, this definitional complexity probably did not exist; modern divergence and debate over the nature of orthodoxy has often been projected back onto these centuries. Walter Bauer, for example, has argued that the theological initiative was invariably in the hands of the heretic, and therefore heresy was antecedent to orthodoxy.[16] Orthodoxy, he claimed, was merely a reflex to and a reaction against what had been proposed by the heretic. The validity of Bauer's contention depends, of course, on how orthodoxy is defined. He is partly correct if orthodoxy is used of the church's interpretation of apostolic teaching, but he is wrong if it is used of the apostolic teaching itself.

This, at any rate, is the contention set forth by H. E. W. Turner in his study on the problem. According to Turner, orthodoxy was temporally prior to heresy because orthodoxy, in the patristic view, was identified with apostolic teaching. That being the case, the relationship of heresy to orthodoxy, Turner argued, took one or more of five forms, each one of which assumed that the relation of heresy to orthodoxy was that of a parasite to its host.[17] These forms are (1) dilution (the infusion of alien concepts into the Christian corpus of teaching); (2) truncation (the reduction of Christian truth to something less than its fullness); (3) distortion (the disproportionate enlargement of some themes to the neglect of others); (4) archaism (the unwillingness to accept further valid insights into the meaning of apostolic teaching or to see that the Old Testament has been extended and in part superseded by the New); and (5) evacuation (the removal of the heart of the Christian system as in Arianism, rather than just a limb). The degree of heresy in these "types" varied, as did its method. But whether the defection was accomplished by addition, subtraction, distortion, imbalance, or outright denial, the body of apostolic teaching had not been preserved intact, and this is what constituted the condition of heresy.

WHAT IS APPROPRIATE LANGUAGE?

The second main problem the church faced concerned language and conceptuality. In seeking to explain the natures of Christ and his personality, the church made use of terms which already had philosophical pedigrees. In the Nicene Creed, for example, the thrust of the orthodox reply to the denial of Jesus' divinity lay mainly in the use of the word *homoousios* (of the same substance). Although this may represent what the apostles intended to teach, they themselves never used the word. Again, in the Chalcedonian Definition the orthodox reply to the Nestorian and Apollinarian heresies was to insist that there were two natures *(phusis)* in one person *(prosōpon* or *hypostasis)*. None of these words appears directly in Scripture either, except in Hebrews 1:3. Consequently, objections were raised that this interpretive work resulted in a type of Christianity that had been infiltrated by an alien philosophy. In the nineteenth century Adolf Harnack was to popularize this misgiving by speaking of the "acute Hellenization" of Christianity in the early centuries. The problem which is raised is whether language that is nonbiblical and, in these cases, philosophical can be used to define and explore the meaning of Christian faith without in some way perverting it.

As a matter of fact, the task of reflecting on apostolic teaching and adapting it to contemporary intellectual needs was not undertaken with much alacrity in the West in the patristic period. The intellectual passivity of early Latin Christianity was quite pronounced.[18] Practical concerns largely replaced intellectual ones; moralism displaced theology. These Christians were witnesses to faith, not often interpreters of it. Exploring the meaning of biblical doctrine was something that was forced upon them by the activity of heretics; it was not something they initiated on their own very often.

The attitude of the East was, however, quite different. Here philosophy came to be viewed as a vehicle of truth, and therefore speculation in matters of a Christological nature was treated at least benignly if not actually welcomed. In the West, however, philosophy was viewed with suspicion, and stern warnings were issued about the dangers of confusing philosophical thought and Christian faith.

The hospitality given to philosophy in the East may perhaps be explained by the fact that the East was predominantly Greek, even as the opposition to philosophy in the West may be accounted for by the fact that it was predominantly Latin. At least it became clear, at a very early stage, that a difference of approach was developing, a difference that over the centuries became so deep that in the eleventh century the Roman bishop excommunicated his counterpart in Constantinople, thus dividing Roman Catholicism from Eastern Greek Orthodoxy.

The approach of Easterners was early signaled when converts such as Aristedes and Clement of Alexandria, both of whom were well versed in philosophy, joined the Christian ranks. In their efforts at interpretation they began to make use of philosophy, trying to show that the best of pagan thinkers rejected what the Christians rejected and wanted what the Christians had. Philosophy was soon providing a bridge to the non-Christian world and traffic, moving in both directions, began to pass over it.

This is seen, for example, in the *Apology* of Aristedes, which begins with a defense of God's existence based on Aristotle's notion of motion;[19] in Justin, who unashamedly appealed to Plato for his view that the mind, if "purified by righteousness," can penetrate "very Being"[20]; in Clement of Alexandria, who argued that as the Jews had the law as their *paidagōgos* (Gal. 3:24), so the Greeks had their philosophy, and whether the antecedent was law or philosophy, an equally good preparation had been laid for the saving work of Christ.[21] In later writers, the mind's way to perfection was patterned on the model of Neoplatonism. The mind, it was taught, ascended from sensible to intellectual, an ascent which culminated in a mystical and ecstatic union with God. Philosophy, then, had found an ample niche in the structure of Christian thought as developed in the Greek East.[22]

This turn of events was not without some advantage. Christian theologians, it must be said, were no longer living in splendid intellectual isolation. But the price for their relevance to contemporary ideas was, at times, a little high. Philosophy, with its penchant for heresy, was being brought into a dangerously close and amiable relationship with orthodox faith.

It is tempting to think that this was not the case in the West, for there were some memorable broadsides fired against the intrusion of philosophy into Christian thought. Tertullian's indignant expostulation about confusing Athens with Jerusalem, the academy with the church, immediately comes to mind.[23] But Latin theologians were more influenced by philosophical notions than they sometimes realized. It is not difficult, for example, to see traces of Stoicism in some of Tertullian's ideas. His notion that the divine essence is merely a refined form of matter hardly finds its genesis in anything which the apostles taught. Western theologians did argue, however, that heresy is always and invariably rooted in philosophy. Their counsel (which they themselves did not always follow) was that the Christian who wants to avoid heresy must avoid philosophy.[24]

The different mentalities exhibited by East and West are plainly apparent in their respective attitudes towards gnosticism, the most pressing of the early heresies. To Eastern theologians like Clement of Alexandria, Christianity was the "true gnosis"; the gnostics had only an incomplete *gnōsis* (knowledge). Clement's point was that the gnostics were correct insofar as they had come. The problem was that they had not come far enough, for they lacked faith. To Western theologians like Irenaeus and Tertullian, gnosticism was wrong because its presuppositions were wrong. Because gnostics started with philosophical presuppositions, in the nature of the case they had to end up with fallacious conclusions. They were completely wrong, and not just partially wrong. Western defenders of the faith, therefore, scoffed at their opponents, mocking them for intellectual pride and uncontrolled speculation. To Irenaeus, the gnostic resembled "the strutting of a cock and the pomposity of a factotum."

Different attitudes between Easterners and Westerners led to different tactics in handling the gnostic challenge. Easterners tried to win them over to a more complete understanding of faith; Westerners tried to exclude them from Christian ranks. The one took up the weapon of reason, the other the cudgel of ecclesiastical censure.

These opposing strategies were symptomatic of a growing polarization in the early church between East and West that became further exacerbated by the difficulties in language that developed. From the second century onwards, Latin become the theological language of the West, while Greek was still retained in the East. The importance of this development was to be seen, for example, in the fourth century when the Trinitarian discussions were at a critical juncture.

In 362, the Council of Alexandria met to resolve some of the theological tensions that had arisen over Arianism, but in the process it brought about some reconciliation caused by these linguistic problems.[25] Until this time there had been three main technical terms used of the Godhead by the Greeks. The first of these was *ousia.* In classical philosophy this was usually used to denote a single existence or individual entity; it was not used of "being." In its Christian setting, however, it began to take on the latter connotation. Origen, who was the first to use it in discussion on the Trinity, declared that there is one reality, one and the same stuff or *ousia,* in which Father, Son, and Spirit subsist. The second term was *hypostasis.* The classical philosophers most commonly used this term to describe the real essence of a thing, that which underlay and which held together its outer, empirical qualities. Origen used this of the Godness which underlay both the Father and the Son.

The third term was *prosōpon.* Originally it was used either of a face or of the face's expression, which revealed what was within the person. It was also used in a legal context for the person who held the right to a property. In its theological context, when used in its former sense, it was applied to the Son who visibly represented what was otherwise hidden in the Godhead; and when employed in the latter sense, it was used of him as having an individual, concrete existence. The contemporary understanding of "person," which borrows heavily on psychology and is largely concerned with self-consciousness and self-understanding, should not be read back into any early discussion on Christ, or for that matter the Father or the Spirit.

The problem then arose over how to translate these terms from Greek to Latin. As a matter of fact, *ousia* and *hypostasis* were so close that they were almost synonyms, and by the time the Council of Alexandria was meeting, the third term, *prosōpon,* was beginning to drop out of use. The need for a term to take its place was assumed by *hypostasis.* This meant, however, that Easterners could speak of God as having three *ousiai*—if by that they meant "persons." But to those seeking a Latin equivalent, that could sound as if the Easterners believed in three *substantiae,* or "beings." Three *substantiae* would be tritheism! Conversely, Westerners could insist that God had one *substantia,* but in the East this could be understood as one *hypostasis* or "person!" One *hypostasis* would be monarchianism!

The Council of Alexandria therefore resolved this terminological confusion, and in so doing put in place the technical apparatus that was needed to discuss the person of Christ relative to the Trinity. It was decided that the East's *ousia* would always be translated by the West's *substantia. Hypostasis* would always be translated by *persona.* God, therefore has one *ousia* or *substantia,* but Father, Son and Spirit is each a *persona* or *hypostasis.* This agreement opened the way for the assertion that the one God is to be worshiped as a Trinity and the Trinity as a unity. The larger questions, however, as to what conceptuality can legitimately be employed in the service of theology, and how close an alliance can be forged with philosophy in this work were never resolved. They have unsettled the church, in different ways, from the second century to the twentieth.

SHOULD THE EMPEROR BE A THEOLOGIAN?

Christologies prior to the fourth century were relatively unaffected by the views of the Roman emperor or his immediate entourage. As a matter of fact, until the emergence of Constantine the Roman emperors concerned themselves with Christian faith only spasmodically, and then their concern was to contain or eliminate it, rather than define it. With the conversion of Constantine in 312 all of this changed. From this point on the views of the emperor significantly affected the balance of power in the Christian world, and this in turn led to the ascendancy of those closest to the emperor in theological attitude.

This is seen, perhaps, nowhere more clearly than in the agonizingly protracted debate over Arianism, the major chapters of which coincided precisely with the shifting fortunes in the emperor's palace.[26] The imperial theologian had become a factor in the church's attempt to define its faith, often fusing a profound knowledge of the workings of worldly power with comparatively little understanding of the intricacies of the faith.

Arius came to prominence early in the fourth century in Alexandria, where he worshiped under the jurisdiction of Bishop Alexander. It was Arius' contention that since the being of God could not be communicated or shared with another without the divine uniqueness being placed in jeopardy, everything else which existed did so by an act of his creation.[27] The Son, therefore, was a creation. He was begotten only in the sense of being created. As created, he had a beginning, as did all other created beings; and as a creation he could neither know his Father directly, nor could he be preserved from the possibility of change and sin. Arius spoke of three Persons, but they were neither coequal nor coeternal, for they did not share the same divine essence.

The Council of Nicea, a new and dramatic procedure for dealing with the outbreak of heresy, was called in 325. The Council was attended by three hundred and eighteen bishops, according to Athanasius, the young assistant to Bishop Alexander. These bishops were divided into four parties. First, there were the two bishops who supported Arius. Second there were the supporters of Bishop Alexander, probably numbering about thirty, who were the real opponents of Arius. They argued that the Son was *homoousion* (of the same substance) with the Father. In between were two parties, the one led by Eusebius of Nicomedia, which tilted toward the left and was semi-Arian and the other, led by Eusebius of Caesarea, which tilted toward the right and was semi-Alexandrian. Given the composition of the Council, it is remarkable that a relatively small minority behind Bishop Alexander was able to sway the vast majority and persuade the Council to adopt the *homoousios* position.

The Nicene Creed, in its reply to Arius, asserted that the Son is *homoousion* with the Father, that his begetting cannot be understood to mean that he was created, and that he was "true God from true God." There was not, as Arius asserted, a difference in the Godness of the Son when compared with that of the Father because they shared the same *ousia* (being). In so saying, Nicea attacked the heart of Arianism and preserved Christian faith from drifting into polytheism.

Or so it seemed. The decision reached at Nicea, however, turned out to be a hollow victory, and it was not until the Council of Constantinople in 381 that the church as a whole adopted the Nicene Creed in practice. Between 325 and 381 ecclesiastical politics, theological misunderstanding, and imperial meddling deprived the church of the clarity of understanding which it had allowed Bishop Alexander to pioneer at Nicea.

During this period four quite different positions on the person of Christ were maintained. The Nicene party, now led by Athanasius following the death of Alexander in 328, argued the position that the Son was *homoousion* (of the same substance) with the Father. They continued to be opposed by the Arians, who became completely ascendant between 353-361 and who argued the Son was *anomoios* (unlike) the Father. Between these old antagonists were the centrists. One group that leaned toward the right argued Christ was *homoiousios* (of similar substance), and the other, leaning toward the left, that he was *homoios* (that he could be compared to the Father), although the term itself omitted any reference to "being" or "substance." Depending on whether it was Constantine, Constantius, Valentinian I, Valens, Gratian, Julian the Apostate, Jovina, or Theodosius I who was in power, these parties either found themselves favored, disgraced, tolerated, or ignored. One thing, however, was clear. These emperors all played the ecclesiastical game, greatly complicating the serious definitional task which the church had been forced to address. Although these intrusions by the emperors were probably undertaken, more often than not, out of political considerations for the empire, the effect was invariably felt at a theological level in the church.

If the emperors were impressed by the advantages to be gained through involvement in ecclesiastical politics, so too were the churchmen of this period impressed by the advantages to be gained through courting the emperor. Each, in their respective way, benefited. Christology therefore became entangled in worldly politics and ecclesiastical manuevering. Indeed a churchman's Christology, his connections in the church, and the favor or disfavor with which he was treated at the imperial level became almost indistinguishable. Those who were unscrupulous exploited these connections for their own advantage but others, like Athanasius, suffered greatly as a result. For seventeen years he was in exile or hiding. Five times he was banished. In refusing to allow political pressure to dictate his theology, and specifically his

Christology, Athanasius sometimes had to stand almost alone. He became the exception to a rule practiced very widely.

In light of these considerations, it would clearly be mistaken to think that the doing of theology in the patristic period, or in those which followed it, was an antiseptic process. It became, in fact, a central ingredient in a political process by which it was often affected and at times perverted. The church, struggling to protect itself from heretics and schismatics, also reached out for conceptual and linguistic tools whose use in the construction of Christology often seriously affected the content of what was believed about Christ. It is this latter theme which must now be explored more carefully and fully.

5 CLASSICAL CHRISTOLOGY: THE PATRISTIC AGE

The main line of Christological development that takes us from the early fathers to the Reformers and into the post-Reformation scholastics constitutes what is here called "classical Christology." Whether it should be regarded as classical in the sense of being standard and authoritative over against that which is unbiblical and unacceptable might be debated. It is, however, classical in the sense that it struggled—and sometimes failed in its struggle—to make sense out of the fact that in the Word incarnate there was both full humanity and full divinity in a single person.

This does not mean, of course, that this conviction was never challenged during this long passage of time, even within the "classical" tradition. Nor does it mean that Christ's humanity and divinity were never compromised, however unwittingly, or that the unity of his person was not at times jeopardized. It does mean, however, that from the fifth century on the church became convinced that justice would not be done to the biblical portrayal of Christ if the theological players in the game had less than a full deck of cards. And that cannot be said of the modern period. Orthodox Christology, Georg Wehrung asserts, "was destroyed by the new world view of the Enlightenment." With it there have risen strong humanistic currents the upshot of which, all too often, has been the feeling that Christ was merely human, though endowed "with extraordinary gifts and outstanding moral character." He bequeathed a system of religion and ethics to the world that "could have been found out without him."[1]

The consensus of the fifth century, associated in particular with the Chalcedonian Definition, was of course preceded by centuries of debate during which time the components of the problem were being formed. Initially the church had to contend with the extreme aberrations in which first Christ's humanity was denied and then his divinity.

These extremes formed the background for the more careful work which was to come. They need to be reviewed briefly.

There were, in fact, many modifications in the way the docetic position (from *dokein,* to seem) was advanced, but by whatever route the argument was followed, the conclusion was that Jesus' humanity was unreal. It was phantasmal. Serapion of Antioch was the first to complain about the docetists and linked them to the Marcionites.[2] Behind the docetists' denial there was usually the assumption, as in the case with the gnostic sects, that all matter is evil. How, then, could God be joined to that which is evil? Allied to this there was also the assumption in many cases that since God is beyond change and suffering he could not, by definition, have formed a union with that which is changing and passible. This, of course, went to the heart of the Christological problem, but prior to the fourth century it was not explored very fully. It seemed sufficient, given the presence of the problem, for the docetists merely to deny that Jesus could have been human. In response, it was sufficient for the church to affirm that he had to have been human, without answering this problem specifically.

On the other side of the Christological spectrum were those who denied that Jesus was divine. The principal protagonists were, in their different ways, Paul of Samosata and Arius. Each pioneered attitudes which have never been fully banished from the church.

Paul of Samosata, the epitome of the vain, worldly, and secularized cleric, authored what a synodical letter described as "new fangled ideas" and "spurious and bastard doctrines."[3] They centered on the belief that Jesus was merely from "below," not from "above." His starting-point was that kind of monarchianism which affirmed God to be one in person as well as in being.[4] If God had his Word, and he did, that Word therefore could be no more than an impersonal attribute. It could not have had personal identity. This Word or power merely came upon Jesus as it had the long line of prophets. It indwelt him. Although there was no union of natures, there was a transferral of power by which Jesus was enabled to perform miracles and even to overcome sin in himself and others.[5] As a reward, God promoted him to divine status and gave him "a name above every name."

Paul's unitarianism, of course, proclaimed a doctrine of human inspiration rather than of divine incarnation. The Word did not become flesh, but rather the flesh became Word. God did not become man, but a human being was elevated to become God. It was a form of unitarianism that had affinities both with Sabellianism and with Arianism. With respect to the latter, it is true, there were differences. Arius spoke of the preexistence of the Son which Paul denied, but both, in their different ways, succeeded in evacuating the divinity of its biblical content. If their Christs were "divine," it was not in any recognizably Christian sense.

Furthermore, both Arius and Paul asserted that the "divine" had displaced an essential part of the nature of Jesus. Arius argued that what was lost was the intellect or rational soul. As stated a little later in Eudoxius' creed, it was believed that the Word was made "flesh but not man," that the flesh was but a veil, God taking the place of the soul. None of the early Arians really developed this idea; they merely exploited it in the interests of arguing that Jesus' Godness was of a different order from that of the Father. Paul of Samosata said the divinity took the place of "the inward part of our nature." Thus, his Christ was only partially human and not divine at all. It was this line of thought that was transmitted to Arius, who was taught by Lucian, one of Paul's pupils.

The church expressed its displeasure with this outlook. The Synod of Antioch deposed Paul in 269[6] and, as we have seen, the Arian challenge was formally addressed at the Council of Nicea in 325, though not actually silenced until the final quarter of the fourth century. In the period from the Council of Constantinople (381) to that of Chalcedon (451) the heart of the Christological problem was laid bare. If the church was to discount these crude aberrations and affirm both the full humanity and full divinity of Christ, how was it to relate the natures to one another and how was it to speak of Christ's unity? It was in this period that the formal lines of debate were set out and the issues explored so profoundly that even when we examine the Reformation period and that of the Protestant orthodoxy which followed, we are still within the same general discussion. Indeed, we often seem to be doing little more than adding periodic footnotes, although the powerful formulation given to soteriological concerns as well as theological methodology in the Reformation did provide a different framework for the older Christological belief.

TWO SCHOOLS

The story of Christological interpretation in the later patristic period is largely, though not completely, the story of two conflicting interpretive traditions.[7] These approaches are usually called the Alexandrine and Antiochene. These terms are not entirely satisfactory. These schools, it is true, were centered in Alexandria and Antioch, but they were not localized theologies. Indeed, these schools of thought have continued to the present day long after their cities of origin have ceased to be focal points on the ecclesiastical map. It is therefore better to speak of these schools in terms of their typical Christology—"Word-flesh" and "Word-man"—rather than the cities in which they first came to prominence.

In the absence of a clear understanding of the Christological problem in the early stages, the church developed ways of thinking about Jesus without always understanding that they had developed from philosophical presuppositions. "Their task," Aloys Grillmeier has said of these two schools, "should have been to uncover their different philosophical frameworks, but this kept on being neglected."[8] With the passage of time, the presuppositions became more deep-seated and the church became less self-conscious about its thought processes at this point.

The *"Word-flesh" Christology,* whose original locus was Alexandria, operated off Platonic assumptions and largely dominated the church's thinking from the time of Origen to about the time of the Council of Ephesus in 431. Typically, this Platonism stressed two cardinal points. First, it underscored the difference between the transcendent God and that shifting world which is contingent upon him. Our world is always and everywhere relative, whereas God is absolute; it is changing, whereas he never changes. Second, it considered each person as a body inhabited by a soul essentially alien to it, and it believed that the soul's incarceration in the body adversely affected the highest life of that soul.

These two charateristics of Platonism shaped the Christology which built on it. Because this form of Platonism stressed the *differences* rather than the similarities between God and his world, its Christology affirmed an uncompromised divinity even in incarnation. "Word-flesh" Christologies were invariably "high" in the sense that they always protected Nicene orthodoxy. They argued for the incarnation of a higher being in a lower order. Second, because of its dualistic attitude toward the person and its belief that the body adversely affected the soul, Platonic Christology removed what was seen to be a necessary point of vulnerability in Christ's humanity. The soul, or "hegemonic principle" or center of direction in Jesus' humanity, it was commonly argued, had either to be removed altogether or at least rendered inert. In the incarnate union, the Word replaced this principle and acted as its surrogate. The Word rather than the soul was therefore the experiencing center of Jesus' humanity. In practice, his was a soulless humanity.

The expression of this Christology followed three paths, two of which were heretical. Already we have noted that the Arians denied a rational soul to Christ, as did Paul of Samosata; and both, in their different ways, added to this difficulty the offense of denying his divinity. Second, in the fourth century Apollinaris, a staunch opponent of Arianism, nevertheless continued this same tradition with respect to Jesus' humanity, also arguing that the Word replaced the human soul. In the process, Apollinaris gave birth to the heresy which bore his name. Third, in a muted form, Athanasius,[9] who also opposed the Arians mightily, aligned himself with this same tendency by asserting that while Jesus' humanity was complete, his soul was not operative and played no soteriological part. Those experiences normally attributed to the soul should be ascribed to the divine Word within him. The outcome of this approach was a denial of the full humanity of Jesus, although Athanasius did not quite cross the border between orthodoxy and heresy.

This kind of Christology secured a far-reaching psychological unity for the God-man, but its philosophical interests also explain some of the typical characteristics of this school, such as a devaluation of the importance of the historical Jesus and a discounting of those suggestions in Scripture that Jesus grew cognitively and psychologically. The Word, after all, is not subject to growth. Platonists, furthermore, had little interest in the empirical world, in which alone the historical Jesus appeared, and much more interest in that world seen to be lying behind it. A human being can give insight merely into that world which is relative and changing, whereas the divine Word could provide access to what is absolute and unchanging. It was, then, the divine Word that held all of the Christological interest for them rather than the historical Jesus.

The *"Word-man" Christology* was centered in Antioch and was forged in opposition to the "Word-flesh" approach. With the defeat of Arianism and Apollinarianism late in the fourth century, it came into full bloom providing the structure for much of the church's thought in the fifth century. It worked off Aristotelian premises. It preferred literal to allegorical interpretation. It was often rationalistic in its temper and opposed to mysticism. If Platonists emphasized the discontinuity and disjuncture between God and his world, Aristotelians argued for their interpenetration and relationship. God is to be understood *through* the empirical world, not antecedently to it. The divine Word is only known within and through the human Jesus and not apart from him. Typically, then, this Christology made a full and complete humanity, and one subject to all of the processes of growth, its starting-point. Whereas those in the "Word-flesh" tradition thought of the life of the divine Word as falling into two chapters, preincarnate and postincarnate, those who propounded the "Word-man" outlook sometimes gave the impression that the Word only came into personal existence at the time of the Incarnation.

The "Word-man" approach actually worked itself out in several quite different directions. This is evident when one notes that its proponents included Eustathius of Antioch, Flavian, Diodore, Chrysostom, Theodore of Mopsuestia, Theodoret of Cyrus, and Nestorius, all of whom loosely constituted the same "school." Most of these thinkers enjoyed the church's approval, the main exception being Nestorius, of course, who suffered its full censure.

In its most orthodox expression, the "Word-man" Christology merely sought to ascribe full reality to Jesus' humanity. This desire, however, easily lent itself to the thought that since Christ's humanity was full and complete, as was his divinity, there were in him two sons joined together, not by personal union, but simply by common purpose. In its most aberrant expression, it began with the recognition of Jesus' full humanity and then dissolved his divinity into a "power" which came to rest upon him and to invest his life with significance. It is the variety of expression within this school of thought that was greatly exploited by its opponents. Those who heard Nestorius arguing for the full reality of Jesus' humanity, for example, set this against the persistent weakness of the "Word-man" approach in being able to affirm the personal union of the God-man and concluded that Nestorius was a secret adoptionist, following in the footsteps of Paul of Samosata!

These two schools became arch-rivals despite the fact that they held much in common. Indeed, R. V. Sellers has developed an elaborate, carefully documented case for saying that "the two parties could not see that they were each contending for the same cardinal principles." What actually divided them, he says, was ecclesiastical politics and personal ambition, which together produced a "spirit of warfare." It was a spirit which searched, not for common understanding, but for "the defeat of the enemy."[10] This is true. It would nevertheless be a mistake to overlook the different philosophical outlooks of each school, the results of which were genuine Christological differences. These differences might have been resolved in a different atmosphere, one that was amiable and conciliatory; in the actual context of rivalry, philosophical differences became the tools for ousting and humiliating the opponents.

Perhaps most fundamentally, the different ways in which soteriological interests were articulated produced Christologies that were different in their substance. The "Word-flesh" Christology was determined by the idea which Athanasius had expounded in *De Incarnatione*, that since the fall had introduced corruption and mortality into human life, the Incarnation needed to produce their antidotes, incorruption and immortality. By joining himself to human nature, the divine Word began that process of reversal which is salvation. To achieve this, however, the divine Word had to work within a human nature spared from those vulnerabilities to which other humans are prone. This, "Word-flesh" proponents believed, was achieved when the Word supplanted or, in the case of Apollinaris, displaced the operating center of Jesus' humanity. It enabled them to say that salvation was achieved, not by the cooperation of a fallible human being with God, but solely by "the unchangeable, invincible power of God, restoring humanity to its true self."[11] It was no accident, in their view, that Nestorius, who seemed to argue for two sons cohabiting the same body and coexisting within it, also refused to take decisive action against the Pelagians. What Pelagius argued for—a salvation achieved by moral struggle and crowned with the possibility of sinless perfection since no one enters this world hampered by original sin—ran parallel to what the "Word-man" proponents argued for. Salvation, they seemed to say, resulted from the earnest cooperation of this man, Jesus, who worked in harmony with the divine Word. Salvation was not something wrought by God alone, but was the result of a cooperative effort with the ideal man, Jesus.

It was also no accident that Martin Luther adopted the "Word-flesh" Christology, although purging it from its Eastern ideas of salvation. Against such mighty powers as sin, death, and the devil, he declared, only another and a higher power could prevail, that of God himself. Almost immediately an abridged interest in Jesus' humanity began to show itself on the Lutheran side of the Reformation. This was aggravated by their need, for sacramental purposes, of affirming the ubiquity (or omnipresence) of Jesus' body. The divine Word, God triumphant, was the dominant interest and the humanity was absorbed into the divinity, taking on its attributes and characteristics. This powerful and consuming interest in Christ's divinity in time produced its reaction. In the eighteenth century the pendulum swung violently to the other extreme. The "Word-man" Christology, allied to the new interest in psychology and anthropology, dominated the later nineteenth century and has controlled most of the twentieth. Today the "Word-flesh" Christology is largely in disgrace.[12] But so, too, are the ideas of a full, complete divinity in Jesus and of a salvation that is all of grace because it is all of God.

TWO CASE STUDIES

Apollinaris did not represent the full range of views that constituted the "Word-flesh" Christology, nor did Nestorius the "Word-man" outlook. They do, however, offer interesting cases for study, for each epitomized many of the tendencies that their schools of thought took for granted.

Apollinaris, who became bishop of Laodicea in 361, had been a staunch defender of Nicene orthodoxy and was, in fact, a close friend of Athanasius. The first foreshadowing of the difficulties to come occurred in 362 when Athanasius chaired the Council of Alexandria. Athanasius declared that Jesus did, indeed, possess a human and rational soul;[13] Apollinaris denied it. Goaded on by his opponents Diodore of Tarsus and Theodore of Mopsuestia, he articulated a more radical form of "Word-flesh" Christology, in the process of which he crossed the bounds of orthodoxy.

Older historians used to think that Apollinaris' real foes were Arians. Arians had employed passages of Scripture stating or implying that Christ was subject to growth, change, and temptation to prove that he could not be divine, for God can neither change nor grow and is not subject to temptation. It is now clear that it was not only the Arians who were the objects of Apollinaris' attack, but also the Syrian proponents of the "Word-man" Christology. Although Apollinaris was diametrically opposed to the Arians on the matter of Christ's divinity, he was one with them in believing that Christ's humanity had no soul. What Apollinaris disliked among the "Word-man" advocates was the opinion that Christ was seemingly two realities, one human and one divine, who, being so divided, could be said to be subject to change in one regard but not in another. This seemed to represent a wholly inadequate yoking together of two persons in Christ Jesus. Not only so, but it seemed to follow that a choice would necessarily then have to be made between the fullness of the humanity and the fullness of the divinity. Because of the "Word-man" propensity for affirming the humanity of Jesus, was it not the case that these teachers would soon be dissolving the divinity into a mere power or grace which alighted upon Jesus? Severing the personal link between human and divine in Christ, as they seemed to do, threatened to destroy a viable soteriology. These were the fears and this the context in which Apollinaris developed his rather roughshod Christology.

Apollinaris' starting-point, as it was for the other "Word-flesh" proponents, was the unity of the God-man. We sense this, he said, in our worship. We do not worship a human being, nor do we distinguish in our worship between what was divine in Jesus and what was merely human.[14] The humanity of Jesus was not something essentially extraneous to and disjointed from the divine, and the divine did not merely fill the human.[15] Rather, God and man actually became one in a unique creation such that the human being who speaks to us in the Gospels is God.[16] Apollinaris spoke of the divine and the human in Christ forming a "compound unity" and, even more daringly, of the two forming "one and the same nature."[17] The divine and the human were fused into one another, the human being absorbed into and subsumed under the divine. In so saying, Apollinaris believed that he had not advanced one iota beyond Athanasius, whose pupil he was. And he was correct.

His heresy lay in the bold and inadvised explanation he offered as to how the human and divine were fused into "one nature." God, he asserted, replaced the "hegenomic principle," the intellect or directing center in Jesus' humanity. Jesus, he said, was "not a human being but like a human being" because "in his highest part," the intellect, he was not "consubstantial with humanity."[18] The Word joined to himself a soulless humanity. This, said Apollinaris, is what incarnation means. To suppose that the divine center of operations in the Word merely functioned alongside rather than replaced the human center of operations would undercut both Christology and soteriology, for only as our autonomous, "self-moved intellect" is assumed into Christ can we be saved.[19] Jesus, therefore, had "God for Spirit."[20] As such, the seat of all sin, the intellect, was removed and the God-man was preserved both from sin itself as well as from the possibility of sin. In other words, condensing the two natures into one, which incarnation required, for these two natures could not merely lie side by side and be joined merely in common action, necessitated the truncation of one of them. Jesus was hominoid but not fully human.

The ecclesiastical storm broke in 375. Condemnations followed in the West in 377 and in the East in 378, 379, and 381. Two main points of objection were made. First, Apollinarianism was a form of docetism, however mild, and to that extent could not be squared with the biblical account of Christ. Nor was it clear why Apollinaris felt driven to assert this position. The core of Jesus' humanity had to be extracted for fear of its power to contaminate the divine. But why was this so? Why could not the human directive principle, the intellect, coalesce with the divine and function, subject to the Word, in total harmony with him? Second, for all of Apollinaris' soteriological interest, he had, in fact, undercut the very principle on which Christian salvation rests. Long before, Origen had asserted that the whole person could not be saved unless Christ had taken upon himself a whole human nature and this soon passed into conventional wisdom, via the Cappadoceans, in the statement that what "has not been assumed cannot be restored; it is what is united to God which is saved."[21] If the humanity of Christ lacked that which most needed to be redeemed—the intellect, which Apollinaris believed to be the seat of sin—then what could be redeemed in those joined to him was their humanity in all of its parts save its center from which all sin arose. Ironically, Apollinaris formulated his Christology to preserve a full, robust soteriology only to be told that the means of preservation had, in fact, become the tool of destruction.

Nestorius, declares G. L. Prestige, was "a heresiarch who in the most explicit terms repudiated the heresy of which he was accused"; he was a teacher deposed for innovation, but he "had not added a single original principle to the common stock of ideas." Perhaps even more remarkably, he was a leader who maintained that "the views which ultimately triumphed in the course of controversy were identical with his own." For all of that, Prestige laments, he was made an outcast and was "the cause of the most extensive schism originating in ancient Christendom."[22] This understanding of Nestorius is a modern development. It grows out of the discovery announced in 1897 of a mutilated Syriac copy of his intellectual self-justification entitled *The Bazaar of Heracleides*. Whether Nestorius was a Nestorian now seems doubtful, and his condemnation as a heretic is probably best explained as the result of power politics between ecclesiastical centers as well as the long-standing feud between advocates of the opposing "Word-flesh" and "Word-man" Christologies.

Nestorius' problems began when the title *Theotokos* (literally, "God-bearer" but understood in popular devotion as "Mother of God") was publicly attacked and then defended in Constantinople where he had been appointed patriarch in 428. Nestorius sided with the attackers. The use of this title, Nestorius thought, made confusion of Christ's natures, and this inevitably led to a diminution of the divine.[23] Not only so, but it made Mary to be a goddess, for who but a goddess could give birth to a god? These criticisms of the use of *Theotokos* were, unfortunately, capable of great misunderstanding, and there were those who were eager to misunderstand the newly appointed patriarch. If Mary was not the Mother of God, they reasoned, perhaps she was only the mother of a mere man who later became God. For all of Nestorius' protestations about the divinity of Christ, perhaps he was a secret adoptionist in the tradition of Paul of Samosata. Nestorius' blunder was rapidly and skillfully exploited by Cyril, who advocated the opposing "Word-flesh" outlook.

In the debate with Cyril,[24] Nestorius, as a spokesman for the "Word-man" Christology, made two propositions central. First, if our salvation is to be effected, the humanity of Christ had to be full and complete and include the possession of a rational soul or intellect. Second, both the humanity and the divinity would be compromised if, in their union in Christ, they did not retain all of their essential characteristics. Each nature, he said, had its respective *prosopon*.[25] This, as much as anything, added fuel to the fires of confusion. He apparently did not mean that each nature had its own personality, although that is what he was widely understood to mean. He used *prosopon* elastically and imprecisely. What he had in mind was "appearance."[26] As the face reveals the mood and character of the person, so Christ, in what he said and did, revealed both his humanity and his divinity.

Cyril, of course, started from a different position, arguing that the personal subject, the experiencing center, of the God-man was one and the same. Cyril employed the troublesome words "one after union" to speak of the relation of the humanity and divinity. What he meant was not that the two natures were merged in and confused with one another, but rather that neither nature expressed itself except in union and in conjunction with the other. Nestorius did not hear in this a principle he himself held. What he heard was the proposition that Christ, being one person, was possessed of only one nature which resulted from a fusion of humanity and divinity. In this situation the divinity would have to be truncated. And, despite Cyril's denials, Nestorius also suspected that the humanity was reduced and lacking, in the tradition of Apollinaris, the central directing principle. Thus Cyril's Christ would be neither fully human nor fully divine.

This dispute was undeniably exacerbated by willful misunderstanding on both sides, by imperial meddling, and by seamy ecclesiastical politics. There were, however, differences of style and substance at the center. Nestorius contended tenaciously for the full humanity of Christ, Cyril for his unity. Nestorius thought of the exaltation of what was human by its union with the divine; Cyril spoke of the condescension of the divine for its union with human nature. Nestorius secured the truth of the two natures, Cyril of the one person. For this reason Cyril employed the *communicatio idiomatum,* the exchange of attributes between human and divine, and Nestorius denied it. To ascribe to the human characteristics that pertained to the divine and to the divine characteristics that pertained to the human resulted, said Nestorius, in confusing the natures. To refuse to do so, Cyril retorted, would result in a dividing of the person. To Nestorius, Cyril was a crypto-Arian; to Cyril, Nestorius was a secret adoptionist.

TOWARD A SOLUTION

For reasons that may not have been entirely laudable, the church sided with Cyril. Nestorius was deposed in 431, the decision being upheld by later councils which repudiated his heresy.

In 451, the Council of Chalcedon was called to resolve the trench warfare to which proponents of both types of Christology had taken.[27] Like so many other councils, Chalcedon began by doing its share of condemning and deposing. It went on to reaffirm the Niceno-Constantinopolitan creed, endorse Leo's *Tome* and some, though not all, of Cyril's letters against Nestorius, and then set about writing a statement which would direct the church in its thought about Christ.

The long period of strife to which the schools of Christological thought had driven the church had at least revealed that heretical aberration was possible on both sides. Chalcedon, therefore, charted middle territory and succeeded in doing so with consummate skill. "Word-flesh" advocates, it asserted, had to be willing to allow against all of their natural theological tendencies that both natures in Christ were fully preserved. These natures, the human and the divine, remained "without confusion, without change, without division, or without separation." Although the human and the divine had a common life, the divine was not merged into the human, nor was the human absorbed into the divine. There was no conversion of the divine, nor adoption of the human, but each retained the properties and functions appropriate to it after union. The Definition asserted that it was to a human nature *(ousia)* rather than a person *(hypostasis* or *prosōpon)* that the divine Word was joined. This means that all of the human qualities and powers were present in Jesus, but that the ego, the self-conscious acting subject, was in fact a composite union of the human and divine.

"Word-man" proponents, on the other hand, had to make peace with that affirmation which sometimes disconcerted them theologically that there was "one and the same Son, one Lord Jesus Christ," "one and the same Christ" who was born of Mary, the *Theotokos.* They could

take comfort from the fact that "the peculiarity of each nature is preserved" and that the "difference of the natures is in no way denied by
reason of their union," but were obliged to affirm that these natures
were joined in a permanent, inseparable union. Jesus therefore had but
one center or principle of operation in himself, and there was in him
but one acting subject who performed miracles and suffered on the
cross. His human nature, therefore, had no existence except in that
union with the divine which had created this single person; apart from
this hypostatic union, the human nature had no personality of its own.
It was in the divine that his human nature lived, and that human life
was not experienced separately from the life of the divine. He had two
natures, one fully human and the other fully divine, but was only one
person.

What was left unexplored in this conception was, of course, the
precise relationship between the natures and whether *ousia* and *prosopon* can, in fact, be distinguished. The Definition identified the area
within which the relationship between Christ's natures is to be found—
without confusion, change, division, or separation—but did not, or
could not, state more positively what the mechanics of that relationship
were. Furthermore, it is not entirely clear how a human nature devoid
of its ego is still human nature; without its *prosopon*, Jesus' *ousia* would
be merely *homoiousion* with ours and not *homoousion*. Would a human
nature merely "like" ours meet the soteriological requirements that it
be "the same"?

The fact that Chalcedon sought to mark out territory that lay
between the two schools of thought has tempted many interpreters to
see in its solution either a compromise[28] or theological bankruptcy.[29]
Indeed, at the time "Word-flesh" enthusiasts in the East believed that it
was a compromise that unduly favored the "Word-man" supporters of
the West. These Easterners rejected the Definition and continued their
Christological reflections as if Chalcedon had never occurred.[30] In
actual fact, Chalcedon succeeded in going beyond the competing
schools of thought even as it wove together the essential concerns from
both sides. It forged a view of Christ that sought to be faithful to the key
elements of the biblical presentation. What it failed to see clearly
enough, however, is what the "Word-flesh" defenders had always insisted upon—namely that there is an interpenetration of Christ's person
and work in the New Testament. It was this that Luther reasserted, and
in so doing he joined together once again what the New Testament had
held together in the beginning.

6 CLASSICAL CHRISTOLOGY: FROM THE DARK AGES TO THE REFORMATION

The period which stretches from the fall of Rome in the early fifth century to the Protestant Reformation in the sixteenth often goes under the designation of "medieval Catholicism." It is a period which has suffered considerable abuse at the hands of historians and theologians.

The Renaissance scholars, who proposed the periodization, spoke of this whole time as being the "Dark Ages." To them, it was a rough and worthless interlude which separated the glories of the classical past, and in particular its humanist focus, from its recovery in the fourteenth and fifteenth centuries. This estimate was continued, albeit for entirely different reasons, by the Protestant Reformers. In 1535 Martin Luther declared in his introduction to Robert Barnes's *Vitae Pontificum* that he had, until that time, contested Rome on the grounds of Scripture, but, he said, an equally good case could be made from history. The Protestants increasingly argued that the Reformation debate was really one between patristic and medieval Christianity.[1] The Middle Ages were often disparaged as marking the point where Christian faith had been derailed. This relentless attack was continued by most scholars in the seventeenth and eighteenth centuries. Their general assessment was also shared by Hegel, who declared in his lectures in 1840 that he had found nothing in medieval philosophical thought except the "base remnants of the Roman world, which on its Fall had sunk in all respects so low that the culture of the world seemed to have come entirely to an end."[2]

In recent decades, however, this negative assessment has been considerably reversed.[3] Many new studies have shown that the high Middle Ages laid the foundation for institutions which have endured to the present and which characterize the essence of Western civilization, such as banking, the jury system, university education, and government. For this reason, the term *Dark Ages* is here restricted to the period from the fifth century to the ninth, although it is recognized that it is sometimes used only of the fifth and sixth centuries and sometimes also of the fifth century through the eleventh. The term *Middle Ages* is here used of the tenth century through the fourteenth, a period that includes the brilliant scholastic flowering in the church.

The fortunes of the church underwent some remarkable changes during the millenium which is in view. At the beginning of the period, the Barbarians were sweeping south from Europe, leaving behind them nothing but a smoldering funeral pyre, and they even attacked and destroyed Rome itself. The lights of Roman civilization began to go out. Many of the structures and institutions of the Greco-Roman world disintegrated. The church withdrew into itself. The flame of learning often flickered only in the monasteries. By the twelfth century, however, the church had reemerged as the mistress and teacher of Europe. It was a wealthy landowner and a powerful institution, wielding the weapons of worldly authority. This transformation did not occur, however, without some loss, the most significant being that of Eastern Christianity.

THE EASTERN TRADITION

From the beginning there had been a potential rift between East and West. Easterners and Westerners developed characteristic ways of thinking. Western theology tended to be more pragmatic, legally minded, down-to-earth, and moralistic. Eastern thinking was typically more mystical, daring, and given to flights of speculative fancy. These differences in mentality produced different theological styles. These styles became increasingly entrenched in opposition to one another as each world looked to competing centers of ecclesiastical leadership, the centers being Rome and Constantinople. These centers and their respective worlds drifted apart from each other politically, linguistically, and culturally. By the fifth century bilingual capacity was already fading, and by the ninth it had virtually disappeared. The Latin West and the Greek East became strangers to one another. This development was heightened by the fact that under Charlemagne, the frontier began to move northwards. The axis of civilization no longer lay east-west as it had in the Roman world. It now lay north-south. Increasingly, Greek Christianity came to be viewed by Westerners as being in the cultural backwaters; and with the triumph of Islam in lands interposed between East and West, Greek Christianity came to be more or less forgotten in the Latin West. The mutual separation and excommunications which took place in 1054 merely cemented long-standing cultural and theological differences which had never been resolved even in the early centuries.

It is this growing bifurcation in Christendom and the increasing ignorance of the East by the Westerners which explains why the post-Chalcedon debates failed to affect the life of the Catholic Church. For

Westerners, Chalcedon resolved the Christological issues; for Easterners, always more speculative and less enamored with legalistic formulae, the Definition merely opened up the Christological question. In the East, this produced extended debates, first over monophysitism and then over monothelitism. In the West there was only a brief recrudescence of adoptionism which was officially subdued at the Council of Frankford (794), although it continued to be a pastoral problem for some time afterwards.

Eastern Christology always had at its center Cyril's dictum that there was one nature after union. This axiom, of course, was susceptible of different interpretations. The more extreme form was monophysitism, which in time spawned monothelitism.

The monophysites[4] contended that Christ could only have had one nature after incarnation, for if he had two, as Chalcedon had insisted, he would have been in two persons. They believed they were protecting the other aspect of Chalcedon's teaching that Christ was one person.

The history of monophysitism became involved and extensive. In the post-Chalcedonian period, it went through three distinct phases.[5] The first period ran from 451-482, during which time the reaction to Chalcedon began to take shape and assume some force. In the second period, from 482-565, it was able to win concessions from ecclesiastical authorities, but these monophysites refused to make their peace with prevailing orthodoxy. In the third phase, from 565-622, they separated, founding their own churches in Armenia, Syria, and Egypt.

The main line of thought in the East was not altogether unsympathetic to monophysitism, but it sought to maintain a stricter adherence to Chalcedon. Two figures who were pivotal in this development were Leontius of Byzantium (485-543) and John of Damascus (c. 675—c. 749).

Chalcedon had merely stated, without supporting explanation, that there were two natures in Christ. This seemed to pose an awkward choice if an explanation were to be sought. Either the natures were joined in hybrid union or they were merely loosely associated in a common personality. Both solutions had their difficulties. Leontius broke through this dilemma by employing Aristotelian reasoning. He argued that nature cannot exist separately from its concrete expression in personhood. It cannot be *anhypostatic* (existing impersonally), but must be *enhypostatic* (finding its expression in personhood). This, of course, challenged the common Platonic habit of imagining that forms could be known apart from their concrete realization in this world. It meant that for Leontius the full humanity of Christ was only completed in its union with the Word. This was, of course, less than what the monophysites hoped for. They contended that Christ's human nature was impersonal. By contrast, the Western Antiochenes argued that it had full personality prior to incarnate union. Leontius' enhypostatic union was a *via media* between these positions.

The Second Council of Constantinople (553) sought to interpret Chalcedon from this new perspective. It endorsed Leontius' view of the enhypostatic union and, in Eastern eyes at least, minimized Chalcedon's insistence on the two natures after union. It also condemned those who had been most insistent on preserving the separate integrity of each nature after union, such as Theodore of Mopsuestia and Theodoret of Cyprus. It also implied that the two natures were mysteriously one without quite adopting the offending formula, and it hinted that the Word was the experiencing center in the God-man.[6]

This Alexandrine tilt to the Chalcedonian formula paved the way for the emergence of monothelitism. If Christ had one nature, then it followed that he had one will. The Third Council of Constantinople (680), however, denied this. There was in Christ only one functioning will, but the Council went on to insist that this resulted from the coalescence of both the divine and human wills.[7] So once again the church had stated that a humanity devoid of any part would not meet the soteriological demands with which Christology must always reckon. Apollinarianism, in this variant form, was still not acceptable.

Nevertheless, the East continued to keep its distance from the West and to develop its own characteristic modes of thought. These were in part the cause of the rupture with the West, and their preservation became an important tool in guarding the distinctive Eastern ways of church life. Political and theological questions constantly played off one another.

The epitome of this development was John of Damascus. His adherence to the Chalcedonian formula was openly expressed. The two natures of Christ were "preserved intact in Him after union."[8] The relation of these natures was seen in the light of Leontius' view of the enhypostatic union. The natures were "united to each other in one composite Person,"[9] and John of Damascus affirmed the presence of two wills working in harmony and concert with one another. Nevertheless, he went on to reason in the Alexandrine mode that while the two natures retained the properties appropriate to each, the divine came to "permeate" the human. Although he said the two natures were "mutually immanent in each other,"[10] it turned out that the divine was more present in the human than the human in the divine! Christ's humanity, he said, was "one with divinity." This meant that as a human being, Christ did not experience the limitations common to human life. The Scripture declares that Jesus grew in wisdom but, said John of Damascus, we should understand by this merely that there was a progressive realization of omniscience in him.

The Eastern way of thought in Christology survived both because it protected convictions that had first surfaced in the exchanges between Cyril and Nestorius and because it was increasingly unchallenged. Political, cultural, and linguistic relations between East and West had broken down. To Easterners, Western theological thought was discounted as being barbarian; to Westerners, Eastern thought was over-looked as being of no consequence. John of Damascus ritualistically attacked the "hellish band" of Nestorius, Diodore, and Theodore of Mopsuestia, but attacks like these were really made for Eastern readers. Communication had died by the eighth century, and the Schism of 1054 became inevitable.[11]

WESTERN DEVELOPMENT

The period of greatest creativity in the West in Christological matters was undoubtedly the patristic age. The Middle Ages was a time, not of creativity, but of codification. Westerners were content to repeat Chalcedonian verities and to reinforce them through a vigorous question-and-answer format. It is, however, difficult to overestimate the importance of the discovery of Aristotle by the Western church in the mid-twelfth century and the new assumptions about reason which this discovery engendered. It is, of course, to Thomas Aquinas that the church was indebted for his role in domesticating Aristotle and forging a new synthesis between philosophy and faith.

The Western interpretive tradition is connected with the names of Boethius (c. 480-c. 524), Anselm (1033-1109), Abelard (1079-1142), Hugh of Saint Victor (1096-1141), Albertus Magnus (1193-1280), Thomas Aquinas (1224-1274), Duns Scotus (1266-1308) and William of Ockham (1280-1349). These thinkers all made distinctive contributions, but they also fall into two quite clear groups. The one, represented by Boethius, Anselm, and Hugh St. Victor, spoke from within the Augustinian-Platonic world. It was a world which was to be shattered by the reentry of Aristotle's works from their Arab custodians into the West. Abelard immediately hailed Aristotle as being the most "perspicuous of all philosophers," but the church was not altogether certain initially.[12] Thomas Aquinas assumed the task of investigating where the legitimate bounds of Aristotelianiam lay. He expressed his enthusiasm for the method of Aristotle, but he infused it with Augustinian content. The church at first condemned Thomas, but then reversed herself, later canonizing him. From the beginning of the fourteenth century onwards, Aristotelian method became dominant, often allied to empirical nominalism. It was this tradition which was represented by Abelard, Albertus Magnus, Duns Scotus, and William of Ockham. In order to set in contrast these two approaches, it is useful to compare the two great rivals, Anselm and Abelard. They do not, of course, represent the entire gamut of medieval thinkers, but they do provide a useful focus for studying scholastic thought.

TWO CASE STUDIES

Anselm and Abelard represented two schools of thought, the one Platonic and the other Aristotelian. The former adopted a rationalistic *a priori* approach to theology, the other an empirical, critical, and innovative one. It is, however, significant to note that Anselm's treatment of the person of Christ was construed within his treatment of the work of Christ. The widespread practice of penance created the context within which Christ's work was understood. Chalcedon's "two-nature" doctrine was accepted as a starting axiom in theology in the West. Attention now shifted in Anselm to its connections with soteriology.

Platonists assumed that the ways of God are rational and that they can be discovered through deductive logic. It was as if there were a network of truths which cover the world, the lower ends of which dangled tantalizingly into the upper reaches of human experience. If the mind could take hold of one of these threads, it could climb above the world of sense experience and link itself with the other threads. More than that, it would now be in a position to understand universals, those world-transcending axioms which are true in all places and times and which are never affected by the changing perceptions of human observers. Knowledge of universals is enduring knowledge; it is the "real" knowledge.[13] The world of sense and time is but their reflection, related to them as echo is to sound.

It was this assumption that produced the *a priori* approach of the Platonist school, and it often led to an odd conclusion. If a Christology begins with supra-temporal, universal principles, it will undoubtedly find that it has answered its Christological questions without having had recourse to the historical Jesus at all!

In general, this approach was evident in Boethius' *The Consolation of Philosophy,* for which he is justly famous, as well as in his lesser known *Contra Eutychen.* In the latter, where he refuted both Nestorianism and Eutychianism, the framework of Chalcedonian Christology was fully accepted. Catholic faith, he declared, "confesses that both natures continue in Christ and that they both remain perfect, neither being transformed into the other. . . . Christ consists both in and of the two natures; *in* the two because both continue, *of* the two because the one person of Christ is formed by the union of the two continuing natures."[14] What is of interest is the content which he infused into the words *nature* and *person,* which was philosophically derived and developed.[15] The formal structure of Chalcedon remained, but its meaning was being determined by philosophical interests.

The same tendency was evident in Hugh St. Victor who equated the Logos of John's Gospel and the Christ of Paul's epistles, the "Wisdom of God," with that Idea in God's mind according to which "all things have been formed,"[16] and which is reflected in all things but especially the human mind. This Word was the point of rational unification of all things, and the human mind is therefore the means for pursuing ultimate knowledge.[17] This assumption was apparent throughout Anselm's *Cur Deus Homo,* where *a priori* reasoning was used to provide the answer to why an incarnation was necessary. The answer Anselm provided was that sin created infinite debt and dishonored God by withholding what was due to him. If this honor had not been satisfied by repayment, God would necessarily have had to punish every offender. Since, however, sin is infinite in its consequences, no human being can repay the debt owed and the honor denied. It follows that only an infinite person could pay such a debt, but since this payment had to be made by a human, the Incarnation of the God-man became a necessity. It was this same kind of approach which led him elsewhere to deduce antecedently that it had to be the Son who was incarnate, rather than the Father or Spirit.[18]

The Son therefore did ultimately what human beings can only do relatively. Penance offered by human beings cannot offset infinite sin, but Christ's act of penance, coming from an infinite person, can. Since he was sinless and did not need to perform such an act, it became a work of supererogation whose merit was passed on to the church in the form of forgiveness. The Incarnation, Anselm proved, was "not a figment but a fact; and not just a fact but a necessary fact,"[19] for without it there could be no forgiveness from God.

The contrast in approaches between these schools of thought is as striking as the contrasts between Anselm and Abelard. Abelard was the brilliant lecturer and debater who trampled recklessly over most conventions. This is seen, not least, in his love affair with the beautiful Heloise through whom he fathered a child, but both entered monasteries to languish for their remaining days.

Abelard did not address Christology in any particular work as did Anselm, but his general approach was evident in *Epitome of Christian Theology* and his *Commentary on Romans*. His approach was empirical and boiled down to addressing an orderly but rigorous set of questions to the biblical and patristic authors. From this procedure emerged the building blocks for a doctrinal structure.

This empirical approach was linked, however, to nominalistic assumptions. Abelard assumed that universals had no reality. The encounter with the empirical world does not lead the mind into a knowledge of eternal verities; these "verities" are simply a creation of the mind. Much later, Hume and Locke would show that particulars can have no meaning in the absence of universals. Nominalism always flirted with, if it was not explicitly wedded to, agnosticism in one form or another.

In Abelard, therefore, there was an abandonment of the Anselmian quest of finding a unifying principle in the light of which theology in general could be comprehended. In its place was simply a method of "scientific" classification of textual data. These approaches could be contrasted as beginning "above" in Anselm and "below" in Abelard. And since Abelard was agnostic as to how the atonement might have affected God, the vertical aspect was replaced by a horizontal interest. The work of Christ was conceived psychologically rather than metaphysically. The interest for Abelard was not its effect upon God, but its effect upon us.

With the ascendancy of the Aristotelian method, the monuments of learning in the thirteenth century therefore became the great compilations of past opinions. These include most obviously Alexander of Hales' *Summa universae theologiae,* Bonaventura's *Book of the Sentences,* Albertus Magnus' *Summa,* Duns Scotus' *Commentary on the Sentences,* and the greatest of them all, Thomas Aquinas' *Summa.*

The one point at which the Chalcedonian heritage came to be questioned was over the nature of the bond between the human and divine. It was not a new question. Three variations emerged, only one of which could be conceived to be viable ecclesiastically. Peter Lombard reported[20] that some people held that it was not merely human nature which was assumed by the divine person, but also a human person. This meant that after union there would be two natures and two persons which was, once again, the characteristic weakness for Nestorianism which Western thought had often displayed. The second view he described was Leontius' enhypostatic union, that the bond between human and divine natures was accomplished in the person of the Word. The third view, which Pope Alexander III condemned in 1177, argued that there could not be a substantial union between human and divine since God is immutable and flesh is mutable. The divine merely put on the human without being substantially linked to it. This argument repeated elements from both Arianism and Nestorianism. Thus, concludes Heiko Obermann, medieval scholasticism "had to find its way through trial and effort back to the formulations of Chalcedon."[21] Nestorianism was once again refuted, and the hypostatic union, now known as the "subsistence theory," was reaffirmed.

THE SYNTHESIS

In many respects, Thomas Aquinas became the epitome of medieval theological piety. His thought has subsequently been endorsed by over one hundred papal encyclicals as being the essence of what Catholic faith means. Thomas' theology also straddled and encompassed the two major traditions that had preceded him. Inasmuch as he was an Augustinian, he was often aligned with the Anselmian school and as such was a conservative, for conservatism was defined by adherence to Augustine at this time. Insofar as he was Aristotelian, his alignment sometimes also lay with the Abelardian school. But Thomas' thought was not merely an aggregate of opinions previously rendered; it was also a brilliant and synthetic reformulation which marked the high point of theological endeavor in the Middle Ages.

Its brilliance lay less, however, in its explicit content and more in the logical threading which ties together this far-flung system. Thomas was, in one sense, a merely passive recipient of teachings and opinions from biblical, patristic, and medieval sources, all of which were assiduously collected and classified. The creativity lay in the logical and theological integration which was formed within his structure of thought. Specifically, his Christology was tied into the doctrine of God as Thomas sought an answer to the question of its necessity; it was related to soteriology as he addressed the question of the nature of Christ's work; and it was integrated into his ecclesiology as he developed his understanding of grace and its bestowal. In formulating these Christological relationships Thomas developed his view of the relation between the human and divine in Christ.

The Incarnation, Thomas affirmed, was necessary. In so saying, however, he departed from Anselm and aligned himself with Augustine because of the way in which he used the word *necessity*.[22] There are two types of necessity. The one is absolute, as when we say that food is necessary to survival, and the other is relative, as when a person might have said that a horse was necessary for travel. Penance, he declared, could have been rendered sufficiently by the sinner, but it is now rendered far more propitiously through the incarnate Word, for now faith, hope, and love are also strengthened. Human nature "has not been made more capable of grace by sin. But after sin it is capable of the grace of union, which is the greatest grace."[23] Thus God chose the method that was most fitting. Thomas' position is in opposition to Anselm's, who contended that God had no choice in the matter. Had he not provided his son, there could have been no restitution from sin. Thus for Anselm, the Incarnation and atonement were related to the *nature* of God, whereas for Thomas they were related to God's *will*, for if they were demanded of God and were not a matter of choice, he would no longer be omnipotent because he would be subject to a higher power outside himself.

The view taken of necessity coalesced with Thomas' view of the atonement. For if the atonement was not necessary in an absolute sense, then it did not have to be accomplished absolutely by the divine in Christ. Thus he argued that it was in his *humanity* that Christ represented sinners and that the presence of the divine merely enhanced the value of that representation.[24] At this point, Thomas was simply reiterating the Anselmian tradition which saw Christ's work as meritorious because he offered penance—not because it was ever required of him, but because of his love. This act of supererogation accumulated merit unneeded by Christ, which is passed on to the church in the form of forgiveness. It was for this reason that Thomas was at pains to argue that Christ's death by itself did not effect salvation.[25] Salvation was accomplished because of Christ's love, the dignity of his life, the sorrows he endured, all of which meant that he had something of great worth to offer up to God.

It is at this point that Thomas' understanding borders on confusion. As a matter of fact, Thomas' mind changed between the writing of his *The Commentary on the Sentences* and his *Summa contra Gentiles* and then again sometime before his final synthesis, the *Summa Theologiae*.[26] In the first of these works he spoke of a human nature so perfectly fitted that it was able to ascend into union with that Word which is immutable. In the last, the direction of his thought had reversed itself. He now spoke of the Word coming down to subsist mysteriously in human nature. He approached Christology from the divine, rather than the human, side. This related naturally and easily to his Augustinian notions of grace, but it clashed with his semi-Anselmian view of the atonement. His doctrine of grace went hand in hand with a Christology constructed from "above," while his understanding of the death of Christ went with one constructed from "below."

These conflicting tendencies, however, were worked out within a formal acceptance of the Chalcedonian orthodoxy. Not only so, but Thomas argued forcefully that of the three views mentioned by Peter Lombard—views which had prevailed since the twelfth century—only the second was viable. The first and third were heretical. Thus he accepted the enhypostatic union. Within this formulation, however, the humanity of Christ was belittled.

Thomas' premise was that the "union of the Word incarnate took place in the nature" and that the Cyrilline formula, "one incarnate nature of the Word of God," should be endorsed.[27] He accepted Boethius' definition of person as "an individual substance of rational nature," but went on to argue, in Aristotelian fashion, that human nature does not exist outside of the individual human being. It was not, therefore, in this nonexistent human nature that the union was effected, but in the person. In the Word, however, the divine nature and human nature were joined.[28]

The Word coming into human flesh, he contended, therefore "hindered" the emergence of personality from that human nature.[29] It needs to be added, however, that the Word apparently not only hindered personality, but also much of the significance of being human. Christ grew neither in knowledge nor in his obedience, since he had each in its fullness.[30] His knowledge was fully and exclusively a "higher supernatural knowledge," which was other than the "natural" knowledge of those seeking to fashion out the meaning of Christian obedience. Thus no development in Christ's inner life occurred.[31] This not only meant that in Thomas' view the human had been absorbed into the divine, at least in part, but also that in some measure it was incomplete. For Thomas contended that the supernatural grace which was first experienced by Christ is the same supernatural grace which is experienced in the church. It is this grace which brings human nature to its fruition and completion. Its presence in the humanity of Christ was consistent with the near-monophysite view of Thomas—namely, that Christ had divinized humanity—as well as with the thought that apart from its presence, Christ's humanity would have been incomplete.[32]

In Thomas, then, we see what had also been central preoccupations for all the scholastics: "the religious question as to the relation between faith and knowledge, authority and reason; the philosophical problem of universals; the theological question as to the nature and conditions of our Lord's redemptive work."[33] On each of these questions, scholasticism also sowed the seeds of its own dissolution. From within nominalism, the church's authority was denied, absolutes were destroyed, and the work of Christ was emptied of serious significance. The church was to be battered first by Renaissance skepticism, in the fourteenth and fifteenth centuries, and then by the Reformation revolt in the sixteenth. And each of these movements capitalized upon the dissent within and the dissolution of the reigning medieval orthodoxy. Theologically, however, it was the Reformation that posed the most serious threat.

THE RUPTURE

The Reformation was a complex social movement. It is important to understand, however, that the political, economic, and ecclesiastical changes which occurred were only the precursors, the context, and the consequences of the Reformation. The Reformation was at heart a religious revolution. It was a revolution which coalesced with and at times increased the tempo of these other changes, but it should not be obscured behind these changes, nor confused with them.

Undoubtedly it is true that the Reformers capitalized upon the social instability and employed it in their own interests. Discontent with the church was widespread and deep. When Luther appeared at the first meeting between Charles V and the German Estates to answer for himself, a document was also presented to the Emperor entitled "The Statement of Grievances presented to the Diet of Worms in 1521." It listed one hundred and one grievances and reminded the emperor of the "oppressive burdens" and of the "abuses" imposed upon the people by the Holy See. This was typical of the entire "grievance literature" which had sprung up at this time protesting the ways of the Church of Rome. There was, too, strong nationalistic discontent. Papal political power and the vision of the Holy Roman Empire were alike being challenged by the emergence of the new nation-states. Germans became especially incensed over their treatment by the emperor and Pope. Their nascent nationalism bloomed into full-blown political discontent. The old medieval order was beginning to crumble, and the former hierarchical structure with kings and princes at the apex and the peasants at the bottom of society looked more and more like intolerable arrogance. Peasant revolts became common and their laced boot, the

Bundschuh, became a feared symbol.[34] All of this was occurring at the beginning of the sixteenth century, and Luther was not above using it to his own purposes. But the Reformation was nevertheless essentially a religious movement.

This insight was pioneered in modern Reformation study by Karl Holl in 1917.[35] He argued that the Reformation began, not in Luther's patriotic feelings or in his political motives, but in his understanding of what it meant to have the Word of God, in his sense of impotence before God's law, his despair before God's judgment, and the overwhelming security from law and judgment which he found in Christ. This is important for our understanding of Reformation Christology, because plainly what was afoot was a radical reshuffling of traditional doctrinal elements in the interests of serving this powerful and dramatically new soteriological concern. What we discover, then, is that the Christology itself was Chalcedonian and traditional. It was in its new religious context that it assumed an importance that set Reformation theology apart from the Middle Ages.

Luther was raised theologically in the briar patch of Ockhamist thought. How much he borrowed off nominalism is a debated point,[36] but his first major theological statement was a fierce repudiation of Aristotelianism. No one, he roundly declared, "can become a theologian unless he becomes one without Aristotle,"[37] for Aristotle is to theology as darkness is to light! There were two immediate consequences of Luther's disaffection. First, he came to distrust deeply all speculative theological systems. Even before his time, William of Ockham and Duns Scotus had worked havoc on the Thomistic synthesis, creating deep fissures in its logic and orderliness. Luther continued this attack, constantly pitting his *theologia crucis* against what he derided in the scholastics as their *theologiae gloriae.* This worked itself out in what sometimes seems like a perverse delight in paradox, in laying side by side contradictory theological elements which are not susceptible of explanation or resolution.[38] It was his way of contesting the sovereignty of alien, speculative systems. The second consequence was Luther's commitment to Scripture as alone authoritative.[39] In Thomas, authority had resulted from an amalgam of Scripture, church teaching, and reason. The nominalists had destroyed reason as an authority, and Luther destroyed church teaching. What remained as alone enduring were the inspired Scriptures.

These convictions became the hallmark of Reformation theology, although the element of paradox was distinctively Luther's. Calvin's reputation is that of a ruthless systematizer who was prone to becoming immediately distraught upon finding any loose ends dangling unconnected within his system; it is a reputation that is unearned. It belongs to the Calvin of myth, not the Calvin of history.[40] His thought was, in fact, stringently and soberly biblical. He derided that kind of religious knowledge which "content with empty speculation merely flits in the brain." We should instead seek, he said, that knowledge which is "solid and faithful" and which will take root in the "heart."[41] Such knowledge is found only in that Scripture which the Spirit inspired and illumines for the reader.[42] He argued this because of two convictions which were foundational for him.

First, he believed that God's nature is so different from ours that we understand nothing about him except what he has chosen to reveal to us. Second, he held that sin has so infected and affected the mind that religious knowledge not founded upon and disciplined by the Word of God is worthless.[43] Together, these convictions secured for him, as it had for Luther, the belief that all theology must be the expression and exposition of the truth which God has revealed in his Word. Tradition may act as guide and counselor, but it could never act as infallible teacher. Reason is to be employed, but its proper use is as a receptacle for God's truth, not as a source for truth about God.

Luther and Calvin as biblical theologians affirmed a Christology which was in full accord with Chalcedon; indeed, the Chalcedonian Definition became an important element in the creedal literature of most of the Reformation churches. Within this historical orthodoxy, however, the tilt of Luther's thought was to the side of the "Word-flesh" Christology and that of Calvin to the side of the "Word-man" Christologies.

Undoubtedly numerous statements can be adduced from Luther showing that he believed in the full divinity of Christ as well as in the full humanity.[44] And his works abound with formal acknowledgments of Chalcedonian orthodoxy—"two natures united in one person," "God and man in one person, undivided and inseparable," "true God of true God, and true man of true man."[45] The question, of course, was precisely how the two natures related to one another.

Luther contended that the essential incompatibility of the natures—the one infinite, unchanging, immutable and the other finite, changing, and mutable—would obviate their union in one person if an interchange of attributes did not occur. The natures would be incompatible with one another. Consequently, he felt it necessary to argue for the *communicatio idiomatum.* He maintained that the union occurred not in the natures, but in the person. On the basis of the unitary person, what properly belongs to the humanity may be predicated of the divinity. Thus he declared that Mary made soup for God and bathed God, and Pilate killed God. Conversely, the helpless infant in the cradle was none other than the mighty God who created heaven and earth.

Luther appeared to have had three motives in mind. First, he wanted to affirm that in Jesus we meet God face to face. He declared the God-man to be both a "veil" and a "mirror," both concealing God

in his sufferings and revealing him in his works.[46] The Pope, he asserted, may believe the correct Christological formula, but he had no sense
of being confronted by the divine, risen, eternal Christ. Although Luther treated Nestorius rather gently, he had no patience with the idea
that the human was simply the bearer of Godness. On the contrary, in,
with, and by the human we are met by God himself.

Second, Luther's soteriological concerns demanded a Christ who
was divine and in whom the divinity intimately and wholly suffused the
human. Gustav Aulén has gone too far in proposing that the "classic
motif" was what alone characterized Luther's view of the atonement,[47]
but there is no question that this was an important element in it.
Luther, in fact, combined both penal and dramatic elements. According to the second motif, God takes triumphant action against sin, death,
the devil, and his own wrath because, according to the first motif,
Christ had made our sin his own and in bearing our punishment for us
turned away God's wrath and destroyed the devil's work.[48] Only *God*
could undertake to bear the penalty of sin, and only *God* could triumph
in the contest with evil.

Third, Luther's view of the sacraments, but especially the Lord's
Supper,[49] required the *communicatio idiomatum*. For Luther's contention was that the bread and wine were the forms under which the actual
body and blood of Christ were concentrated, although he denied the
Catholic teaching that the substance of the bread and wine was miraculously transformed into the body and blood. Luther's view required that
he affirm the ubiquity of Christ's body, for how else could the Lord's
Supper be celebrated in this way worldwide? The argument for the
omnipresence of Christ's humanity was necessarily an argument for the
transfer of divine attributes to the human.

It is, of course, true that the person and work of Christ had been
linked in the past. But in Luther they were joined as they seldom had
been before. Indeed, he came close at times to making the work of
Christ determinative of the person, for he wanted to underscore, as
Paul Althaus put it, that "God has opened his heart to us in the person,
activity, and history of Jesus Christ and thus gives us certainty about
how he feels about us and what he intends to do with us."[50] This was
the "new meaning" of the Deity which emerged from Luther's Christology. It did, however, raise serious problems. Luther had argued that
human nature, though itself finite and limited, was capable of receiving
the infinite. This in turn flowed later either into a pantheistic view
(that all human nature receives and is transformed by the divine), or
into one which posited that Christ's humanity, precisely because of its
capacity for the divine, is unlike that possessed by any human being.
This was the undoubted tendency of later Lutheran thought. It is
ironical to note, therefore, that Luther's Christology held within it
tendencies whose outcome would be the destruction of that biblical

soteriology which his Christology had originally been constructed to protect and articulate.

The later debates between Lutheran and Reformed theology have often left the impression that Calvin and Luther were themselves fiercely opposed to one another. This is not the case. Calvin's theology was quite as Christocentric as Luther's, Francois Wendel believes,[51] and certainly a full Chalcedonian orthodoxy was present in Calvin's belief. Despite their similarity of approach, there were some differences, however, that need to be noted.

First, Calvin worked his understanding of the Trinity into the other aspects of his theology,[52] and especially his Christology, more vigorously than did Luther. The difference was one of style and emphasis rather than specific substance. Calvin's theology presents us with the way in which the actions of Father, Son, and Spirit have been united in the same task of saving the same men and women infallibly. Those whom the Father chose are those for whom the Son died,[53] and it is those same people who are regenerated and called by the Spirit. Salvation is a divine work in its plan, execution, and application.

Second, Calvin united the person and work of Christ by presenting him under the threefold rubric of prophet, priest, and King. This was not entirely novel. Thomas Aquinas alluded to the idea, and before him Eusebius had made mention of it. Calvin, however, was the first to structure his entire presentation around this rubric.[54] In doing so, he was attempting to hold together what Scripture holds together, the person and work of Christ—what God has said and what he has done. And it enabled him to set out his Christology in the light of his conviction about God's incomprehensibility. For God's nature is so much higher than ours, and our sin has so closed us off from fellowship with him, that outside of this Mediator, there could be no healing of the divine/human breach.[55]

Third, Calvin always affirmed the full integrity of each nature within the unity of the person. To say that is to say no more than that Calvin was Chalcedonian. The truth is, however, that it was possible to be Chalcedonian in theory but to formulate principles concerning the relation of the natures which in practice subverted the orthodoxy which was believed. Where Luther insisted on the unity of the person, Calvin was unyielding on the integrity of the natures. This he did, as much as anything, to protect the divinity of Christ, for any suggestion of an interpenetration of one nature by another could only mean the elevation of the human to a position in which it was no longer human and a degradation of the divine to a position in which it was no longer divine.[56] It was possible to destroy both natures by an undue insistence on the unity of Christ's person. For this reason, he opposed the use of the *communicatio idiomatum.* No conversion of humanity into divinity or divinity into humanity occurred, but each retained the properties native to them. The human was not capable of being divinized, and the divine could not be mutilated through union with the human. As a matter of fact, the human was not capable of absorbing or containing the divine, and the divine in Christ was in no way limited by the human, for then it plainly would no longer be divine. "Here is something marvellous," Calvin concluded, "the Son of God descended from heaven in such a way that, without leaving heaven, he willed to be borne in the virgin's womb, to go about the earth, and to hang upon the cross; yet he continuously filled the world as he had done from the beginning."[57] This view, which seems to belittle the reality of Christ's self-emptying, is known sometimes as the *extra calvinisticum.*

The problems that were latent in Reformation thinking should not obscure the importance of the greatness of their achievement. They derived their doctrine of God centrally from their Christology. "He who has seen me has seen the Father" could have been a text on which the Christologies of Calvin and Luther in Europe, as well as Cranmer and Knox in Britain, were all built. This "Christianized" the knowledge of God. In Jesus we meet God, face to face, and through him our sovereign and great God has taken triumphant action against sin, death, and the devil by yielding himself in substitution for his people on the cross.

Part 3: Modern Interpretation

7 THE ENLIGHTENMENT AND ITS AFTERMATH

The word *modern* has curiously elastic limits and rather imprecise content. If the limits are set chronologically, then it would be difficult to speak of pretwentieth century theology as being "modern." Indeed, some even reserve the word merely for post-World War II thought. If, however, the word is being used generically, then it encompasses a much greater part of the post-Reformation period. For it is undeniable that much contemporary theology is echoing and implementing the revolutionary intellectual changes which occurred in the Enlightenment. The twentieth century has not cut itself adrift from the eighteenth; the eighteenth continues to lay hold upon the twentieth. It is for this reason that the word *modern* is here being used widely and will be understood as a synonym for that period which stretches from the beginning of the eighteenth century to the present, a period which largely cut itself loose from both the medieval synthesis and the Reformation outlook, and which has often sought to build a view of life that is without religious foundations. It is in this period that a decisive break with classical Christology has frequently occurred. The rise of Enlightenment rationalism coincided, as it turned out, with the decline in religious vitality in both Protestantism and Catholicism. In part this was no doubt due to the religious wars which followed the Reformation and which did much to undo the Christian world view over which battles were being fought. The wars discredited Christian faith, not war. And in part this decline reflects an almost predictable cycle which has recurred many times. Religious life ebbs and flows rhythmically, periods of great activity being followed by periods of retraction and decline. This is true on both a micro and a macro scale.

This pattern was noted, for example, in the pre-Reformation period. The patristic era was one of great creativity and vitality. It was followed by the Dark Ages in which much of the Christian world view and its culture was destroyed. The Middle Ages was a time of partial recovery and of conservation, of consolidating the patristic gains. The church as an *institution* flourished, but its theology was largely involved in codifying past gains. This, in the end, led both to sterility and dissolution. In the Reformation there was once again an extraordinary irruption of creative energy, and within a fifty-year period what had taken Europe a thousand years to accumulate was rejuvenated, reorganized, or discarded. The Reformation, like the patristic era, was followed by the "Dark Ages" of the Enlightenment, in which much of the world view the Reformers had fought for was disbanded and denigrated. Theology during this time busied itself surviving. It did this by consolidating and codifying past gains. The scholasticism which resulted was not without its merits, but it is also undeniable that it often produced sterility in mind and spirit.

It is this situation, a situation of intellectual hostility in the culture and of the exigency of survival in the Christian churches,[1] which goes a long way to explaining some of the significant trends in modern theology. Much of the Christian tradition has continued to maintain its identity with the past, at times perhaps wistfully hoping that modernity will be like the chaff which the wind will blow away. This identity is forged in different ways. In Roman Catholicism it is accomplished through the understanding of tradition and authority in the church; in Eastern Orthodoxy, there is almost a tangible link with the past in the ethos of its worship and the life and language of the churches; in more conservative Protestantism it is accomplished through the insistence on doctrinal continuity across the ages, beginning with the Bible. This, however, has produced problems in terms of the "morality of knowledge,"[2] for it sometimes has led these Christians to believe matters which are considered unbelievable in the modern world. It is this tension which has, of course, produced for other Christians a quite different strategy for survival. Modernity is viewed as a condition that should be embraced rather than shunned and, in some cases, as a condition which is the direct result of divine involvement. Theology therefore needs to be written in terms of modernity and perhaps by employing its substance. Where this occurs, theology takes on the appearance of the secularism and humanism which is now at the center of most Western cultures. It then takes on the same kind of hostility toward traditional forms of theology as does this culture. This, quite obviously, has a profound effect on the shape of the resulting Christologies.

CLASSIFYING CHRISTOLOGIES

Theologies in this period have tended to fall into one of two categories. They are either constructed around *discontinuity* between the being of God and the created order, or around their *continuity*.[3] The former recognizes the alienation of faith from the Enlightenment culture, and the latter minimizes it. This is, to be sure, a classification to which there are some exceptions, and sometimes it may not be immediately evident into which category a theology is to be placed. The chapter which follows is itself an example of this, for while it is indisputable that Barth's Christology is built around discontinuity and Pittenger's around continuity, Schillebeeckx's is far less easy to categorize. The distinction is, nevertheless, a useful one.[4]

Theologies which are built on discontinuity accent the differences between the natural and the supernatural and, in one way or another, present their Christology as the invasion of the divine into that domain which is natural and created. These are almost invariably "high" Christologies, which may even employ the older "Word-flesh" language and which yield not one iota on the divinity of Christ. Their world view easily accommodates the presence of miracles, and it affirms the need for divinely initiated revelation.

Theologies which stress continuity argue that the "supernatural" is revealed within the natural, and therefore "miracles" are often equated with the workings of natural law. To those with eyes to see, a beautiful sunset or the regeneration of nature in spring are "miracles," whereas for those without eyes to see, sunsets and springtimes are simply sunsets and springtimes.[5] Because human nature is seen as a natural receptacle of the divine and as being infused by the divine, human insight is often thought to be the means of divine revelation. In biblical hermeneutics, therefore, the interpreter will often assume an autonomy from the control of the text in the interest of giving "revelation" which is contemporary. This "revelation," in the nature of the case, generally accords with or, at least can be made compatible with, operating norms in the society. This is precisely what one would expect, for there is no metaphysical or noetic disjuncture between God and human nature, the supernatural and the natural. Christologies in this framework, therefore, generally depict Jesus as the perfection of an existing religious consciousness that is common to all or most people. These Christologies usually fall into the "Word-man" pattern, but one in which significant Chalcedonian elements are lost. They are Christologies which are constructed from "below." They usually begin with whatever can be known of the historical Jesus, and the divine is conceived within the limits of what is human. This, of course, often results in what is divine being equated with and thereby defined as extraordinary insight or profound moral consciousness. There is little or no substantial and personal union between the human and divine, but rather an infusion of the latter is seen to have taken place in the former, so that an atmosphere or aura is created within the human Jesus such that it can be said God dwelled in him.

Roman Catholic thought does not fit comfortably into this classification. In some ways it represents an approach of discontinuity, but in others of continuity. An argument can be advanced for the former on the ground of the clear distinction which is made, especially in Thomistic thought, between the natural and the supernatural with the corresponding need for divinely initiated revelation. The church endorses miracles both within and without the biblical period and, as we have seen, is officially committed to full, Chalcedonian orthodoxy. In practice, however, the Thomistic understanding of natural theology has provided a bridge that not only leads from the natural into the supernatural, but also tends to blur the distinction between them. This was why Barth fulminated against this view, declaring it to be the invention of the Antichrist himself! In a traditional Catholic context, this breach in the pattern is not large enough to move Catholic thought out of the category of those theologies building on discontinuity. In the contemporary situation, however, it may. In Karl Rahner's theology, for example, traditional Thomistic categories have been filled with existential substance, and the result is that Thomas often dances to the tune piped by Heidegger. Thus Rahner has taken the old distinction of "nature" and "grace," which was originally designed to protect their mutual differences, and so reworked it that these differences are never revealed in practice. Nature, he argues, has never been dislocated from grace. It has always breathed the supernatural atmosphere of grace. It has always been graced. This is what he refers to as the "supernatural existential." This means that divine, supernatural grace is a factor in and a working component of all human nature everywhere. In theory, Rahner's theology builds on discontinuity, but in practice it asserts a continuity between God and the created order.[6]

Theologies which articulate the themes of discontinuity are almost invariably Chalcedonian in their outlook. The modern intellectual world is seen as the context within which this Christology is to be affirmed, but not one from which this Christology should borrow any of its substance. The chief representatives of this approach would be from traditional Roman Catholicism, Anglo-Catholicism, Greek Orthodoxy, conservative Protestantism, and some parts of neo-orthodoxy. Theologies built upon continuity accept modifications within the Chalcedonian framework and see the modern world as providing not only the context, but also the source for their Christology. This means that the degree of modification in Chalcedonian orthodoxy will vary in direct proportion to the extent to which modernity has become determinative theologically. Proponents of this approach are to be found in the older Protestant liberalism as well as in its current recrudescence in such people as Langdon Gilkey, Edward Farley, and Gordon Kaufman, in Catholic modernism, in some post-Vatican II Catholic theology, in process thought, and in some of the liberation theologies.

This bifurcation, which is rather clearly established and defined in the twentieth century, was largely formulated in the nineteenth century, although it is the direct outcome of the Enlightenment in the eighteenth. There were two important developments for Christology in the nineteenth century which revealed the diverging paths. These were the emergence of kenoticism and the "lives of Jesus" movement. Protestant liberalism and Catholic modernism were the broader theological expressions in which some of these Christological tendencies came to expression. This chapter therefore will trace the shift in emphasis from the Reformation Christologies, which build on discontinuity, to the liberal theories which assumed an ontological continuity.

KENOTICISM

The historical origins of kenoticism lie mainly within the debates generated by post-Reformation Lutheranism and Calvinism. Lutheranism, it has already been noted, moved within the "Word-flesh" Christology, while Reformed theology articulated the "Word-man" approach. Lutheranism, therefore, was vulnerable to the charge of having confused the natures of Christ and Reformed theology to having divided his person. Fuel was added to these existing fires in the speculative period which followed the Reformation.

Martin Luther's interest in Christ's ubiquity seems to have been limited to its sacramental context. It was important to Luther to affirm this because of his belief in consubstantiation, although the term itself is not always liked by Lutherans. The words of institution and in particular the expression, "This is my body," he believed, should be understood with a degree of literalness which neither Calvin nor Zwingli would allow. In the next generation, however, ubiquity became a matter of Christological importance too, and the result, A. B. Bruce judged, was that Lutheran Christology became "a vast pyramid resting in a state of most unstable equilibrium on its apex, Christ's bodily presence in the Supper; which again rests upon a water-worn pebble,— the word of institution." Bruce went on to note that this massive pyramid was held upright "solely by the strong arms of theological giants," and when they died it tumbled into "irretrievable ruin."[7]

The giants in question were not without some differences among themselves, but they were agreed in giving an interpretation to Lutheran Christology which led to a double discontinuity, one that was not only at a divine level but also at the human. This occurred through their employment of the *communicatio idiomatum* by which the human in Christ took on the characteristics of divinity, thus breaking continuity with the human race.

This Christology, however, was formulated in two different ways, sometimes referred to as the "Brentian" and "Chemnitzian" after the two respective fountainheads. John Brentz's starting premise was that Christ's two natures were not merely joined in a common person, but were forged into a common person. Without their infusion in one another, there would have been no person. This being the case, what were later to be called the relative attributes also extended to his humanity. Brentz argued, for example, that there were different forms of the omnipresence of Christ's humanity, which meant that it could be both localized (ubiquity *in loco*) and universalized (ubiquity *in Logo*). That meant that the divine majesty of the second person of the Godhead was not in any way diminished or minimized for the purposes of incarnation. Thus in Christ there was little, if anything, to distinguish his self-emptying from his exaltation. Rather, two modes of existence coincided in him. The difference between his ascended state and his incarnate state is merely that in the former the outward circumstances of humiliation are absent, whereas in the latter they were present.

Martin Chemnitz's work was far more moderate and cautious, but still the characteristic form of Lutheran thought was clearly affirmed. Again the personal union was the centerpiece of his thought, its expression accompanied by the almost ritualistic complaints that Reformed Christology presented Christ's natures as two boards merely glued together! He nevertheless asserted that Christ's humanity is permanent and will always be localized. And the *communicatio idiomatum* he interpreted not so much as the permanent transfer of qualities from the divine to the human as the use of the human by the divine in ways that went outside the bounds of normal human limitation. Reverting to a familiar patristic image, he declared that as heat infuses and invests the iron with its presence, so the divinity has given to the humanity extra physical powers and graces. However, the humanity, he went on to say, is always in the Logos, and therefore the Logos can make it present anywhere in creation that he so chooses. Thus the exchange of attributes appears in Chemnitz's thought to have been intermittent, whereas in Brentz it was constant and a necessary result of the personal union of the Incarnation. In time this difference produced two schools of thought, the one arguing that the attributes of omniscience, omnipresence, and omnipotence were present, albeit concealed, and the other proposing that though present in capacity, these attributes were seldom if ever used.[8]

The *Formula of Concord* (1576) attempted to reconcile the schools of thought on this and a number of other matters on which the Lutheran divines had parted doctrinal company. It was a document of compromise which enjoyed the advantages that such compromises provide and suffered from the disadvantages which they always produce.[9] The opposing schools of thought were affirmed in what they maintained, and their differences were largely passed over in silence. The *Formula* affirmed the *communicatio idomatum* not merely as a linguistic form (such as in the expressions "God died" or "Mary is the mother of God"), but "in very fact and very deed."[10] But what did this mean?

Once again familiar images reappeared. The two natures of Christ were not like boards glued together, but in their relationship more like heat suffusing iron.[11] The human nature came to possess divine properties, and the divine "majesty" was present in Christ from the time of conception onwards. Christ was always in possession of it, but in one place the *Formula* asserts his use of the attached attributes and in another their concealment in his human nature![12]

The compromise was not a stable solution. It was merely an interim settlement. When the matter[13] was again revived in the nineteenth century, it was not with the intent of discovering when, where, and how Jesus might have had access to the attributes or actually became omnipresent, omnipotent, and omniscient. Now the question was whether it was possible and biblically proper to see him having access to these attributes under any circumstances. What, after all, did it really mean to say the Word became *flesh*?

The kenotic outlook flourished "like a green bay tree in Germany during the middle quarters of the nineteenth century."[14] And then, just as it began to die out there, it was revived in the latter part of the century in Britain. In general, kenoticists maintained, according to F. J. Hall, that "the Divine Logos, in order to take our nature upon him, and submit in reality to its earthly conditions and limitations, abandoned somewhat at least of what was His before He became incarnate."[15] The Logos reduced himself to human dimensions and accommodated himself to human nature for the purpose of incarnation. Most commonly it was argued that this denuding process led to the loss of the relative attributes: omniscience, omnipotence, omnipresence.

There were, as A. B. Bruce has said, three questions which kenoticists inevitably had to address.[16] First, was this denuding, this stripping of the divine of all except its essential core, a condition that was relative or absolute? Did Jesus have recourse at any time to these attributes, or were they denied to him from birth to death? Second, into what relation with the man Jesus did the divinity enter? Stripped of his power and scaled down to the dimensions of humanity, did the Word fill the human soul, exist alongside of it, or replace it? Third, was this denuding or depotentiating partially or totally completed? If it was totally complete, then Jesus was always and everywhere a mere human being; if it was partially completed, then at moments he would be semidivine while being also fully human.

Kenoticists answered these three questions in a variety of ways. For some, the divinity was stripped of its relative attributes permanently; for some, this occurred only partially. For some, the Word thus depotentiated took the place of the soul, and thus these proponents came close to reviving Apollinarianism; for others, the Word coexisted with the soul, and the danger of Nestorianism once again became a possibility.[17]

Some were absolute and others relative kenoticists. Of these various forms of kenosis, two will be considered as case studies, those of Thomasius and P. T. Forsyth.

Gottfried Thomasius (1802-1875), a Lutheran in the Erlangen school, began with what was a common distinction among kenoticists, that between the "moral" attributes (love, justice, holiness) and the "physical" attributes (omniscience, omnipotence, omnipresence). The self-emptying of Philippians 2:5-11, he then postulated, must be understood in terms of the emasculation of the relative or "physical" attributes. What forced him into seeing this passage in this way appears to have been logical necessity rather than exegetical conclusion. A Christ composed of the infinite and finite, the absolute and relative, was, from the point of view of logic, an impossibility. The older Lutheran theologians cut the Gordian knot by converting the finite into the infinite via the device of transferring attributes; Thomasius reversed this and converted the infinite into the finite. This, however, was conceived within both Chalcedonian orthodoxy and the characteristic Lutheran interests in Christology. Thomasius was as insistent on the *communicatio idomatum* as had been his Lutheran forebears. In his case, the problem did not produce a resolution in which Christ's humanity was transformed and lost its inherent limitations because the divinity whose characteristics were infused in it had already lost the attributes that would have violated the genuineness of the humanity. The divine "mode of being" was divested in favor of "the humanly creaturely form of existence" of space, time, and development.[18] He asserted, as a good Lutheran would, that human nature is structured to receive the divine *(natura humana capax divinae)*,[19] but of course the human nature into which the divine was received was one subject to growth, change, and development.

The divine appropriated and penetrated the human, participated in the human, and imparted itself to the human.[20] The Word, stripped of the customary prerogatives of divinity but not devoid of anything essential to being divine, took on a human ego. Because the self-limitation of God was voluntary, the Incarnation did not destroy his being divine; because it was a whole humanity which was embraced, soul with body, metamorphosis could be denied. Jesus' consciousness was that of a human being even though the divine ego had "made human nature its own."[21] There was, of course, only one "unitary center" in him. In this "center" the divine consciousness was present, but exhibited itself within the bounds of human possibility and under the conditions of human growth. Thomasius therefore offered a moderate kenosis as a way of reconciling a genuine humanity with the idea that the divine was indeed incarnate. Others such as Gess, for example, went much further, postulating that the divine consciousness was entirely expunged.

In Britain it was Charles Gore[22] who made the kenotic view a factor to be reckoned with although typically his views were far less speculative than those advanced in continental Europe. The British expression also appealed more obviously to devotional concerns. The work of the British theologians—in particular H. R. Mackintosh,[23] A. M. Fairbain,[24] and P. T. Forsyth[25]—was therefore rather different in tone and temper from much of what had gained attention in Europe a little earlier.

Forsyth's key assertion was his denial of the adequacy of the term "nature" in earlier Christological discussion. This, he said, was a metaphysical category, and it had led Christological thought into a thicket of unnecessary problems.[26] It served the purpose in the early church of fending off competing and erroneous conceptions, but it had contributed little of positive worth. Forsyth also believed that earlier kenoticists had been lured into formulating their views in metaphysical categories, distinguishing, for example, between the absolute attributes (which could not be abandoned) and the relative (which could be abandoned). Natures, he countered, were not substances, and Christology was not an exercise in chemistry in which one tried to understand how the natures might react upon each other. The question, rather, was how two "modes of being" were related to one another.[27] The category was moral, not metaphysical; its accent was religious, not speculative.

In the Incarnation, therefore, the attributes of the eternal, divine Word contracted from a condition of being actual to one of being potential. This contraction was itself the result of a monumental moral act within the Godhead, and the slow, progressive recovery of Godness in its wholeness within the life of the human Jesus was itself also an act of moral conquest. Forsyth therefore rejected Thomasius' view that the relative attributes could simply be severed off, and he also rejected the idea that these attributes were hidden but always within reach, as it were, for use by Jesus. The self-reduction, self-retraction, and self-emptying were genuine. It was a reduction that was possible only because God's greatness is, in fact, so great that his self-limitation becomes a possibility, for his greatness is moral, not physical. This self-divestiture, Forsyth went on to insist, must be complemented by an understanding of Christ's emergence into the full potentiality of Godness in the cross and resurrection.[28] The humbled God has as its coefficient the triumphant God. Kenosis and plerosis are therefore the complementary truths of Christ's life—self-sacrificing love joining with royal, redeeming holiness.

Forsyth's aversion for the older categories also led him to modify the way in which he saw the human and the divine being yoked in Christ. The human and divine did not meet in a "person." They met, rather, in saving action. They were the components, the coefficients, of that action, the "mutual involution of two personal movements raised by the whole scale of the human soul and the divine."[29] What distin-

guished the human was the emergence of personality by moral struggle, and what distinguished the divine was the self-retraction by an act
of moral expression, human and divine coexisting and coworking in
the common cause of saving lost men and women. We therefore face in
Christ "a Godhead self-reduced but real, whose infinite power took
effect in self-humiliation, whose strength was perfected in weakness,
who consented not to know with an ignorance divinely wise, and who
emptied himself in virtue of his divine fullness."[30]

Kenotic theories, of which only two have here been considered, in
general had several notable and praiseworthy features. First, they all
began with a divine, preexistent Word. What they sought to explain was
how an incarnation was possible. The problem could be resolved by
denying the preexistence or modifying the divinity of the second person, but in the nineteenth century kenoticists refused to do this. Second, kenotic theories sought to ascribe full reality to the historical
Jesus. The humanity was not simply the garment by which the divine
could masquerade as being human. The humanity of Jesus was as real
and full as any other expression of humanness, and also subject to the
same finitude and limitations. Third, kenotic theories invested the
divine love with significant moral content. The Incarnation and not
merely the cross was costly to God. The historical life of Jesus was itself
an act of sacrifice by God, and as such it is to be an incitement to
devotion.

There were, however, some troubling dimensions to the theory, the
degree of difficulty being related to the precise form which any particular kenotic theory took.

First, it was not clear to critics that it is possible, as Thomasius and
others proposed, to sever some of the attributes of God from the essence of God. The only God of whom Scripture speaks is one who is
all-powerful, knows everything, and is everywhere. By definition, a god
who has diminished power and knowledge is not the biblical God.
Forsyth tried to evade the force of this criticism by refusing to use the
language of the discussion, but whether the evasion was successful is
questionable. Scripture nowhere encourages us to think that there is an
irreducible minimum to what is divine and that there are acts and
characteristics normally associated with being divine which are simply
optional extras.

Second, kenotic theories all implied a disruption in the internal
relations of the Trinity. Some theorists proposed their views in moderate terms, others in radical ways, but what was held in common was
that for a period, be it short or long, the divine self-consciousness of the
incarnate Son was expunged. Not only so, but the divinity was also said
to be contracted into mere potentiality. This potentiality, however, became synonymous with divine passivity, and divine passivity can only
be distinguished from divine impotence in theory. In practice, a necessary passivity is an operating impotence. In many kenotic theories this

was virtually admitted in the large role that was invariably assigned to the Holy Spirit in the nurturing of the human Jesus. The Spirit became a surrogate for the extinguished, depotentiated Word. In practice this meant that during the incarnate period the divine circuitry was broken, the second person was on a leave of absence from Godhead, and the Trinity was at best reduced to a "binity."

Third, the contraction of the divine inevitably led to a vitiation of that love which it was the chief purpose of the kenotic theories to exhibit. "The love which moved the Son of God to become man consumed itself at one stroke,"[31] declared Bruce, for the love of which the Incarnation as the result was lost for years until at length Jesus began to find its first yearnings within himself and at the end was able to say "Amen" to it. The divine Word lost his consciousness for much of Jesus' life, and in that loss lies much that the kenotic theories claim to exhibit.

Fourth, most kenotic views led to a conversion of Godhead into manhood, violating Nicea's prohibition on supposing the Son is "subject to change," and in the process removed any serious element of unity in Christ. For if this Logos, stripped of divine characteristics, infused himself into a human ego or took upon himself human nature, what coalesced was what was essentially compatible. If the Logos was reduced to the dimensions of humanity, then in joining with humanity there is little reason to speak of the need of unity when the possibility of disunity is no longer there! The self-reduced Logos and the human center of the man Jesus simply become the coordinates of the same self-consciousness. The one person could never be a composite of elements essentially contradictory or different, and therefore to say that Christ was "one" was as unexceptional as saying that people today are "one."

Fifth, kenotic theories misplaced the element of humiliation. Undoubtedly they were correct to emphasize the costliness of incarnation for the one who surrendered his riches for our poverty. It is possible, however, to make too much of this, perhaps even to leave the impression, however unwittingly, that there is something degraded and reprehensible about being human. If the emphasis of Philippians 2:5-11 is to be sustained, the element of humiliation is to be associated, not with Christ's incarnation, but with his atonement. What is degraded and reprehensible is not the flesh to which he was joined, but the sin which he took upon himself as our substitute to effect our reconciliation to God. Christ emptied himself for the purposes of incarnation, but he had to humble himself for the work of redemption.

THE "LIVES OF JESUS" MOVEMENT

The most tangible result of this new mood in biblical study in the nineteenth century was the rash of "lives" of Jesus that were produced. The nineteenth century as a whole was dominated by a dramatic renewal of interest in things historical as well as in "breakthroughs" in historical methodology. The eighteenth century had shown little interest in these matters. Descartes argued that history had neither the certainty of philosophy, nor the precision of science. Voltaire, by reputation the greatest historian of his time, spent most of his life in philosophy and only at the end turned to matters of history. Kant was not merely disinterested in history; he also depreciated it. The nineteenth century saw a dramatic reversal of these attitudes.

In Hegel and Marx, history became the means of doing philosophy. For Hegel, it exhibited how the rational principles by which reality is structured have been unfolded for our study; for Marx, history exhibited those principles by which all societies have been determined and in the light of which the future can be predicted. Although Marx boasted that he had stood Hegel on his head, his high estimation of the significance of history for human understanding was very similar to Hegel's. This renewal in turn stimulated the search for more acceptable methods of study which would win respectability for the subject. In scholars like von Ranke it resulted in vigorous analysis of source material, a confidence that scientific techniques and objectivity could be transferred to historical analysis, and oftentimes an extraordinary confidence in the capacities of human nature. The problem, of course, is that human affairs are not susceptible to "scientific" analysis in the same way that the laws of gravity are. The "objective" techniques which the positivist historians used yielded a diversity of interpretations, which became as much an embarrassment as it would if scientists today kept reaching entirely different conclusions about how gravity works.

In the meantime, however, the new enthusiasm for history, coupled with the new techniques for its study, crossed over into theology where they were merged into the critical studies being done on Scripture. It was this cross-pollination of disciplines which produced the "lives of Jesus" literature.

It is also important, however, to note the mood in which this literature flourished. It was nowhere better expressed than in Harnack's *What is Christianity?*, published at the turn of the twentieth century. Harnack's book was nurtured within an almost tragic sense that for masses of modern people Jesus had become an irrelevance. He was as irrelevant to them as to the age in which he lived. What Harnack tried to do, therefore, was to capture the meaning of Christianity as an "Idea," an Idea which had been realized in and expressed through Jesus, but was not itself defined by and limited to Jesus. Here lay the nub of Harnack's analysis, and this was the program of Protestant liberalism. Christianity was historical in the sense that it came to focus in Jesus, but it was not historical in the sense that Jesus defined its meaning. This formulation was carried out with apologetic motives, the hope being that the Christianity which resulted would accord more easily with the assumed norms of its "cultured despisers." What is of interest, however, is that Harnack claimed that he reached his conclusions by "the methods of historical science" and not as an "apologist" or "religious philosopher"!

In both continental Europe and Britain, writing lives of Jesus became a vogue. Among the Victorians, says Daniel Pals, this was a subject "to which every type of writer—devotional, radical, clerical, or eccentric—was sooner or later attracted."[32] In Europe it produced now well-known works by David Strauss, Christian Weisse, Bruno Bauer, Ernest Renan, and Maurice Goguel, among others. In Britain, the studies by J. R. Seeley, Richard Hanson, F. W. Farrar, and Alfred Edersheim were among the more widely circulated. Albert Schweitzer was the one who took it upon himself to ax this movement. After a thorough and at times tedious review of works written mainly in Germany, he concluded that the authors had "played fast and loose with true history," reading into the Gospel accounts an imaginary and idealized picture of Jesus. Indeed, the Jesus who emerged from most of these studies was so like the liberal authors who wrote them that Schweitzer observed that they must have been looking down the long well of human history and seen their own faces reflected at the bottom! Their Jesus was "a figure designed by rationalism, endowed with life by liberalism, and clothed by modern theology in an historical garb." It was a figure which has now "fallen to pieces," battered by "the concrete historical problems" which resulted.[33] This "half-historical, half-modern Jesus," Schweitzer concluded, would never be able to meet the theological expectations which had inspired his construction. The fundamental mistake, Schweitzer charged, was to suppose that Jesus could mean more if he were dressed up as a "modern" person than if he were left as he really was.

The real significance of the movement was not in its historical discoveries. These were, at best, minimal. This enterprise was, in fact, an elaborate attempt at breaking the bonds of traditional doctrine, an attempt undertaken on Enlightenment premises. History, it was thought, was the key to reality. This was an extraordinary, naive supposition which foundered on the hard rock of reality and had its demise unceremoniously declared by Schweitzer. The abysmal failure of the movement, however, wounded the theological community.[34] It is a wound that to this day has refused to heal.

LIBERAL PROTESTANTISM

The nineteenth century belonged to Protestant liberalism in Europe. In North America, but especially the United States, the liberal era only began mid-century, and it ended later than in Europe. There, its demise was marked by both the beginning of World War I and the rise to prominence of Karl Barth. In North America, liberalism flourished into the 1930s when it became the victim of both the Depression and the influx of neo-orthodox ideas from Europe. On the Roman Catholic side, Christology was not an issue over which there was dissension or, for that matter, much creative thought. The Council of Trent (1545-1563), which met to rebuff Reformation theology, made no pronouncement on Christology. This was not a point of controversy. In the counter-Reformation period which followed, Catholic theologians merely repeated and refined previous schools of thought.[35] The single exception to this was the irruption of Catholic modernism (1890-1910). The modernists, though always insistent that great differences existed between themselves and the liberal Protestants, actually reproduced many of the ideas current in liberalism. The movement was snuffed out, but after a suitable interval some of the same ideas were accepted by the Second Vatican Council (1962-1965) and have become a part of Catholic orthodoxy.[36]

The nineteenth century, of course, also belonged to the heirs of the Enlightenment thinkers. This was an important factor in the formation of Christology in both Protestant liberalism and Catholic modernism. Both movements were apologetic in nature. Both were occasioned by the fear that modernity was passing Christianity by. Proponents of these movements countered that it was not the essence of Christian faith that was antiquated but its doctrinal encasing. Schleiermacher therefore sought an accord with its "cultured despisers," not in common doctrinal agreement, but in a common inner core of consciousness which could be identified as religious and with which an amalgam of Christian elements could be formed.[37] This consciousness was, however, shaped by the culture in which it was formed, and therefore the kind of faith of which Schleiermacher spoke was essentially one which stressed continuity between Christ and culture. Likewise George Tyrrell, the prophet of English Catholic modernism, spoke of their strategy as necessitating the creation of a synthesis between faith and modernity in which what was essential to both would be preserved. To understand the "synthesis," therefore, we need to keep in mind the essentials of modernity to which faith was allying itself.[38]

There were at least three broad impulses that were central in the formation of the nineteenth-century consciousness which were bequeathed to it by the Enlightenment. These were first, an antiauthoritarian bias; second, the emergence of human autonomy; and third, the focus upon inner consciousness.

The antiauthoritarian mood, of course, took many different forms, but anticlericalism and a distrust of the Bible were among the more important. Both the Bible and the church were seen to be part of an older order whose removal was necessary for the emergence of the new. This produced mockery of Christian faith by intelligentsia like Thomas

Paine, and in Europe it also resulted in violence against the church. In the place of the church, as a source of meaning, was substituted the empirical world. This, too, took many forms. Some, like Hegel, looked to history; others, like Freud, to human nature; and others, like Darwin, to the natural world. The point was, however, that meaning and values were being sought in ways other than those that had prevailed in medieval and Reformation Europe, and they were being sought in realms other than the traditionally religious.

Concurrent with this development was the emergence of human autonomy. The interpretation of life and the world was now being sought, not from the church or from the Bible, but from the perspective of the unaided human interpreter. It was, after all, in the interpreter that, according to Descartes, we can find the one thing that is certain in the world. It is, he argued, possible to doubt and question everything else, but when this doubting process had run its course, one thing remained unscathed and that was human consciousness. It was, then, in human consciousness that a point of integration was sought from which understanding of all of the diverse elements of experience would result. The shift from outward authorities such as the church and Bible to the authority of the interpreter therefore moved on into an elaborate discussion on inner consciousness.

The sanctity and inviolability of this consciousness was, however, severely undermined from two entirely different directions. In the late eighteenth century Kant demolished the confidence in reason which the rationalists had maintained, and in the nineteenth Freud shook the confidence in the innocence and simplicity of consciousness. Kant's argument,[39] of course, was that reason only functions in conjunction with the stream of sensory perception. This means that we can know no more than our senses can deliver to us. And what we know is not to be directly equated with what exists, for reason categorizes and organizes the information received from the senses. Reason is interposed between the object which is perceived and what the object is perceived to be by the person. It is a screening device whose function is to organize sensory perception. The consequences of Kant's philosophy were enormous, but the most important for theology were those that followed from his empiricism. Nothing can be known except what reaches us through our senses or what is constructed as meaning and imposed upon the world by our reason, an example of the latter being cause and effect by which we make sense of what occurs in the world, but which is not made known to us from the world empirically. The senses cannot know the relations of things to one another, only their empirical qualities such as size, shape, texture, and position.

In Kant's sequel,[40] however, what had been taken away from religion with one hand was now reintroduced with the other! Given his strictures on reason, it would have appeared that "God-talk" was quite impossible. On the old basis Kant had argued that it was. But then he went on to assert that the presence of moral consciousness, which is in itself both undeniable and inexplicable, leads us to postulate that there is a God who is the explanation of this consciousness. Kant's conclusion was awkwardly ambiguous but seminal for the modern period: unless we postulate the existence of God we cannot explain the fact that we are moral creatures; but in explaining ourselves we cannot utilize the knowledge of God, for God has located himself beyond the range of reason.

Protestant liberalism flourished largely in the period between Kant and Freud, which undoubtedly made its task a little easier, for Freud in fact demolished the naivete with which Kant had spoken of this moral consciousness. Morality, Freud argued, is simply the artificial barrier which society forms in its members to protect itself from the dark, subterranean forces that lurk beneath the surface of consciousness. The moral sense is but a trick of our nature and of society.

These currents have, of course, flowed into the twentieth century. Kantian thought, which is the basis of virtually all modern epistemology, has easily bent itself to scientific habits of mind in which experience is treated as if it were composed of atoms as is matter. Experience has been broken down into discrete, isolated units which impinge upon the experiencing subject as atoms do upon atoms. This is the assumption that runs through Russell, much of Wittgenstein, and into A. T. Ayer and most of the current linguistic philosophy.[41] This has been rapidly followed by a comparable dissolution of the self; it, too, is treated atomistically. Indeed, in the process thinkers it is perceived to be changing in a way that is comparable to the way atoms move and change. The dissolution of the self, and especially of its significance as created in the image of God, has made meaning hard to find. In the twentieth century we have seen Nietzsche's "supermen" arise, dictators of both the political left and right, who believed that they could impose totalitarian rule because people had no intrinsic worth or meaning. Experience and the experiencing subjects have been dissolved, and their place has been taken by dark impersonal forces arising out of history and moving relentlessly to the predestined goal. And interestingly enough, the most vigorous protest that has been made against this situation, which is that of existentialism, still concedes the point that human nature has no reality. This final outcome, however, was far from clear when liberal theology entered into a partial alliance with this kind of thinking.

The movement, of course, came to focus in several different schools of thought. In Europe, these were principally the Schleiermacherians on the one side and the proponents of the Ritschl-Harnack emphases on the other. The differences between these schools have, I believe, been exaggerated. Although the schools cannot be equated with one another in all points, the Ritschlians and the followers of Harnack will not suffer unduly if Schleiermacher is considered as representative of liberal Protestantism. In America the leading proponents, people like Washington Gladden and Walter Rauschenbusch, accepted the axioms of liberalism, but often allied these to social activism.

Schleiermacher is justly described as the father of modern theology, because of the method he established for doing theology.[42] Where Kant had argued that religious predications must be built upon the moral consciousness, Schleiermacher substituted for the moral consciousness a religious consciousness. There is, he argued, within all people a sense of dependence which is absolute. It is this which Christianity clarifies, but its presence is not exhaustively contained within Christian communities, nor is it alone described by Christian theology. For Schleiermacher, therefore, the disclosure of God within the historical Jesus was not the sole, dominating center of his theology; and though this Jesus is to form and reform the meaning of faith, he does not exclusively define it.[43] It was this contention that aroused more of Barth's ire than perhaps any other.

Although Schleiermacher was not entirely explicit about the generic relationships of his theology, it seems reasonably clear that his operating assumptions were derived from romanticism, and in many ways these brought him into line with the earlier Greek theology. He assumed that human nature—all human nature—is the natural receptacle of the divine, that the divine infuses and suffuses the human morally, psychologically, and epistemologically. In this sense, human nature is sacramental inasmuch as that to which it points, the divine, is itself communicated in and through human nature. Jesus, therefore, was important because in a measure unparalleled in anyone else he focused, identified, and then submitted himself to the divine. In him we see the clearest exposition of what the divine is like—though it is not an exclusive exposition. And because of the divine, we are also able to recognize what our own nature is like as it reflects its Adamic purity.

The specifically Christological section in *The Christian Faith* is astonishingly brief, and Schleiermacher's comparative indifference to the questions which had troubled earlier thinkers laid the groundwork for the barrage of criticism which came later from the neo-orthodox scholars. Obviously, Schleiermacher thought of Jesus as the perfection and ultimate exemplar of that God-consciousness which is, in varying degrees, in all people. What set Jesus apart from others was not his humanity but "the constant potency of His God-consciousness, which was a veritable existence of God in Him."[44] Schleiermacher equated the "absolutely powerful God-consciousness" with the "existence of God in Him."[45] This represented what he understood by incarnation. The incarnation of God was his overwhelming self-communication within and through this man Jesus. Schleiermacher was at some pains to distinguish this from pantheism, and his argument was that God does not come to such expression in all things but only in people, and then he has only come to this ultimate expression in one person, who is Jesus. He then struggled to assert that this consciousness of God in all people cannot, in fact, be called an "existence" of God, because it is always insufficiently focused and realized. Only in Jesus was it an "existence," and in this sense he was unique. Whether Schleiermacher was successful in combining the Enlightenment notion of universalized religion with the Christian conception of the uniqueness of Christ is most doubtful.

Schleiermacher did not favor the historic Christological statements such as, "the two natures, divine and human, inseparably united in one Person are one Christ." He contended that the name "Jesus Christ" could only be used of the earthly period of life, and that it could not be extended backwards into eternity as had become common practice. He felt it was inappropriate to use the same word *nature* to describe both the divine and the human, and that this was the source of all the confusion in the past. The aboliton of the two-nature doctrine was the condition for theological clarity. And, since he was out of harmony with the traditional understanding of the Trinity, Schleiermacher could not look with favor on the use of the word *person*.

Schleiermacher also took issue with some of the proponents of the enhypostatic union who had argued that the human nature in Christ, though full in every respect, did not come to completion outside of the person. What we can affirm, he declared, is that in ordinary people there is only "the germ of the imperfect and obscure God-conscious-ness," but from the very beginning of Christ's human development there was "the absolutely powerful God-consciousness."[46] Thus the "divine influence upon the human nature is at one and the same time the incarnation of God in human consciousness and the formation of the human nature into the personality of Christ."[47] For this develop-ment to have occurred, no virgin birth was necessary, nor are the New Testament stories relating to this to be considered as doctrinally signifi-cant.

How, then, were the "natures" related to one another? Schleier-macher argued that the divine was active, taking the human into itself, and the human was passive, allowing itself to be filled and directed by the divine. The *communicatio idomatum*, however, needs to be "ban-ished from the system of doctrine,"[48] because the communication of divine qualities to the human nature or of human qualities to the divine would result in contamination of their essential characteristics. The human would be other than human, and the divine less than divine.[49]

What Schleiermacher really presented was not so much a doctrine of incarnation as of inspiration. It was a view of Jesus as a God-filled man. Undoubtedly Schleiermacher was able to elude most of the problems inherent in traditonal formulations. He did not have to address the problem of the relationship between a nature that was divine and one that was human, between that which was absolute and that which was relative. Nor did he have to formulate the relation between these natures and the single person in which they were united. Jesus was simply a man with a powerful sense of God. The immediate gains for Christology were, however, serious losses for Christian faith. Struggle as he did, Schleiermacher never quite succeeded in saying how Jesus was unique. Jesus was not a unique invasion of the divine in the human, but only the perfection of what was already present in all people. Not only was the uniqueness of Christian faith thereby forfeited, but it was not clear why Jesus was really important to faith. It is true that Schleiermacher saw him as the clarifier of God, the expositor of the divine par excellence, but in the end what was important was the Idea, not the person in whom it came to expression. And this Idea and the consciousness by which its presence is registered is a common human possession. Schleiermacher's theology was, therefore, an admirable statement of the common nineteenth-century assumptions about human life, but it was profoundly out of touch with the essence of the apostolic witness. It was on this point that Schleiermacher was called to account by the neo-orthodox thinkers.[50]

8 TWENTIETH-CENTURY TURMOIL

The cacophony within twentieth-century Christological thought has arisen, not primarily out of Christological considerations, but from factors that are more generally theological in nature. Theology itself is in disarray. Three times in the present century it has collapsed. This occurred first in the demise of Protestant liberalism and in its replacement by Barthianism in the early part of the century. It happened again in the late 1940s or early 1950s when Barthianism was eclipsed by Bultmannianism, and it happened once more at about the end of the 1950s when Bultmannianism dissipated, to be replaced by fast-moving fads, some with little depth, some with little duration, and others with little of either. These include the death-of-God theology, the schools of Pannenberg and Moltmann, and process thought. The mass of political, liberation, and ethnic theologies presently in vogue have still to prove that they have staying power. Each of these systems has construed the theological task in a different way, each has functioned with different theological principles, and each, correspondingly, has addressed specific Christological issues differently. This far-reaching instability, the pervasiveness and rapidity of change in theology even at its most fundamental levels, makes it impossible to speak in generalities of twentieth-century Christology. It is important for us, therefore, to discern more clearly what the reasons for this confusion are and then, with these reasons in mind, to take some soundings. Three thinkers have been chosen for this, each representing a distinct tradition of Christological thought: Karl Barth, Norman Pittenger, and Edward Schillebeeckx.

REASONS FOR CONFUSION
There are four factors which are central and germane to all Christological thinking which have become highly controverted in the twentieth century. These are, first, the role of Scripture in the construction of a Christology; second, the place of history—specifically that of Jesus—in

this task; third, how the doctrine of God is to be formulated, but especially whether it is tenable any longer to speak in terms that are Trinitarian; finally, what should be understood as being encompassed by the human flesh to which the Word was allied at Bethlehem. It is the enormous diversity that is evidenced at each of these points which inevitably has led to widely differing Christologies.

The first factor to be considered is the changed role which Scripture is now assuming in the work of many twentieth-century theologians. The Christological task is, therefore, rather different now from what it was in much of the past. In the patristic period, for example, the debates were over what Scripture taught about Christ or what was believed to be implied in the biblical narrative, and how best to protect these affirmations of Scripture. Despite differing hermeneutical principles which were applied to the biblical Word and despite the intrusion of philosophical interests into its interpretation, Scripture was viewed as normative. That is no longer the case.

The change in the normative function of Scripture came, not in the twentieth century, but in the eighteenth; and its source of origin was England and not, as we are in the habit of assuming, Germany. It began with the confluence of deistic skepticism about the possibility and veracity of biblical revelation and the emergence of imagination as a prime means of finding truth. It was not long before the integrity of the biblical narrative began to be eroded and imagination began to assume some of the tasks of defining the meaning of Christian faith which had formerly been yielded wholly to the biblical text. This, in time, produced elaborate treatises and a fierce accompanying controversial literature on the rules of interpretation, the place of literal meaning, ostensive reference, and a growing category generally entitled "meaning." The debate moved to Europe, and German scholars added their own contributions. In the nineteenth century, these small beginnings were to issue in a fundamental cleavage between the theology of the "pre-critical" era and that which followed it. In the former, the assumption always was that the biblical text was accessible to the interpreter, who could discover what, in fact, it meant; in the latter, this assumption has been largely destroyed. The focus now became, as Hans Frei has put it, "the unitary structure of understanding [in the interpreter] rather than the written text as such."[1] Bridging the gap between text and interpreter had become increasingly "complex and uneasy." The biblical narrative passed under the eclipse of critical theory, and meaning was emancipated, in a significant degree, from the control of the text. Imagination, what Bishop Butler in the eighteenth century had called "that forward delusive faculty," had won a large role for itself in the doing of theology.

This has produced a variety of views in contemporary theology on how the biblical text should function relative to the synoptic statements which theologians have formulated.[2] These views more or less fall into two categories. In the one category are those scholars who view the biblical text as being identical with God's disclosure of himself, be this identification in whole or in part; and in the other category are those who disengage the revelatory element from the text and see a different role from the traditional one for the biblical text. In the first category would be conservative Protestants and Catholics who make a complete identification between the text and God's disclosure of himself, as well as some who make a partial identification. These would include, for example, G. Ernest Wright,[3] and perhaps Karl Barth and Oscar Cullmann.[4] By contrast, Bultmann locates the authoritative meaning in the interpreter, Paul Tillich in the interpretive community, much post-Vatican II theology in the Spirit of God as he reveals himself in tradition, the written Scriptures, and the contemporary people of God, and much liberation and ethnic theology in the sociological realities in which the theology was born. The biblical text is then relegated a role alongside these other sources as part of a wider and more complicated *discrimen* within which theology is done. Given these widely differing perceptions on how Scripture should be used, it is inevitable that widely differing Christologies should result.

Second, it is difficult to overestimate the trauma which resulted when the "quest for the historical Jesus" had to be aborted. It is also difficult to overestimate the importance of the consequences this has had in twentieth-century Christologies. Barth dismissed the entire movement as being theologically unworthy because it was bent on finding a Jesus behind our literary sources who, in fact, cannot be discovered. And what was probably worse, the Jesus who was reconstructed in accordance with these historical techniques was quite unable to sustain the love, faith, and hope which people are asked to reside in him. In Barth, therefore, a violent reaction began, not merely against liberalism, but against every effort which endangered and entangled the Christ of faith in the historical Jesus.[5] This, too, has had a variety of expression which, on the one end in Barth, identifies as one person Jesus and the Christ, but disparages the knowledge of the historical Jesus in favor of the knowledge of the resurrected Christ, and on the other end, in Bultmann, disengages the Christ of faith from the historical Jesus and seeks to bury the latter in total obscurity.[6]

Whether in its more moderate or its more extreme forms, this sentiment has at its center the adage that the uncertain truths of history cannot yield the certainties of faith. In order to articulate this, history is often spoken of in two ways. *Historie* describes the empirical network of events which is understood by reason and within a natural cause and effect framework. *Geschichte* relates, not to the empirical data, but to the divine realm of meaning. It is grasped not by reason and research but by faith. *Historie* is always subject to revision and, as a human enterprise, is without any ultimate certainty. *Geschichte,* by contrast, has a divinely sanctioned certainty. The difference between Barth and Bultmann was not over their desire to preserve Christ *(Geschichte)* from the vagaries of historical research on Jesus *(Historie)*. In this they were agreed. Their differences, rather, were that in Christology Barth believed that *Geschichte* was found within *Historie* and Bultmann thought it was found apart from *Historie*. This is not an issue which has yielded to a commonly agreed solution.

There are, in fact, two sides to it which are often confused. The one concerns the relation of faith to the historical events of the life, death, and resurrection of Jesus. The other concerns the relation between faith and historical methodology.[7] With respect to the latter, scholars ask what devices are available for finding the facts. How do we devise explanations of those facts, explanations which are comprehensible enough to include all of them, and flexible enough to accommodate the presence of those factors which are unique in Jesus' life for which no contemporary analogies exist in our experience? To what extent was God *incognito* in Jesus, and what kind of control should the historical Jesus exercise over the Christ of faith? Is it possible to be encountered by Christ in the absence of any knowledge of the historical Jesus? Is Christ himself now *incognito* and revealing himself perhaps within other religions?[8] None of these questions has been resolved to everyone's satisfaction, and the result is that Christological thought is as diverse and as scattered as is that on methodology.

The third problematic question concerns the nature and identity of God as conceived within contemporary theology. An incarnation, in a classic theological sense, is only possible where a Trinitarian conception of God is operative. In the absence of this, the Incarnation becomes merely an instance, however variously described, of the divine filling of the man Jesus, a filling that differs in degree but not in kind from any other fillings of which human experience provides the record. In the contemporary scholarly context, defenders of a traditional Trinitarian conception are relatively scarce.

The root cause of the difficulty is, of course, the ambiguity which is so prevalent about the role of Scripture in determining theological constructs. If this biblical Word is to be displaced from its normative function, then it might be easy to agree with Cyril Richardson that the New Testament offers three predominant symbols of God which, in fact, do service for a whole multitude of relations which God sustains to the world. That being the case, to restrict God's relationship with the world to its traditional formulation is, Richardson believes, untenable. The doctrine of Trinity, he declares, "is an artificial construct" which forces these multiple relations into "an arbitrary threeness."[9]

It is, of course, true that the intrusion of philosophical interests in the early church had a significant effect on the way the Trinity was understood. In the early postbiblical period, it was common to distinguish between the first two persons of the Godhead as "God" and "Messiah." The intent of this was to show that Old Testament monotheism, even in its Christian context, was still intact. At the time when the use of "Son" became prominent, a subtle shift in understanding did take place. The use of "Father" and "Son" took place in a context where the fundamental problem that these terms addressed was philosophical. The problem was how the infinite can be related to what is finite, the absolute to the relative, the eternal to the temporal, the one to the many. The solution that emerged with wide consensus was that the "Father" was to be identified with all that was transcendent and the "Son" with all that was immanent. The "Father" was veiled, remote, unknowable, beyond reach, alone, and the originator of all that exists. The "Son" became the agent in creation, and in his Incarnation the divine remoteness was broken, transcendence broke through into immanence, the infinite into the finite, eternity into time, what was unknowable into that "which we have heard, which we have seen with our eyes, which we have looked at and our hands have touched" (1 John 1:1). Thus was the philosophical problem resolved.

If this is indeed the issue which the doctrine of the Trinity is designed to address, then it might well be asked today whether this is still the central issue and whether the Trinitarian conception is any longer a viable concept. The fact that the doctrine of Trinity actually arose for entirely different reasons, as the response to an ineradicable part of biblical revelation, is not one that commands wide attention. Even the most notable defender of this doctrine in the twentieth century, Karl Barth, is not without his equivocations on this point. That being the case, it has become extremely difficult to find even general unanimity on what might be meant by saying that the second "person" of the Godhead was incarnate.

The final question out of which theological discord has been generated concerns the meaning of "nature." To affirm Chalcedon is to affirm that two "natures" were joined in a single person. But what content is to be put into such a term, and how does it relate to our modern forms of knowledge?

When the nineteenth century began, as was noted, some form of Cartesian dualism was held by most people in the intellectual world. Descartes argued that mind and body were, in their essence, distinctive realities which operated on one another while retaining their own characteristic life. Mind and body resembled two clocks so perfectly synchronized that the respective "tick" of each coincided.[10] They coincided, not because the one's workings were the cause of the other's ticking, but because of their perfect manufacture and synchronization. So it is with body and mind. The nineteenth-century materialists attacked this notion vigorously, arguing that the mind is simply a part of the body's matter. And in our own century, Gilbert Ryle has ridiculed this notion as the "ghost in the machine" theory.[11]

Not only has the mind come under attack, but the entire notion of "human nature" is in philosophical disfavor.[12] This, in large measure, is also a legacy of the nineteenth century. Darwinian evolution made a mockery of the thought that human nature is an unchanging and enduring reality in all people, that the *imago Dei* has given to all people, in all cultures, in all times the same internal shape. Karl Marx, of course, enthusiastically endorsed Darwin's theories and went on to work out their social consequences. Marx began with the presupposition to which Darwin's work had arrived: there is no such thing as human nature. History, for Marx, became the blueprint in which we see unfolded the principles by which our societies are slowly being organized. These principles are inherent within human life; they are absolute, and their effect is deterministic. It is these principles which are shaping individual people and molding them into collective units. The moral responsibility and personal accountability which has passed into the legal system of the West and which was originally predicated on the biblical notion of human nature created in God's image was dismissed by Marx as a creation of capitalism. Capitalism needs the individualistic, entrepreneurial spirit to survive, and it created the belief in personal accountability. It is this spirit which creates the illusion of individual worth, of private morality. The role Marx gave to the state could be sustained only if human nature, as biblically conceived, did not exist.

In the twentieth century B. F. Skinner has reached similar conclusions. Skinner's approach builds on what he perceives to be the collapse and bankruptcy of psychoanalysis. Freud, and those who followed him, had sought the meaning of the person within the inner consciousness of the person. The search for this consciousness, and the diagnosis of its components, have become mired in futility, Skinner believes. Psychoanalysis does not work, its inflated claims not withstanding. Skinner therefore looks for the meaning of the person from society, not from inner consciousness or some sense of what it means to "have" human nature. What explains human behavior can be identified only in social environment. People have the illusion of being free from that environment, but it is only an illusion. Skinner, therefore, has proposed a radical program of social engineering, the point of which is to change people.

The existentialist thinkers in our century have, of course, bitterly opposed all philosophies and philosophers who see the human being as merely an object moved and shaped by external and impersonal forces. Jean-Paul Sartre typically attacked this whole approach by arguing that "existence precedes essence." The individual is not the product of something that has preceded him or her. Sartre attacked the supposition that impersonal forces are determining human nature. There is no such thing as human nature, he contended. What we have is individual human beings in the process of shaping themselves by their choices; and the choices they make are either authentic, in which case the person moves toward having an individual shape, or inauthentic, in which case the person allows himself or herself merely to mouth and imitate what are conventional norms in a society, be they of a moral or religious nature. Sartre, and the existentialists who stood with him, were adamant that the argument for human nature was an argument against personal freedom and authenticity. It was, he thought, the contention that each person in life is merely the outworking of an antecedent human nature from which the person cannot escape and over which the person cannot exercise control that doomed every attempt to find meaning and authenticity.

Given this broad consensus, it is no surprise to encounter the argument within theology that "nature" and "person" "have become ambiguous and, perhaps, unacceptable concepts." Because of this, G. C. Berkouwer declares, "One can speak without exaggeration of a far-reaching crisis in the dual-nature doctrine" of Christ. The old confession "that Jesus Christ was truly God and truly man, has increasingly become the object of radical criticism."[13] It is now our purpose to examine some of this criticism by taking our soundings at three different places in the stormy waters of Christological formulation.

KARL BARTH

It was, of course, Karl Barth who called the dominant liberal theology of his time back to a Christological focus. For the liberals, Christian faith was without a focus. It had become synonymous with a universalized Idea, a felt presence in human nature. Its connections with the historical Christ were never more than tangential or slight and never really necessary. Barth's *The Epistle to the Romans* violently repudiated this development, and his *Church Dogmatics* is a far-reaching attempt to restructure the whole of theology around a Christological axis.

In 1938 Barth himself spoke of the "Christological concentration" in his thought. This would, of course, expose him to the charge that he had developed a "christo-monism." The term, Barth allowed, was hardly beautiful, and he asked "whether a Christian theologian can with a good conscience and a joyful heart do anything else than put 'Christ only' first and last in his thinking?"[14] Had Barth merely reasserted the Reformers *solo Christo* motif, Berkouwer, Brunner, Paul Althaus, Cornelius Van Til, and many others would not have assailed him as they did on this point. To his critics, however it appeared that Barth's theology as a whole had been distorted in order to uphold the unusual way he developed the role that he had assigned to Christ. This goes to the heart of the matter. Barth's Christology was distinctive, not so much for its specific substance as for its place in his theology as a whole.

The Christology itself was unashamedly Chalcedonian. Christ, the second "mode" of the divine Trinity, preexisted and, at a point in time, chose the humanity of Jesus for his enfleshing within the virgin Mary. Barth was not a Sabellian, for he held that each "mode" was permanent within the triune being of God.[15] And in line with the Augustinian tradition, he insisted that the whole Godhead was present in human flesh, although the soteriological task was assigned in particular to the Son.[16] This meant that he gave an unqualified and unabridged statement of Jesus' divinity. It was "true God of true God." No diminution of this Godness occurred in the process of incarnation, nor did any conversion of divinity into manhood result, but "Jesus Christ is very God and very man."[17] This meant that even within the infant Jesus, as well as in the Christ dying on the cross, no loss of divine attributes occurred. In him, from start to finish, we meet God, in all of his veiled greatness and majesty. Barth returned to this theme repeatedly, never yielding any ground in his insistence that in Jesus there is a Godness which is *homoousion* with that of the Father. To say otherwise, he insisted, is to undercut both the giving of revelation[18] and the possibility of salvation.[19] To accede to the argument of the docetists or even the kenoticists would be to attack the central pillar of the Christian affirmation. To yield here is to cease to be Christian.

Barth was likewise insistent on the virgin birth by which the eternal Son took to himself a full humanity.[20] To say that the Son "became man" is to say that he took human nature to himself. It was a nature that was complete and consubstantial with that of all human beings. Indeed, so complete was this identity that Barth even equivocated over Jesus' sinlessness. He insisted that in being incarnate, Christ had assumed an Adamic nature. "He does not avoid the burden of this state and position but takes the conditions and consequences upon himself."[21] The virgin birth was not the means whereby God intercepted the transmission of this nature in its fullness; the virgin birth was important because it underscored Christ's humanness. Although human and bearing Adam's nature, Christ was nevertheless incapable of sinning because God is incapable of sinning. Barth therefore came close to saying that Jesus was a sinner simply and only because he was human, but at the same time Barth insisted that in practice Jesus was without sin, for in him "the Son of God appropriated and actualized his special possibility as Man."[22] How, then, were this true humanity and true divinity related to one another?

That, of course, is a question which Barth did address, but it needs to be noted that his interest in it *per se* was modest. Barth's concern was to see how Jesus Christ effects the relationship between sinful men and women and their Creator. He complained, as a result, that the person of Christ in its constitutive parts had often been viewed statically, almost like the components of a chemical reaction, rather than dynamically.

The "two-nature" doctrine became a thing in itself, rather than being seen as the means of God's own humbling and of the exaltation of humanity through the incarnate and risen Word. Barth's insistence on the functional aspect of Christology, however, was never advocated, as it often is in other scholars today, at the price of the ontic. Again and again Barth returned to the same theme that if Christ was not true God of true God, one who never ceased to be God, one who never ceased to be fully God from cradle to grave, then he could not act on behalf of apostate humanity as only God can act.

On the other side of the question, Barth argued that it is not made clear from Scripture what the exact components of Jesus' human nature were. What the Scriptures affirm is that Jesus Christ was a part of our human existence and shared our history. When Jesus pointed to himself, it was not as a moral ideal or an example of human nature. He pointed to "the Way which is as such the Truth and the Life, to the true Light, to the one Door, to the heavenly Bread, to the faithful Shepherd."[23] There was a particularity about his human existence. He was human in a concrete, historical way. He was not a human abstraction. And in his particularity, he was God made present to us.

The humanity of Jesus, therefore, exists and takes its form within the sovereign action of God, "of which he is born and by which he is sustained and preserved and upheld."[24] There is not, then, a human reality and a divine in Christ, juxtaposed alongside each other. Nor is the one absorbed into the other, but the human finds its place while retaining its full integrity within the divine. What constituted this Christ was and is "the one, divine reality, in which as such the human is posited, contained and included."[25] Barth therefore affirmed the patristic doctrine of enhypostatic union, which he interpreted to mean that "the man Jesus came into being and is by the Word of God, it is *only* by the Word of God that He came into being and is. Because he is the Son of God, it is only as such that He is real man."[26]

The speculative accompaniments of this doctrine, however, held little interest for Barth. Barth agreed with both traditional Lutheranism and Calvinism on the ubiquity of Christ's body, albeit in different ways. With the Lutherans he also asserted the fact of ubiquity because of the unity of Christ's person; with the Calvinists he shared a common concern that each nature of Christ be preserved in its integrity and that neither lose its distinctiveness. The problem is that each side had a legitimate concern, and, given the terms of the debate, neither could prevail without doing injustice to the course of biblical orthodoxy.[27] Barth's solution was to propose that there is a general ubiquity of Christ, a corporeal presence, in the world (because he is one, divine person), but this does not erase the particularity of the Jesus who lived, died, rose, and ascended to a particular place (because his natures retain their integrity). It is possible, therefore, to speak of a particular presence of Christ's body which is limited and a general presence which is universalized.[28] And it is necessary to affirm the latter because the church and the world cannot have his Spirit and his grace "if He is not there as a whole—the one undivided Mediator between God and man."[29]

In its substance, then, Barth's Christology falls clearly within the "Word-flesh" school. Like them, he has made the unity of the person fundamental, and he has construed this unity in terms of the divine, sovereign action in salvation. Although penal motifs are present in Barth's formulation of the atonement, the determining element is that of divine conquest.[30] It was at the cross that God triumphantly acted against sin, death, and the devil whom Barth collectively refers to under the term *das Nichtige*. In this action God employed the human, necessarily incorporating it in his saving action. God used the existence of the human Jesus, but this is at its most fundamental level *divine* work. There can be no thought of the human creature cooperating in the divine action, nor of Jesus acting representatively and in the place of sinful humanity in a work of cooperation. Barth's deep-seated antipathy to every form of synergism found Christological expression in his "Word-flesh" formulation.

In this, Barth swam steadily upstream against the almost overwhelming sentiment in recent decades that the "Word-man" Christology is alone sufficient in giving an account of all the New Testament data. He was Alexandrine when it had become fashionable to be Antiochene. Yet this is not the most distinctive aspect of his Christology. Its distinctiveness lies, rather, in the role which it plays within his system as laid out in the *Church Dogmatics*. Because of the complexity of this function, only a few aspects of it can be dealt with in this brief treatment.

There were four factors that were important in defining and shaping this role. The first of these was Barth's belief that theology as a whole should attempt to give a comprehensive statement of the substance, meaning, and implications of biblical revelation. This belief was often stated with a polemical edge to it. It meant, for example, that there could be no principles or established antecedent to the study of Scripture which could determine the nature of biblical revelation for it. There is no "essence of Christianity," no sifting device which enables us to take seriously some parts of this revelation and disregard others, as Barth believed Harnack had proposed.[31]

It is the character of this revelation which distinguishes such work from a merely religious enterprise. Religion, Barth argued, is the human enterprise which attempts to think thoughts about God. The movement is from earth to heaven. The content of it and the authority which accompanies it can never be more than merely human. It is an activity of fallen, human *Erōs*. Theology, by contrast, is the restatement of the Word of God, that Word which is in its content and authority divine. It is, in fact, the Word which Jesus Christ employs to address his people. The movement is from heaven to earth. The initiative is God's. It issues from the divine *Agapē*. The words of the biblical revelation are not themselves revelatory. They do *become* God's revelation as Christ uses the Word and employs it afresh. The interconnection between the divine, sovereign Christ and the totally indispensable place of biblical revelation was important. Other theologians might follow Schleiermacher in distilling out of their experience a knowledge of God with its resulting Christology. Barth could not. And when he perceived Bultmann, Gogarten, and Brunner beginning to move in this direction he accused them of returning to "the fleshpots of Egypt."[32]

What was as important as this conviction, however, was the Kantian epistemology in which it was interpreted. This is the second of the factors that determined the shape of his Christology. Already it has been noted that the general tendency of this epistemological outlook was to isolate the self, the knowing subject, from the world. Existentialists like Sartre and Camus took this tendency to its radical conclusions and constructed an entire philosophy around this sense of isolation within a world whose meaning had dissipated. In Barth, however, it led in another direction. The meaning of the created order is something only God can give. Meaning can be had only if it is both given and received. Barth denied that God had given meaning to the created order or that it could be received. In his famous debate with Brunner, he denied the existence of both natural revelation and the *imago Dei*. In the *Church Dogmatics* he speaks of this *imago* in two different forms, one of which is retained subsequent to the fall and one of which is lost. What is lost is the innate capacity to know God, for then, Barth felt, a knowledge given by the living Word in encounter would simply be an addition to what was already possessed. This, once again, would result in synergism. And the supposition that God has disclosed himself in the created order would, Barth feared, open the door to natural theology whereby the fallen creature builds up a knowledge of the Lord merely by human industry and astuteness. A works salvation was always just around the corner from this kind of presupposition, as Roman Catholicism had so often shown.[33]

Having thus destroyed every possibility of any natural theology, Barth utilized his Kantian epistemology to highlight the awful isolation of the self, an isolation which can only be broken by the in-breaking of the living Word. By this in-breaking, these revelatory insights given personally and coming from "above," epistemological links are reestablished first with the triune God and then with the created order. Kant's destruction was not assailed. Barth accepted the work of demolition Kant had carried out and used it to buttress the role assigned to Jesus Christ. It is *only* in Jesus Christ that we have any knowledge of God at all, only in him and because of him and through him that we can recognize God as Creator and assign meaning to the creation. The Word therefore became the surrogate for the epistemology Kant demolished.

Third, Barth always carried with him a sense of horror over the "lives of Jesus" movement. It translated into a lifelong fear of jeopardizing the absolute, divine Christ by concealing him in the obscure and uncertain truths of history. For Barth, then, there was an emancipation of the Christ of faith from the Jesus of history which was necessary, *Geschichte* from *Historie*. This emancipation was partial, unlike Bultmann's program in which it was complete, but it did mean that once again a knowledge of Christ could not be had by diligent human research into the historical life of Jesus. By the same token, it could not be jeopardized by such research either.

Finally, Barth also carried throughout the *Church Dogmatics* a profound antipathy towards all synergistic forms of salvation, the two most important expressions of which had been given in Protestant liberalism and Roman Catholicism. Barth attacked every possibility of supposed cooperation between sinful humanity and God. His Christology, as much as anything, was used as a tool in this warfare. It was constructed in such a way that God's sovereign initiative is everywhere upheld, and the sinful proclivity to which all are prone, of self-justification and self-salvation, is everywhere struck down.

These factors came together in prescribing a role for Christology which was distinctive in Barth's thought, not to say unique.[34] Christ, then, is the agent of God's sovereign initiative in creation, revelation, and salvation. In order to articulate this in an appropriate way, Barth completely reworked the theme of election.[35] In traditional Protestant thought, the objects of God's decrees—one to salvation and the other to damnation—are sinful men and women. The two decrees, in Barth's theology, terminated not on sinful people, but in and on Christ. Christ is the bearer of the divine Yes to humanity and, in his death, of the divine No. The elect Man is the rejected Man. He who was God was struck by the judgment of God. Christ is the agent and the object of this double predestination. Although this almost certainly resulted in a universalism in Barth's thought, despite his occasional protest to the contrary, it was one predicated wholly and only on the triumph of God's grace. The gospel, he declared, "is not a mixed message of joy and terror, salvation and damnation. . . . The Yes cannot be heard unless the No is heard. But the No is said for the sake of the Yes and not for its own sake. In substance, therefore, the first and last word is Yes and not No."[36]

This sovereignty with its corresponding destruction of all human involvement was preserved in Barth's threefold understanding of the Word. The most fundamental expression of this revelation is Jesus

Christ. This revelation, however, is not accessible by diligence or research, but only by faith. If Christ could be found by research, then God could be manipulated by sinful beings. However, God's freedom from all such manipulation was exactly what the doctrine of the Word was set up to protect. The biblical revelation or sermonic formulations of it, therefore, have no divine disclosure within them until the primary form of the Word of God, Jesus Christ, gives it to them. A knowledge of God cannot be distilled from or constructed out of the biblical materials. It is given in conjunction with the biblical text, but is not identical with that text. It cannot be searched out; it must be given. It is only Jesus Christ who can give it, and he does so personally, directly, and from "above."

This same concern worked itself out in Barth's soteriology where the traditionally "subjective" aspects were subsumed under the "objective." Gustav Wingren has contended that all Barth has done has been to turn the liberals on their heads. They had no divine transcendence; he had no immanence. They functioned within the Abelardian tradition and imagined the work of Christ was wholly interior; Barth presented it as wholly exterior. Consequently, Barth argued that "Christ in you" should never be understood as an experiential reality, but only as an objective reality forged in Christ's history.[37] Conversion and even sanctification, he argued, refer to what Christ achieved on behalf of sinners and not to what he does in sinners based on his death on their behalf. What this means, then, is that ultimately what distinguishes people is not that some believe on Christ and have received forgiveness because of his death in their place and others do not. The difference, rather, is that some know that in his death all humanity was redeemed and others do not.[38]

Barth's neo-orthodoxy, then, is strikingly revealed by his Christology. In its substance Barth's Christology is, to a high degree, "orthodox"; in its function, however, it is "neo," constructed out of concessions to Kantianism and reactions to the multiple failures of liberalism. Its virtues, which are considerable, come from its orthodoxy. Barth unflinchingly asserted the full, unqualified Chalcedonian doctrine and yoked together, as Scripture consistently does, the person of Christ and his work. And in so doing, he rightly insisted on the sovereignty of God, his freedom in grace to act without constraint by the cooperating creature. This great virtue turned, however, into vice. Barth's grasp of this truth was distorted by his violent reaction to liberalism and his capitulation to Kantianism, as a result of which the world was illicitly and unbiblically denuded of divine meaning, human nature stripped of its divine capacity. Christ was severed from a meaningful relation to the historical Jesus; the biblical words were, in and of themselves, evacuated of revelatory content; and soteriology was so truncated and distorted that great biblical themes like faith, regeneration, conversion, and sanctification were emptied of their proper significance. To Barth's view of Christ's person, Scripture says Yes; to his view of Christ's role, it says No.

NORMAN PITTENGER

Pittenger's contribution is important for at least two main reasons. First, he is an exponent of a philosophical outlook whose presence has affected much recent theology. Broadly speaking, there have been two predominant philosophical outlooks on how human nature should be conceived and epistemology structured. The fountainheads were Kant and Hegel. The expressions given to these outlooks have been diverse, but each has had discernible characteristics. The outlook flowing from Kant always tends, as we have noted, to isolate the knowing self from the world; that originating in Hegel always tends to confuse the knowing self with the world, perhaps even merging the two together ontologically. It is this latter tradition, sharpened and refined in Alfred North Whitehead, that has provided the framework for Pittenger's thought.[39] As an exponent of it, he has forged a distinctive place for himself and has won acceptance for Whiteheadian process thinking in contemporary theology.

Second, Pittenger stands almost alone among process thinkers in having given concerted attention to Christology. His first attempt at reconstructing Christology in terms of process philosophy came in his *Christ and the Christian* (1941). This interest was developed in his *The Word Incarnate* (1959). This was further refined, he says, "in the light of criticisms and comments on my views by several distinguished theologians in Britain and the United States,"[40] and expressed in his *Christology Reconsidered* (1968).

Christology is also dealt with tangentially or partially in other works, such as his *Reconceptions in Christian Thinking, Christ in the Haunted World,* and *Catholic Faith in a Process Perspective.* Working on his Christology is especially satisfying because he has also produced several studies on related themes, such as the Trinity[41] and sin,[42] which give full-bodied coherence to what he says on Christology. For these reasons, Pittenger's work deserves serious attention.

In moving from Barth to Pittenger, we not only move from the Kantian to the Whiteheadian tradition,[43] but also from a proponent of the "Word-flesh" Christology to an advocate of the "Word-man" Christology, from a supporter of Chalcedon to one of its opponents. Pittenger takes aim in particular at the enhypostatic formula, in the light of which he believes Chalcedon is consistently misunderstood. To argue, as its proponents do, that the humanity of Christ only finds its "personal center" in the Word, that it lacks its own center, is to say that it lacks what is essential to being human. This sounds to Pittenger like the old Eutychian heresy in which the Word replaced the personal center of the humanity rather than acting alongside of it.[44] Pittenger would rather be in jeopardy of dividing the person by appearing to offer two personal centers, one in the Word and the other in the humanity, than he would diminish the humanity.

To Pittenger's critics, his views appear more than a little Nestorian! There is, however, a very large and significant difference between the form of the entire patristic discussion and the form of Pittenger's ruminations. The early fathers, barring the heretics, all functioned within Nicene orthodoxy on the doctrine of the Trinity; Pittenger does not. They understood Christ's divinity to be a supranatural reality, ontologically distinct from the created order; Pittenger does not. Pittenger may affirm, indeed he does affirm, that Christians must believe in the divinity of Christ, but what he means by this is something entirely different from what the early fathers, let alone the writers of the New Testament, meant.

The movement from Barth to Pittenger is also a movement from a profound antiliberalism to a repristination of it. It is no surprise that Pittenger returns again and again to the luminaries of the older movement. They constitute the trough from which he drinks with appreciation. It is to people like F. D. Maurice, C. E. Raven, J. F. Bethune-Baker, W. R. Matthews, C. C. J. Webb, and on the Catholic side, to Friedrich von Hügel and George Tyrrell that he looks. And once again, the old liberal ideas reappear despite the fact that process theology is supposed to be "post-liberal." Christianity is one of the more remarkable illustrations of the evolution of reality,[45] albeit in a Whiteheadian sense; the supernatural is found in the natural and merged with it; God is found in human nature in a bond of mutual reciprocity and involvement between the human and the divine; sin is simply the failure to develop into what we could be; the biblical miracles are simply metaphorical ways of speaking; Christ is the exemplification of the divine, but not its exclusive disclosure;[46] and his work was the epitome and symbolic representation of what God can do in all people more generally. This is classic liberalism. The strictures of Barth and Brunner against it are brusquely dismissed as being "extreme." That may be so, but it is odd that one who has made so much of the need to be "modern" should have replicated views that are both so dated and so thoroughly discredited.

In any process framework, the classical Christological problems are necessarily dissolved.[47] The historical debate has, as we have seen, been about the relations of the human and the divine, how it is possible to have unabridged humanity and divinity within unitary personhood. In process thinking, all of the elements in this "problem" disappear. First, there is no such thing as pure divinity or pure humanity. God is seen to be both absolute and relative, infinite and finite, Creator and created. He casts his "lure" into the natural order, eliciting from it its hidden potential, and then absorbs this potential into himself in order that his own potential might come to fuller expression. Between God and the world there exists a symbiotic relationship. Each is dependent on the other, each comes with the other, each lives by the other in an unending process of unfolding. Natural reality is never purely natural, and the divine is never experienced as, nor indeed in its own life is it, dislocated from the natural. This has led process thinkers "to place their emphasis upon 'becoming,' as a dynamic movement of development in relationship," says Pittenger, "rather than on 'being'; here, they insist, is the best 'model' for our understanding of God."[48]

Second, this means that there cannot be a uniqueness to the person of Christ in any traditional sense. The world is the visible story of the dynamic movement of God. It is a movement with its ebbing and flowing. Jesus was a remarkable effulgence of the divine, but one which differed from other such expressions in degree but not in kind.[49] Every actuality in the world—both in human and nonhuman forms—is an incarnation of God. It is, of course, for this reason that process thinkers have a deep affinity for much Eastern thought.

Third, there is no such thing as substantive personhood. The "person" is, in fact, dissolved into a series of swiftly changing "particles of experience." A person is nothing more than the events and activities of any particular moment in which that "person" is engaged, events and activities which themselves are always changing.[50] As these change, so the "person" changes. That being the case, there is nothing purely divine to be incarnate, nothing purely human in which it could be incarnate, and no such thing as a "person" in whom they could be joined and expressed! Within human life there are multiple intimations of the divine as it struggles to find expression within a reality which is inextricably, inevitably everywhere and always both human and divine.

It is this context which needs to be borne in mind when Pittenger enumerates the fundamentals of any satisfactory Christology. This first involves the full humanity of Jesus; and since Pittenger is Antiochene in outlook, this is made fundamental. Second, he affirms that Jesus must be divine, but what he appears to mean by this is that the accomplishments of Jesus were more than merely human. Third, the human and the divine must be seen as essentially harmonious with one another and never pictured as a duality. Fourth, Christ must be related to the work of God throughout the cosmos.

Pittenger is uneasy with the language of incarnation because it usually carries with it the connotation of uniqueness. He contends that if the divine Word were incarnate only once, in the historical Jesus, the humanity of Jesus would be completely unlike ours. To restrict the Incarnation to Jesus, he declares, leads inevitably to "making the incarnation a docetic exception to human conditions, circumstances, and situations."[51] Rather, Jesus should be seen as a specific and especially important instance of the divine act of incarnation which is generally experienced throughout the created order.

The man in which this divine work was exemplified was fully human with a "true çentre" or ego which is not in any sense displaced or minimized.[52] But this itself breaks down as Pittenger continues his analysis, because the word *person* implies a kind of static core or prescribed shape to the interior capacities of human being. Pittenger believes this conception is derived from Greek philosophy. The person is not an unchanging substance, but a process of successive events and experiences. This process, in all human beings, "is nothing other than the reflex of the divine action in and on and through manhood."[53] The insistence on a full humanity in Jesus, orthodox-sounding as it is, really becomes an insistence on a Jesus who experienced the divine as we do, his experience merely differing from ours in the degree of clarity and its intensity. Despite the infusion of process categories, this argument is identical to Schleiermacher's that God's presence is registered in all people, but in Jesus this presence, "the constant potency of his God consciousness," became so powerful as to constitute an "existence" of God within him.[54] Not only so, but this insistence on a full humanity is also an insistence on a figure who was as fallible and prone to misconception as we are.[55]

The distinctive thing about Jesus was that in himself he unveiled the divine. What was disclosed was not the "being" of God in any conventional philosophical or theological sense, but the "act" of God, God in motion in relating to the human creature and the creation, giving and disclosing his nature of love while eliciting from his creation its own potential. As such, however, "Jesus is not *exhaustive* of Deity,"[56] but merely exemplifies and manifests the divine.[57] The person and the work of Christ are therefore bonded more closely than in most theologies, for Jesus is what he does; but what he does differs only in degree from what other humans do and not in kind. He is not unique; he is merely a forerunner, Pittenger asserts, that of which "other men, each in their own small way, are the adumbration and intimation."[58]

Despite the engaging way in which Pittenger writes and the often provocative forms in which he puts old problems, it needs to be observed that what he has presented is not a Christology. His Christology is simply a statement about the means and objectives of the inspiration of the human Jesus. Jesus was a God-inspired man who differed from other people in the degree of his God-inspiredness. All of the elements which necessarily make up a Christian understanding of Christ are gone. Gone is the conviction that the triune God is other than and independent of the creation, that the second person in the Godhead took the humanity of Jesus in a union which was unlike his relation to any other being, that Jesus as a result is a unique disclosure of the divine and the unique bearer of human sin in his substitutionary work on the cross. Gone, too, is the biblical understanding of the *imago Dei*, of a self whose worth is not simply that of the accumulation of momentary events and experiences, of a world in which there are absolute norms and an unchanging God. There is, in fact, no reason at all, no logical reason at least, why Pittenger should hold any allegiance to *Christian* faith, for he is quite unable to explain why God should have made this special disclosure in Jesus, or why, given Pittenger's evolutionary perspective, we should not expect greater and more intense disclosure in other people as the being of God comes to greater and greater realization within the natural order. This possibility is unwittingly anticipated when Pittenger argues that Jesus never believed himself to be divine and never acted in any way that was inconsistent with our own humanity. And the trace which Jesus' life left behind was not that of a unique person who acted in terms of his inner substance, but rather one who was an accumulation of changing experiences and was borne along by those experiences as much as he was their shaper. The experiences and events are, in Pittenger's process thinking, the substitute for what has classically been described as the person. How can one exercise saving faith in this succession of events and experiences? In the end, what Pittenger has offered as a Christology is really only a theism[59] constructed on process lines, whose cardinal interests are antithetical to biblical theism and whose substance is actually hostile to the exercise of faith in any discernibly biblical way.

EDWARD SCHILLEBEECKX

Of the three theologians who are being considered in this chapter, Schillebeeckx probably presents the largest number of difficulties to most readers. These difficulties arise, first, from his ambiguous standing in the Roman Catholic Church; second, from the convoluted and sometimes confused form of reasoning he has produced; and, third, from the fact that, in stark contrast to the situation in Europe, he is little known in Britain and North America, with the result that there is relatively little literature of a secondary and reflective nature on his work available in English. He nevertheless warrants attention, despite the fact that only two volumes have appeared in his planned trilogy on Christology.

Schillebeeckx, a Dutch Dominican priest, has been prominent in shaping the "New Catholicism"[60] that was first given visibility and legal standing by the Second Vatican Council, but he has contributed his own distinctive ideas to this. His approach, presupposed by his volumes on Christology, is one which has strong affinities with both existentialism and process thought, but this is worked out within Catholic convictions. It is his philosophical approach, quite as much as the specifics of his Christology, which appears to have landed him in serious trouble with the Congregation for the Doctrine of Faith in the Vatican. In 1980 the documents from "the Schillebeeckx case" were published.[61] They reveal that there is considerable dismay over and suspicion about his views in the Vatican, and the possibility of further disciplinary action is suggested. Given this difficult political situation, it is not easy to discern where the rock bottom in Schillebeeckx's thinking lies and how far he has had to modify his views to achieve greater accord with what is judged to be orthodoxy in the Vatican.

Schillebeeckx's thought is, in any case, difficult. His books suffer from an exuberance which will not be disciplined by or contained within the question at hand. A text or a problem elicits a mighty cascade of words and knowledge, much of which has the effect of obscuring the original text or problem. It is no surprise that after Schillebeeckx had completed the first two studies[62] in his trilogy, he was obliged to write a book explaining and clarifying what readers had failed to understand sufficiently or accurately in these volumes![63] In my own approach to Schillebeeckx, it is this explanatory volume which will be used as a key to his Christological studies, but these will necessarily have to be placed also in the larger framework of his thought.

As it turns out, the novelty of Schillebeeckx's approach is simply a matter of appearances coupled with the language of Catholic spirituality which he employs. The underlying ideas are all too familiar. His operating assumption, he declares, is that the experience of modernity not only provides the context within which biblical teaching is heard, but also determines what contemporary people can hear from that teaching. Our task is not one, he argues, of discovering what Scripture teaches and then applying that knowledge to the modern world. We "have become increasingly aware that no one is in a position to rediscover precisely what the message of the gospel now means to us, except in relation to our present situation."[64] This is, of course, a proposition that is foundational to the new hermeneutic and has been variously developed on the Protestant side by the Bultmannians and post-Bultmannians. What it means for Schillebeeckx is that *experience* is the key to Christology.

Schillebeeckx, therefore, begins with contemporary experience, that sense of alienation which modern people have, the jarring and discordant elements within it which leave behind them a residual sense of things being adrift and wrong, that haunting fear of "the precariousness of our existence." It is this experience which is either incorporated into a larger experience which is religious or leads us into a negative affirmation about life. Experience underlies both faith and unbelief. It is, in fact, the thread which also leads us back to Jesus, for in his day, too, it was experience which provided an *entrée* to understanding who he was.

This, of course, raised the question as to whether or not there are divine elements in human experience and, if so, how these might be described. This is a matter to which Schillebeeckx has given considerable thought, although it is not always communicated with clarity. His deepest conviction is, however, that God is the ground of our being, that he is "found," not by penetrating obscure realms above, but through and within human relations. God is the foundation and ontological substratum of those relations. He is therefore experienced "in and through our love towards our fellow men and the world, realizing fully that we ourselves are not the ultimate source of this human love and this secular involvement."[65] The reality of God which shines through the cultural matrix is, however, determined by that matrix. Thus the link to Jesus (experience[66]) is a link which is divine, but it is divine in terms which are comprehensible within a secular society. And, in measure, it is revelatory, for it is, as a process, an explication of the mysterious presence of God.[67] In this, of course, Schillebeeckx is merely broadening the categories with which Catholics have always worked. The truth about God is derived not only from Scripture, but also from experience, and not merely the experience of the magisterium, or even of the church, but of human beings. Thus the category of tradition has been broadened to include experience of a nonmagisterial and even nonecclesiastical kind.

Schillebeeckx's view of human experience as revelatory leads on to the question as to how far sin has destroyed the *imago Dei* and to what extent it is a barrier to God's presence in human life. After reviewing the teaching of the Second Vatican Council on this matter, Schillebeeckx declared that this "new humanity" applies to all men of "good will," since God knows only one destiny in life, the same for all men. In this, the Council affirms most explicitly that the man renewed in Christ is not a monopoly for Christians.[68] The conclusion from this seems to be that all people are sustained by and are in relationship to God, that the experiences of evil in life call this into question and either lead us to affirm our relation to God or provoke us into a denial of it, but insofar as this relation is affirmed it provides the context for understanding Christ. Experience is our link with him.

How this experience should relate us to Christ is minutely explicated in both his *Jesus* and his *Christ*. It is the experience of suffering which is the door through which others first passed,[69] and in particular is this true of the women whose expectations were destroyed by Jesus' death and who found, in that destruction, the occasion for finding life.[70] It it this same kind of experience which Schillebeeckx also believes lay behind the text which records the apostolic thinking about Christ, which is delivered in more formal terms. Who, then, was this Christ? Who was this core within the human affirmation of life? And where lies the distinction between this core experience and the doctrinal interpretation which is given to it? These are not easy questions to answer.

The framework for understanding Jesus, Schillebeeckx asserts, are our convictions, first, that it is God's design to save people from the pains and calamities of suffering; second, that his Rule, in which this occurs, is being realized; and third, that this saving Rule is experienced in our own "Easter encounter." This last element is especially obscure in Schillebeeckx. What he appears to have in mind is some form of experience which occurs within the church and, in particular, in connection with the sacraments, in which transubstantiation (albeit understood in non-Aristotelian terms) does occur. The message of Christian faith is that of liberation from the oppression of suffering, and Jesus is the liberator.

Much of the first book, *Jesus,* is devoted to an historical analysis of the source who lay behind the Christian and post-Easter experience. Schillebeeckx accepts without argument that a knowledge of Jesus reconstructed from the historical materials cannot by itself lead on to a belief that he was and is Christ. That belief comes from elsewhere, specifically from our own experience, which is revelatory. In the New Testament period, it was to produce the images in which Christ was pictured, such as "Son of Man" and "Son of God."[71] The important question which is left to be decided, of course, is the extent to which these images are merely cultural or confessional and the extent to which they were determined by Jesus himself. This remains a problem that hangs, like unbroken cloud cover, over the entire second book, *Christ.*

It is perhaps for this reason that Schillebeeckx is astonishingly spare in his comments on the specifically Christological issues. What he has done, in fact, is to turn over the exegetical soil without gathering the results into a succinct statement as to what precisely should be asserted about the person of Christ. What can be said is only this: God's general purposes in creation are exhibited with clarity in Jesus, who was fully human.[72] Within this humanity was apparent a relationship to God characterized by familiarity and intimacy. In Jesus was another reality. This reality, this divine reality, was, however, only disclosed by Jesus partly. God is much bigger than the glimpses Jesus gives us of him. What we do see—and of this Jesus is the prophet—is a God intent upon overcoming the world's suffering, liberating men and women from their pains and calamities. Indeed, our own experience carries within it intimations of such conquest, of the positive overwhelming the negative, and this is the context from which we draw the conclusion that the Jesus discovered by historical research was, in fact, the Christ.

What Schillebeeckx has attempted to do is write a systematic theology from the point of view of Christology in much the same way (albeit with radically different conclusions!) as Carl Henry has done from the vantage point of biblical revelation. These are entirely legitimate ventures, for theology is a circle which can be entered at many different places. The extraordinary thing about Schillebeeckx, however, is that the point of entry—Christology—is the one thing that is conspicuous by its absence in the seventeen hundred pages of his two main Christological volumes! Schillebeeckx's performance is not unlike the liberal biblical scholars Karl Barth excoriated because they imagined that dealing with matters of prologomena such as authorship, recipients, and destination of the New Testament letters was itself the writing of the commentary on those letters!

There are two elements which are seriously deficient in Schillebeeckx's methodology. The first relates to biblical revelation. Schillebeeckx locates the real substance for Christology not within the text, but behind it; the text, made normative by the process of canonization, is simply the outward recognition of the important "events" that had occurred. Access to these "events" is made through a reconstruction of the biblical materials and by our experience. This is the second flaw. Schillebeeckx has little understanding of the way sin has affected human nature, distorted human perception, and ruptured relations with God. He refuses to accord Scripture integrity as a source for knowledge of Christ and instead transfers this confidence to human experience.

It is this same deficiency that distorts everything else Schillebeeckx says. It leads him to think of salvation, not as reconciliation to a God who is really angry about sin and who is committed by his own nature to destroy it, but as overcoming suffering and anxiety. Because he thinks all people are in saving relation to God, the meaning he attaches to Christ's cross is, to say the least, vacuous. The truth is that on Schillebeeckx's terms Christ had no need to die in the way that he did. This means, then, that grace, saving grace, is not especially connected with Christ, but is something that flows from God's overall relationship to and ontological involvement with all human nature.

In this scheme of things Jesus becomes merely a prophet, one who points toward the nature and acts of God and who exemplifies these in what he does. He does not exhaustingly disclose the divine, nor does he exclusively reveal his Father. So in the end, what we encounter in Schillebeeckx is what we have already found in Schleiermacher and Pittenger. Jesus differs in degree but not in kind from religious people everywhere. He is the perfection of what is imperfectly revealed and made known generally. He is not a unique break-in, a new species, doing for us on the cross what we could never do for ourselves. He is but a prophet who sees clearly where we see dimly, who acts with perfect love where we love only sporadically and imperfectly.

Is such a figure large enough to sustain and explain the faith of millions of people worldwide and people in cultures vastly different from that of the West? The answer is that such a figure might be admired by some, he might be followed in some ways by others, but he could only be believed upon as Christian faith requires us to do by those capable of extraordinary gullibility and naivete. Why, one is left pondering, would the martyrs have died for such a person? God's grace was accessible to them without him. God's revelation could be had without him. God's intention to overcome the world's sorrow has already been explained, and the execution of God's intention is not dependent upon him. Schillebeeckx remarks that once a person has found this salvation, "it is natural (and proper) that he should project his own expectations and ways of envisaging the 'true being' of man on to Jesus."[73] That is the Achilles' heel in Schillebeeckx's treatment. Jesus has become a figure, in part, constructed out of the consciousness of twentieth-century people. Schillebeeckx, too, is looking down the long well of human history and seeing his own face reflected at the bottom.

9   CONCLUSION

There are two kinds of orthodoxy. This is what was argued earlier in connection with the patristic period. There is the "right opinion" with respect to the biblical material, and there is the formulation of the "right opinion" in the light of current challenges and prevailing norms. The second orthodoxy has obsolescence built into it inasmuch as it is geared into specific contexts, theological interests, and cultural norms. The first, though it has to be formulated by fallible minds always subject to error, does not change and is never obsolete.

The precise relationship between these orthodoxies has become obscure in the modern context. Roman Catholicism and, for that matter, liberal Protestantism have, in their different ways, identified biblical orthodoxy with the experiential or ecclesiastical; the former orthodoxy disappears in the latter. What is ultimately authoritative in these traditions is not the biblical Word—protestations not withstanding—but the interpretive authority in the church in the one case, and the dominant cultural and experiential interests in the other. By contrast, more conservative Protestant thought has tended to absorb itself in biblical orthodoxy and to overlook the importance of contemporary formulation of the meaning of this orthodoxy.

While there is much to be said, for example, for using and affirming the Chalcedonian Definition today, the truth is that this expression of ecclesiastical orthodoxy is some fifteen hundred years old, and it may not pass as a substitute for the hard work of theological definition which we ought to be doing for ourselves. In this connection, a satisfactory Christology for today—one that coheres with and is disciplined by the biblical material, that is consistent with the historic consciousness of the church, and which is articulated in a conceptuality native to this age—must build upon the following four principles.

First, the conceptual framework in which Christ must be understood

171

is that of the eschatological "age to come." The Gospels speak of this
largely under the language of the Kingdom, but in the epistles it is
developed in other ways. The conclusion, however, is the same. This
"age" which is dawning is one which God alone can establish, for in it
realities are brought into being that only God can effect. It is an "age"
that is essentially discontinuous with the present "age" in its nature,
although it overlaps with it chronologically. The "age to come" is from
"above," while the conditions of the present "age" are from "below."

Jesus was the one in whom this "age to come" was realized,
through whom it is redemptively present in the church, and by whom
it will be made cosmically effective at its consummation. He is the
agent, the instrument, and the personifier of God's sovereign, eternal,
saving rule. As such, he is in a category by himself. In the nature of the
case, there can be no human analogies to, nor parallels for the person
we are looking at. He is the point and means of divine invasion into this
world for the purposes of salvation and judgment. At this one place, and
only at this one place, do we touch divine transcendence in human
bones. Here we see, and only here do we see, the awful resolution of
God to take upon himself our guilt and sin and to wage war on all that
blights and darkens creation. Here is heaven's immunity broken for
earthly sorrows. His eternal resolution to be the "one mediator" is
fulfilled through that obedience which called him to enter into the
near oblivion of human flesh, to veil his heavenly glory, to become God
incognito, and, in his poverty, to make us rich.

It is not possible to construct such a figure from "below," to create
him out of the fabric of human experience. There are no analogies in
human experience for this role. Christologies constructed from "below"
produce only a larger-than-life religious figure, the perfection of what
many others already experience. The common assumption of these
Christologies is that diligent theological workers can build a tower the
point of which will pierce heaven itself, if only they sweat and toil over
it long enough. They will not succeed. Their towers, their Christologies from "below," are never more than pictures of the ideal religious
person, pictures which all too often merely personify their fabricators.
Their christs might be admired, but they cannot be worshiped. They
might inspire religious devotion, but they cannot sustain or explain
Christian faith. They tell us very much about their authors and very
little about Jesus. They are, inevitably, half-breed christs. They are half
ancient and half modern. They are constructed on the mistaken assumption that a christ who is as baffled as we are about existence, who
is as secular as we are, and who is the victim of change and circumstances as we feel ourselves to be is somehow more appealing than one
who is not. These christs are impotent, and their appeal is superficial.
Their appeal is not that of the biblical Christ, the One who was God
with us, the means of forgiveness for our sin, and the agent of our

reconciliation. Forgiveness and reconciliation are what we need centrally. We need to know there is someone there to forgive us, someone who can forgive and heal us, and that was why the Word was incarnate. Our Christology, then, must be constructed from "above."

In our modern context, this approach requires that we give special attention to the matter of Jesus' divinity and to the categories in which we understand him. The New Testament, to be sure, is insistent upon the fact that the Son of God was consubstantial with the Father in terms of his Godness and consubstantial with us in terms of our humanity. To say, then, that special attention needs to be given to his divinity appears to place undue or inappropriate stress on one side of any Christological construction. It needs to be remembered, however, that whereas initially the thought of a fully human Christ was so problematic, in our time the difficulty is with a fully divine Christ. We assume as a matter of course that he was fully human, but a figure who was at the same time also fully divine seems incomprehensible. What is incomprehensible about it is that we have no empirical analogies for it, and in a scientific age all knowledge must rest on an empirical basis or be prepared to run the gauntlet of skepticism and derision. Furthermore, a secular culture is one in which the divine may be acknowledged as existing in general but never in specific relationship to daily life. At most, *God* is a synonym for what is otherwise inexplicable, but it is always assumed that life as we know it is self-enclosed, self-sustaining, and self-interpreting, and therefore God is neither needed in nor relevant to its processes. That being the case, the overwhelming tendency in those theologies in which there is interpenetration between Christ and culture is to build a Christology in such a way that a divine invasion is not necessitated. A christ constructed from "below," whose "divinity" never breaks the bounds of ordinary humanity is, in fact, a christ who, even in his divinity, is like ourselves. Such a christ fits in well with our pluralistic age, which is intolerant of and unforgiving about every Christological proposal in which a unique break-in of the divine in the human has occurred.

The secular impulse, with its low cognitive horizon and its rejection of the religiously unique, often comes to expression at an unexpected place in Christological discussions. It often takes on the form of orthodoxy, insisting that Christ must, first and foremost, be said to be fully human. The word *human* is then transformed into a synonym for twentieth-century, secular modernity. It is then assumed that to be human, such a christ must be as fallible as we are, as confused, as filled with doubts, as unsure about the future, as agnostic about the purposes and plans of God, as diffident about the possibilities of knowing God, and as baffled about ethical norms and the possibility of absolutes. To present a Christ who is the exegesis of God's character and plans, who acts and speaks as God, who knows from whence he came and why, and who did on the cross what only God could do is, it is argued, to present a Christ who is not human!

The problem is not so much what should be understood by words such as *human* and *divine* as the presuppositions of modernity in which they are understood. What is human is understood within an evolutionary framework where change and development are fundamental. This has led us to think more of becoming and less of being, more of existence and less of essence, more of involvement and less of intellectualizing, more of the subjective and less of the objective. We think of reality as slowly unfolding itself rather than as something outside of ourselves which is there to be examined. That being the case, our understanding of what is divine is cast, not in terms that are germane to its own nature, but in those that arise from our modern consciousness. As religious people, we allow for the presence of the divine within human life, but its reality we suppose cannot be registered as something intrinsically different from or alien to that life as it unfolds. The divine is what we experience in becoming, in existence, in involvement, and in the subjective. Christ is important because he clarifies for us what we understand from within ourselves only dimly and inchoately. But where has the category of understanding such a christ come from? It is the product of the dim and inchoate experience it is seeking to illumine! It is the fruit of modern consciousness, not of biblical revelation. It is a sociological reality, not a theological verity. This consciousness is the myth, and the world of which it is a part needs to be demythologized! Our categories of understanding, then, must be as divinely given as was the Son whom they explain.

It is important to observe that this stricture is applicable to the new liberation and ethnic theologies of Asia, South America, and North America, as well as to the European Bultmannians and post-Bultmannians. In the case of the Europeans, the interpretive category is internally shaped and is the product of interaction with those aspects of a culture that is existential in its outlook. In that of the Asians and South Americans—with a few expressions in North America—the interpretive category is shaped sociologically and is the outcome of political realities. The process, however, is the same; Jesus is interpreted in categories other than those which he himself provided. To the European existentialists, he has emerged as a person of striking insight who united in himself the conditions of estranged existence. He did on the religious side what Heidegger has done on the secular side. Heidegger and the other existentialists saw only dimly what he saw very brightly. To the proponents of liberation, Jesus was the agent through whom the overthrow of oppressive and unjust conditions in society would occur. The fact that Jesus did not attempt to overthrow the oppressive and unjust order to which he belonged seems inconsequential to liberationists, and the reason is that Jesus has been co-opted to a political ideology. South American and Asian theologians may be correct in diagnosing their societies' ills as they do. They may be correct in working for the rectification of what they see is wrong. But they are quite mistaken in rewriting traditional Christologies to reflect their programs for change. The issue over the intrusion of philosophical categories which surfaced in the patristic period is one which has not abated and which has a pertinence as large today as at any previous time.

Second, the person and work of Christ must constantly be linked, each interpreting the other. What Jesus *did* was possible because of who he *was.* Who he was cannot be divorced from or confused with what he did. In the patristic period, the Chalcedonian Definition inadvertently separated the person of Christ from his work because the church was driven to focus all of its attention on Christ's person. In our own time, the person and work of Christ are often separated deliberately because we are ruled by a pragmatism which asserts that a person is known only in action, that it is in action that personality emerges, and therefore what Jesus did is our only access to understanding who he was. Ironically, those most intent upon making the functional aspect determinative of the ontological are also those who are most offended by the intrusion of philosophical interests into Christian thinking in the early church. It is a mistake to imagine, however, that such an intrusion is wrong when others do it, but that our own philosophic interests have an immunity from criticism if they are sufficiently modern and completely *au courant!*

The Incarnation can only be understood aright when we see it within God's overarching purposes of salvation. Speculative schemes and systems have their intrinsic interest, but none will do justice to what occurred through Christ until we view it from within Christ, from that position in which a saving trust has placed us, a position created by the Holy Spirit in the presence of faith in accordance with that Word which the Holy Spirit himself inspired. In Christology, then, we can only philosophize from faith, not to faith, and our thought must resonate with what Christ reveals himself to be through Scripture, with the revealed purpose of his coming, and not with the ways we might like to see him as modern people. This means that to understand Christ aright, we must also know something about our own guilt. We must know ourselves to be sinners. We must have hungered and thirsted after righteousness. The New Testament, after all, was not written for the curious, for historians, or even for biblical scholars, but for those, in all ages and cultures, who want to be forgiven and to know God.

Third, the Christ whom we meet, in whom and because of whom we find forgiveness, is personally identical with the Galilean whom the Gospels describe. The content of the Christ is defined by the historical Jesus, because the person of the one is identical with the person of the other. Christ is not other than or different from Jesus.

In the modern period, as we have seen, there has been considerable apprehension among theologians that the meaning of Christian faith will be violated if its truth content is tied into the flux of human life at any point in history. Given the presence of this fear, two quite different reactions have been evident in Christology. Some, notably conservative Roman Catholics, have taken the position that historians should be told what they may find in the Christian past. Others, however, have decided that historians should be allowed to roam freely through the past, but that their findings should never be allowed to impinge on the meaning of faith. The Christ of faith has therefore been disengaged from the Jesus of history. The word *Christ* has been filled with content and defined by present religious experience and within current epistemological assumptions rather than by the historical Jesus. Both reactions are mistaken.

On the one hand, it is inescapable that the Son of God was joined bone to our bone, flesh which was our flesh, and it is through this incarnation that he disclosed himself. On the other hand, this joining in no way means, as Lessing claimed, that we can know nothing certain about the God involved in this work and this disclosure. Lessing's argument asks us to agree that if we cannot have everything cognitively, then we cannot have anything. As mortal, fallible human beings we never have everything cognitively, but that seldom prevents people from making ultimate decisions. One of Paul Tillisch's real achievements, I believe, was to show that however agnostic and cognitively diffident a person may be, he or she has ultimate concerns that necessitate ultimate decisions which are tantamount to religious commitments, and these are made every day. The decisions we make based on the historical Jesus are neither less certain nor more ultimate than the decisions that are constantly being made by nonreligious people in our secular, humanistic culture all the time. Christ cannot be allowed to float free of the historic disclosure recorded in the Gospels because of this fear, but the identity that exists between Jesus and Christ must be realized, Christ being defined by Jesus.

In this regard, both the liberal and the neo-orthodox Christologies have been woefully inadequate. The liberal Christology identified the entrance of the divine, not so much with one person, as with human nature in general. It was against this distortion that the neo-orthodox protested, oftentimes with force and brilliance. On the issues defined by liberalism for debate, few volumes have given a more potent affirmation to biblical interests than Emil Brunner's *The Mediator.* What the neo-orthodox theologies sought to put in place of the liberal Christology was, from the opposite point of view, also inadequate. If the liberals merged Christ into human nature, the neo-orthodox so distinguished between the divine and the human that the historical Jesus is scarcely allowed to define for us the meaning of Christ. If we look to the neo-orthodox to expose the liberal Christology, we need to look mainly to the evangelicals to expose the neo-orthodox. This is certainly true of the Christological section of Carl Henry's substantial series entitled *God, Revelation and Authority,* and at this point we need note also the incisive work of some of the British Anglo-Catholics who share a common outlook, such as E. L. Mascall's *The God-man, Theology and the Gospel of Christ,* and even his *The Secularization of Christianity.*

Fourth, it seems inescapable that some form of the enhypostatic union must be employed if justice is to be done to the full range of New Testament teaching. It is true that this doctrine is itself extrabiblical, but that does not mean that it is necessarily unbiblical any more than does the doctrine of Trinity. There is no Christ without Christology; even the Synoptic Gospels have their Christology despite the fact that their prime concern is not with Christology *per se,* but with the process whereby Jesus revealed himself. The question, therefore, is whether this Christology, as well as the other Christological lines of thought represented in the New Testament, can be sufficiently represented by the enhypostatic doctrine.

The cruder expression of this kind of doctrine appeared first in Cyril and is properly termed anhypostatic rather than enhypostatic. His argument was that the person of Christ was that of the Son of God. This divine person assumed a human nature that was without its own person. This produced discussion about the "impersonal humanity" of Christ, discussion which traded on a sharp distinction existing between "nature" and "person." Such a position effectively eliminated any Nestorian interpretation of Christ, but the question has to be asked whether it did sufficient justice to Christ's humanity. Can one really have human nature that is devoid of a personal center? And if it is devoid of this center, is it not lacking the very thing which needs most to be redeemed? Does the Cyrilline doctrine, if understood in this way, not also fall under the same condemnation as did Apollinarianism? The more refined view of this doctrine, outlined by Leontius of Byzantium, employed by some of the Reformers, and recently given fresh currency by H. Maurice Relton, argues that human nature is accorded its personal identity in the divine Word, by whom it is assumed and to whom it is joined. This means that Christ's human nature was not "impersonal," but that, though fully human, it reached its personal completion in the divine Word because of the action of God in effecting a union with it. As such, it is "in-personal."

This doctrine undoubtedly has often been allied to the older philosophy of "substance" as explanation is sought for the meaning of personality, rather than the modern understanding of the person as an acting subject, but the doctrine does not require either conceptuality. In actual fact, the key to it is the *imago Dei* rather than any particular philosophy or psychology. The *imago Dei,* to be sure, has been understood in a variety of ways, but at the heart of most views is the idea that what constitutes humanity, what sets it apart from mere animal life, are capacities and perhaps resultant roles in creation the originals of which are to be found in God. Human nature as created is the echo of which the Creator is sound. He is original, and we are derivative. Whether it is then appropriate to speak of the "humanity of God" may be questionable, as questionable as speaking of the "divinity of man"; yet the thought is not entirely awry. If God is the original, then the derivative only finds its meaning in relation to the original. What it means to be truly human is revealed in and by God himself. That being the case, a perfect humanity, one unspoiled by sin, would not only coalesce naturally with the divine but would, in fact, find its perfection in the divine from which it was derived.

To speak, then, of the humanity of Christ coming to personal completion in the divine Word in no way diminishes or belittles the full reality of that humanity, but simply recognizes that in this instance the original intention of creation has been fully and finally realized. The central constituent in the God-man is therefore God for the same reason that the central constituent in the creation is the Creator. In Christ we come face to face with God. We meet him, not subsumed under human flesh, not merely associated with it, not merely accompanying it, not merely shining through it, but in undiminished moral splendor, giving to that humanity the moral completeness which has been missing from the time of that fall. Though human, Jesus is properly accorded our worship, for he is God; though human, his is the world and his is the church, for he is God. Though human, he is the conqueror of sin, death, and the devil, for he is God. He is God in whom our human nature, without its sin, has come to perfect realization, to moral completion, to perfect union.

The divine Word, then, was not united to a human nature that was antithetical to its own life, but rather the divine Word already possessed everything that was necessary to be human. This must be so, for the most human person is never other than the image of God, the pale and emasculated copy of what is originally in God. The Incarnation is the expression of the image, the embodiment of it in the course of our life and existence, in which the ideal human life and the ideal of the divine coincide. They coincide, not because the human has grown into the divine, but because the divine has taken the human into itself in an action in which the human reaches its fulfillment. In Christ we see all that Adam was intended to be, but never was, all that we are not but which we will become through resurrection. In him we see the dawning of that redemptive "age," an age not of this world, but one in which human life finds in Christ its fulfillment, its creation ideal. This is the eschatalogical harvest of which he is the cause and firstfruit.

Such an understanding escapes the charge of Apollinarianism, for it sees the humanity of Christ as having a completeness which even ours presently lacks because of sin. It escapes the heresy of Nestorianism, for it is insistent that the person of the God-man is the person of God and not some form of hybrid union between a divine "center" and a human "center." It accords with the New Testament insistence that Christ's work was work that only God could do, and that he could only do it in union with flesh that was ours. It explains why monotheistic Jews in the New Testament knew that in Jesus they had come face to face with the one God. And it explains why in Christ men and women in all ages and cultures have found that for which deepest impulses of their nature cry out. In him they have found their Creator and their Redeemer. They have found the exposition of God's character and ways, the declaration of his love and judgment, the fulfillment of his intention for creation. In him and through him and because of him they have found God or, rather, have been found of him.

NOTES

Introduction

1. John Hick, ed., *The Myth of God Incarnate* (Philadelphia: Westminster, 1977), p. x. In the continuation of the discussion Michael Goulder, one of the essayists in Hick's book, made the same point. "There can be no doubt," he said of the original book, "that its message had often been stated before, and sometimes better stated. . . ," Michael Goulder, ed., *Incarnation and Myth: The Debate Continued* (Grand Rapids: Eerdmans, 1979), p. vii.
2. See John Macquarrie, "Christianity without Incarnation? Some Critical Comments," *The Truth of God Incarnate*, Michael Green, ed. (Grand Rapids: Eerdmans, 1977), pp. 140-144.
3. Van A. Harvey, "The Alienated Theologian," *McCormick Quarterly* 23 No. 4 (May 1970), 234.
4. *Ibid.*, 235, 236.
5. Van Austin Harvey, *The Historian and the Believer: The Morality of Historical Knowledge and Christian Belief* (Philadelphia: Westminster, 1966), pp. 68-163.
6. An excellent introduction to the Christological implications of form criticism is provided by Norman Perrin, "Recent Trends in Research in the Christology of the New Testament," *Essays in Divinity, Vol VI: Transitions in Biblical Scholarship*, J. Coert Ryladrsdam, ed. (Chicago: University of Chicago Press, 1966), pp. 217-233; Patrick Henry, *New Directions in New Testament Study* (Philadelphia: Westminister, 1979), pp. 120-152; William G. Doty, *Contemporary New Testament Interpretation* (Englewood Cliffs, N.J.: Prentice-Hall, 1972), pp. 52-86.
7. Green, *The Truth of God Incarnate*, p. 59.
8. For brief introduction to the issues, see Michael F. Palmer, "Can the Historian Invalidate Gospel Statements? Some Notes on Dialectical Theology," *Downside Review* 95 (January 1977), 11-18; K. Schubert, "Geschichte und Heilsgeschichte," *Kairos* 15 No. 1-2 (1973), 89-101.
9. Donald Dawe, "Christology in Contemporary Systematic Theology," *Interpretation* XXVI No. 3 (July 1972), 260.
10. Harvey, *The Historian and the Believer*, p. 104.
11. See, for example, his book coauthored with Thomas Luckman entitled *The Social Construct of Reality: A Treastise in the Sociology of Knowledge* (New York: Doubleday, 1967); Peter L. Berger, Brigitte Berger, Hansfried Kellner, *The Homeless Mind: Modernization and Consciousness* (New York: Irvington, 1974). The themes explored in these volumes reappear frequently in different contexts in his other writings.

12. Peter L. Berger, *Facing Up to Modernity: Excursions in Society, Politics, and Religion* (New York: Basic, 1977), pp. 162-181.

13. Baptista Mondin, "New Trends in Christology," *Biblical Theology Bulletin* IV No. 1 (February 1974), 33.

14. Joseph Sittler, "The Scope of Christological Reflection," *Interpretation* XXVI No. 3 (July 1972), 332.

15. Cf. Rahner's essay "Christology and an Evolutionary World View," *New Testament Themes for Contemporary Man,* R. Ryan, ed. (Englewood Cliffs: Prentice-Hall, 1969), pp. 217-225; see also T. Pearl, "Dialectical Panentheism: On the Hegelian Character of Karl Rahner's Key Christological Writings," *Irish Theological Quarterly* 42 (April 1975), 119-137.

16. Even such a conservative thinker as G. C. Berkouwer has been forced to reckon with this fact. The opening chapter in his volume *Studies in Dogmatics: The Person of Christ* (Grand Rapids: Eerdmans, 1954) is entitled "The Crisis in the Doctrine of the Two Natures." Today, he declares, we have a "far-reaching crisis" in the traditional, Chalcedonian formulation.

17. For a brief introduction to this development, see Richard Lucien, "Some Recent Developments on the Question of Christology and World Religions," *Eglise et Theologie* 8 No. 2 (Mai 1977), 209-244. Among the more important books reviewed are Paul Tillich's *The Future of Religions,* George Rupp's *Christologies and Cultures: Toward a Typology of Religious Worldviews,* John Cobb's *Christ in a Pluralistic Age,* Schubert Ogden's *The Reality of God* and *Christ Without Myth,* John Hick's *God and the Universe of Faiths,* Charles Davis's *Christ and the World Religions,* and Raymond Panikkar's *The Unknown Christ of Hinduism.*

18. A brief introduction to the context of this movement is found in Alec Vidler, *The Church in an Age of Revolution: 1789 to the Present Day* (Harmondsworth: Penguin, 1961). The decisive history of it is still that of Albert Schweitzer, *The Quest of the Historical Jesus: A Critical Study of Its Progress from Reimarus to Wrede,* W. Montgomery, trans. (New York: Macmillan, 1948). There are however, some interesting perceptions of it in Werner Georg Kümmel, *The New Testament: The History of the Investigation of Its Problems,* S. McLean Gilmour and Howard C. Kee, trans. (New York: Abingdon, 1970).

19. See James M. Robinson, "Hermeneutic Since Barth," *New Frontiers in Theology,* Vol. II: *The New Hermeneutic,* James M. Robinson and John B. Cobb, eds. (New York, 1964), pp. 1-77.

20. The first accounting of this quest in English was James M. Robinson, *A New Quest of the Historical Jesus* (London, 1959). For subsequent discussion see J. Benjamin Bederbaugh, "The First Decade of the New Quest of the Historical Jesus," *The Lutheran Quarterly* 16 No. 1 (August 1964), 239-267. An analysis of issues is found in Ralph P. Martin's essay, "The New Quest of the Historical Jesus," *Jesus of Nazareth: Saviour and Lord,* Carl F. H. Henry, ed. (Grand Rapids, 1966), pp. 23-46.

21. Erst Fuchs, "The New Testament and the Hermeneutical Problem," in *The New Hermeneutic,* p. 117.

22. Norman Perrin, "Recent Trends in Research in the Christology of the New Testament," in *Transitions in Biblical Scholarship,* pp. 220-223. The redaction-critical procedures are succinctly described in Norman Perrin's *What Is Redaction Criticism?* (London, 1970). An important aspect of this procedure is the criteria by which material is judged to be authentic or inauthentic. On these issues see R. T. France's essay, "The Authenticity of the Sayings of Jesus," *History, Criticism and Faith,* Colin Brown, ed. (Leister, 1976), pp. 101-143.

23. The issues raised here can be explored in many different ways and directions. Some of these other aspects are made evident in the following brief surveys: J. S. Beer, "The Changing Face of the Liberal Christ," *Modern Churchman* 19 (Winter 1975), 6-12; C. E. Braaten, "Lordship of Christ in Modern Theology," *Dialog* 4 (Autumn 1965), 259-267; F. E. Crowe, "Christologies: How Up to Date is Yours?" *Theological*

Studies 29 (March 1968), 87-101; D. Griffin, "Essential Elements of a Contemporary Christology," *Encounter* 33 (Spring 1972), 170-184; P. C. Hodgson, "Christology: A Future?" *Religion in Life* 42 (Spring 1973), 8-24; N. H. G. Robinson, "Future of Christology," *Expository Times* 77 (February 1966), 136-140, 167-170; Adrian Thatcher, " Some Recent Developments in Christology," *Baptist Quarterly* 26 (October 1976), 335-343; Illtyd Tretharan, "Christology Again," *Downside Review* 95 (January 1977), 1-10; E. W. H. Vick, "Liberal and Radical Attitudes to Christology," *Modern Churchman* 15 (July 1972), 224-235.

24. Arguments for thinking this is the case are summarized in John Charlot, *New Testament Disunity: Its Significance for Today* (New York, 1970), pp. 79-88, but developed less radically yet with much more sophistication in James D. G. Dunn, *Unity and Diversity in the New Testament: An Inquiry into the Character of Earliest Christianity* (Philadelphia: Westminster, 1977), pp. 201-308. These matters have to be considered in detail later.

Chapter 1: The Framework

1. "The research into the life of Jesus of the Liberal theologians of the last century unconsciously confused the rational-ethical and religious humanitarianism of their own ideal of religion with the thought and purpose of Jesus; the result was that this school of thought succeeded in representing Jesus as a teacher of general ethical and religious truths, a man who was distinguished from others by the fact that in his own life he exemplified these general and religious truths in an unusual way. . . . This Jesus never existed; further, the Gospels never give any occasion for this historical error to arise." Emil Brunner, *The Mediator: A Study of the Central Christian Doctrine of the Christian Faith,* Olive Wyon, trans. (Philadelphia: Westminster, 1947), pp. 189, 190.

2. Johannes Weiss, *Jesus' Proclamation of the Kingdom of God,* Richard Hyde Hiers and David Larrimore Holland, trans. (Philadelphia: Westminster, 1971), XII.

3. *Ibid.,* p. 133.

4. *Ibid.,* pp. 81-92.

5. Albert Schweitzer, *The Kingdom of God and Primitive Christianity,* L. A. Garrad, trans. (New York, 1968), pp. 102-129.

6. Moltmann's work is heavily influenced by the revisionist Marxist, Ernst Bloch. Though Moltmann has attempted to balance the overwhelming emphasis upon a this-worldly "millennium" which is completely future, the acceptance of a Marxist ideology constantly hamstrings the effort. It further cements the alliance between the coming of this "Kingdom" and the use of revolutionary tactics. See David F. Wells, *The Search for Salvation* (Carol Stream, Ill.: 1978), pp. 119-139; Rubem Alves, *A Theology of Human Hope* (Washington, 1969), pp. 55-68.

7. See also Geerhardus Vos, *The Pauline Eschatology* (Grand Rapids: Baker, 1979), pp. 1-62. The equivalent of Dodd's "realized eschatology" in some of its aspects was what Vos called "incipient realization."

8. For a critique, see W. G. Kümmel, *Promise and Fulfillment: The Eschatological Message of Jesus* (Naperville, 1956), pp. 19-25.

9. See, for example, *ibid.,* pp. 57, 58, 81, 83, 101-104, 125-127, 134-136, 144-146; I. H. Marshall, *Eschatology and the Parables* (London, 1963), pp. 26-47.

10. Thus Kümmel sums up by saying that "Jesus connects the present, being *by its very nature* an eschatologically *fulfilled* present, with the expected future, because the encounter with the man Jesus in the present demands a decision which will be the determining factor for the eschatological verdict of Jesus when he comes as the Son of Man." Kümmel, *Promise and Fulfillment,* p. 142.

11. Mark 1:15; 4:11, 26, 30; 9:1, 47; 10:14, 15, 23, 24, 25; 12:34; 14:25; Matt. 5:3 (Luke 6:20); 6:10 (Luke 11:2); 6:33 (Luke 12:31); 8:11 (Luke 13:29); 10:7 (Luke 10:9); 11:11 (Luke 7:28); 11:12 (Luke 16:16); 12:28 (Luke 11:20); 13:33 (Luke 13:20); 5:10, 19, 20; 7:21; 8:12; 13:19, 24, 38, 43, 44, 45, 47, 52; 16:19; 18:1, 3, 4, 23; 19:12; 20:1; 21:31, 43; 22:2; 23:13; 24:14; 25:1; Luke 4:43; 9:60, 62; 10:11; 12:32; 13:28; 17:20, 21; 18:29; 21:31: 22:16, 18. It is assumed, as has frequently been argued, that there is no distinction to be made between *Basileia tou theou* and *Basileia tōn ouranōn, hoi ouranoi* being simply the periphrasis for God. In a broader context we note that *Basileia* by itself is used fifty-five times in Matthew, twenty in Mark, and forty-six in Luke; *Basileus* is used twenty-two times in Matthew, twelve in Mark, and eleven in Luke.

12. I am here adopting Bultmann's terminology of the Kingdom in which he regularly employs the word Rule rather than Reign, *Gottesherrschaft* rather than *Gottesreich*.

13. Norman Perrin, *Jesus and the Language of the Kingdom: Symbol and Metaphor in New Testament Interpretation* (Philadelphia: Westminster, 1976).

14. Herman Ridderbos, *The Coming of the Kingdom*, H. de Jongste, trans. (Phillipsburg, N.J.: Presbyterian and Reformed, 1962).

15. George Eldon Ladd, *Jesus and the Kingdom: The Eschatology of Biblical Realism* (Waco, Tex.: Word, 1964), p. 189.

16. *Ibid.*, p. 167.

17. R. Schnackenburg, *God's Rule and Kingdom* (New York, 1963), p. 213. Cf. a statement of Bornkamm: "The story told by the Gospels signifies the end of the world, although not, it is true, in the sense of an obvious drama and a visible catastrophe. On the contrary, it is not the world which ends here obviously and visibly; rather it is Jesus on the cross. And yet, in this story the world reaches its end. . . . For life, world and existence of each individual, now stand in the sudden flash of light of the coming of God, in the light of his reality and presence. This is the theme which Jesus proclaims." Günther Bornkamm, *Jesus of Nazareth*, Irene and Fraser McLuskey, James M. Robinson, trans. (New York: Harper and Row, 1960), pp. 62, 63.

18. Robert Henry Lightfoot, *History and Interpretation of the Gospels* (London, 1935), pp. 66-88.

19. Stonehouse has argued that Matthew's emphasis on the Kingdom is larger than that of the other Synoptic authors because he was especially concerned to see Jesus in the larger context of God's dealings with his people in the past. Ned B. Stonehouse, *The Witness of Matthew and Mark to Christ* (Philadelphia, 1944), pp. 229-234. This point has been developed by Jack Dean Kingsbury in his *Matthew: Structure, Christology, Kingdom* where the inauguration of the reign of God, in its redemptive aspect especially, is seen both as the fulfillment of Old Testament promises and the context of his Christology. A summary of this line of argument can be found in his essays, "Structure of Matthew's Gospel and His Concept of Salvation History," *Catholic Biblical Quarterly* 35 (October 1973), 451-474; "Form and Message of Matthew," *Interpretation* 29 No. 1 (January 1975), 13-23.

20. For a brief review of the distinctives of the Acts Christology, see S. S. Smalley, "The Christology of Acts," *Expository Times* LXXIII (1962), 358-362.

21. I. Howard Marshall, *Luke: Historian and Theologian* (Grand Rapids: Zondervan, 1971).

22. The important argument of Conzelman, however, in his *The Theology of St. Luke* should not be overlooked, namely that eschatology played a significant role in the shaping of Luke's Christology.

23. It is the argument of R. H. Fuller in his *The Foundations of New Testament Christology* (New York, 1965) and Ferdinand Hahn in his *Christologische Hoheitstitel* (Goettingen, 1963), among others, that each New Testament author was addressing a different Christological question, as a result of which different Christologies have emerged. Indeed, competing Christologies have even been found in the same author! See Albert C. Sundberg, "Christologies in the Fourth Gospel," *Biblical Research* 21

(1976), 29-37. Most commonly, however, these supposed differences tend to coalesce into two competing models, the adoptionist viewpoint—as reflected it is argued, in Romans 1:3, 4; Acts 2:36—and a "Divine man" model as seen, for example, in 1 Timothy 3:16 and John 1:1-18. In the first the flesh becomes Word, and in the second the Word becomes flesh. The redactional presuppositions behind these assertions are not, however, entirely self-evident, and it is not difficult to argue for a more coherent understanding than is represented in these books. Cf. Mark L. Lane, *"Theios Anēr* Christology and the Gospel of Mark," *New Dimensions in New Testament Study,* Richard N. Longenecker and Merrill C. Tenney, ed. (Grand Rapids, 1974), pp. 144-161.

24. The chief words employed by the New Testament are *chronos* (time), *aiōn* (age), *hēmera* (day), *hōra* (hour), and *kairos* (season).

25. Oscar Cullmann, *Christ and Time: The Primitive Christian Conception of Time and History,* Floyd V. Filson, trans. (Philadelphia: Westminster, 1950), pp. 37-68; James Barr, *Biblical Words for Time* (London, 1962), pp. 47-81. See also the appendix in John Marsh, *The Fullness of Time* (London, 1952), pp. 174-181.

26. R. T. Fortna has argued that John's concept of life was not understood in the setting of the new age or of the overthrow of sin and death; this is his thesis, based on supposed redactional work of the "signs source," in his book *The Gospel of Signs: A Reconstruction of the Narrative Source Underlying the Fourth Gospel* (Cambridge, 1970). It should be countered, however, as David L. Mealand does, that "we do violence to the evangelist's work if we only ransack it for older traditions, and do not attempt to listen to the totality of *this* gospel's presentation of the significance of Jesus." David L. Mealand, "The Christology of the Fourth Gospel," *Scottish Journal of Theology* 31 No. 5 (1978), 449. On the concept of life, see Raymond E. Brown, *The Gospel According to St. John (i-xiii)* (Garden City, 1966), pp. 505-508; George Banker Stevens, *The Johannine Theology: A Study of the Doctrinal Contents of the Gospel and Epistles of the Apostle John* (London, 1894), pp. 241-263, 312-354.

Chapter 2: The Identity of Jesus

1. In answer to the question as to what the origin of Paul's conception of Christ was, Wrede wrote: "For those, indeed, who see in Jesus what Paul saw, a supramundane, divine being, no problem arises. But those who take Jesus for what he was, an historical human personality, perceive an enormous gulf between this man and the Pauline Son of God. Not a generation had passed away since the death of Jesus, and already his form had not only grown into the infinite, but been utterly changed." W. Wrede, *Paul,* Edward Lummis, trans. (Boston, 1908), p. 147.

2. *Ibid.,* p. 151.

3. *Ibid.,* p. 92-121.

4. Albert Schweitzer, *The Mysticism of Paul the Apostle,* William Montgomery, trans. (New York, 1931), p. 54.

5. *Ibid.,* p. 66.

6. *Ibid.,* p. 90.

7. Rudolf Bultmann, *Theology of the New Testament,* Kendrick Gobel, trans., Vol. I (New York: Scribner, 1951, 1955), pp. 33-42.

8. *Ibid.,* Vol. II, pp. 6, 12, 66.

9. R. H. Fuller, *The Foundations of New Testament Theology* (New York, 1965), pp. 102-141.

10. James D. G. Dunn, *Christology in the Making: A New Testament Inquiry into the Origins of the Doctrine of the Incarnation* (Philadelphia: Westminster, 1980).

11. Cf.: "The hard and fast distinction between Palestinian and Hellenistic Judaism, and therefore between Palestinian and Hellenistic Christianity can now be seen to be based on two fallacies: that the Mishnah is normative for first-century Palestinian Judaism, and that Philo is normative for the Judaism of the Diaspora. Qumran has given the *coup de grâce* to the first of these. As to the second, we have it on the evidence of Philo himself that there were at least three types of Jew in Alexandria in his day—the literalists, the progressive and the middle-of-the-road men like Philo himself; and we also know that the Diaspora synagogues maintained close touch with Jerusalem, and that there were plenty of Hellenists living in Jerusalem and throughout Palestine." C. B. Caird, "The Development of the Doctrine of Christ in the New Testament," *Christ for Us Today*, Norman Pittenger, ed. (London, 1968), pp. 68, 69.

12. Fuller is explicit in his rejection of the narrative portions; Dunn does not reject them, but handles them in such a way that they shed little light on Jesus' self-consciousness.

13. Cf. Luther's comments on Galatians 3:13—"Here you see how necessary it is to believe and confess the doctrine of the divinity of Christ. When Arius denied this, it was necessary also for him to deny the doctrine of redemption. For to conquer the sin of the world, death, the curse, and the wrath of God in himself—this is the work, not of any creature but of the divine power. Therefore it was necessary that He who was to conquer these in Himself should be God by nature. . . . Hence those who deny the divinity of Christ lose all Christianity and become Gentiles and Turks through and through." Martin Luther, *Luther's Works*, Jaroslav Pelikan, ed., 54 vols., Vol. XXVI (St. Louis: Concordia, 1963) pp. 282, 283.

14. Morna Hooker, *Jesus and the Servant: The Influence of the Servant Concept of Deutero-Isaiah* (London, 1959), pp. 69, 70.

15. C. K. Barrett, *The Holy Spirit and the Gospel Tradition* (London, 1966).

16. Jack Dean Kingsbury, *Matthew: Structure, Christology, Kingdom* (Philadelphia, 1975), p. 40.

17. M. J. Down, "The Matthaean Birth Narratives: Matt. 1:18-2:23," *Expository Times*, XC No. 2 (November 1978), 51, 52.

18. Vincent Taylor, *The Person of Christ in New Testament Teaching* (London, 1958), pp. 161, 162.

19. W. D. Davies, *The Sermon on the Mount* (Cambridge: Cambridge University Press, 1969), pp. 15, 16.

20. Taylor, *The Person of Christ*, p. 164.

21. Cf. Günther Bornkamm, *Jesus of Nazareth*, Irene and Fraser McLuskey and James M. Robinson, trans. (New York: Harper and Row, 1960), pp. 153-157.

22. See Charles H. Talbert, "An Anti-Gnostic Tendency in Lukan Christology," *New Testament Studies* 14 No. 2 (January 1968), 259-271.

23. The most exhaustive recent treatment of the birth narratives is Raymond E. Brown's *The Birth of the Messiah: A Commentary on the Infancy Narratives in Matthew and Luke* (New York: Doubleday, 1977). On the general subject, see D. Edwards, *The Virgin Birth in History and Faith* (London, 1943); H. von Campenhausen, *The Virgin Birth in the Theology of the Ancient Church* (London, 1964). Two older volumes are still worthy of study: J. Orr, *The Virgin Birth of Christ* (London, 1907); J. Gresham Machen, *The Virgin Birth of Christ* (London, 1930).

24. Joachim Jeremias, *The Prayer of Jesus*, John Bowden and Christoph Burchard, trans. (Philadelphia, 1978), p. 57.

25. Joachim Jeremias, *The Central Message of the New Testament* (London, 1965), pp. 23-26.

26. Willoughby C. Allen, *The International Critical Commentary: A Critical and Exegetical Commentary on the Gospel According to St. Matthew* (Edinburgh, 1907), pp. 122, 123. Allen suggests the same thought underlies the use of ἦλθον in Matthew 5:17 and ἀποϐτείλαντά in Matthew 10:40.

27. D. E. Nineham, *Saint Mark* (Philadelphia: Westminster, 1963), pp. 309-311.
28. Cf. Rudolf Bultmann, *The History of the Synoptic Tradition,* John Marsh, trans. (New York: Harper and Row, 1968), p. 326.
29. Vincent Taylor, *The Gospel According to St. Mark* (London, 1966), pp. 472, 473.
30. C. F. D. Moule, *The Origins of Christology* (Cambridge, 1977), p. 8.
31. Richard N. Longenecker, "The Messianic Secret in the Light of Recent Discoveries," *The Evangelical Quarterly* XLI No. 4 (October-December 1969), 210.
32. Although somewhat dated, the study by Wilbert F. Howard is still a helpful analysis of the work done on John. See his *The Fourth Gospel in Recent Criticism* (London, 1961). In this present chapter, I have not been able to give consideration either to the substance of the Book of Revelation or the critical questions which have arisen concerning it. The standard bibliography is to be found in Raymond Brown, *The Gospel According to John,* esp. Vol. II (New York: Doubleday, 1966-70).
33. See Raymond B. Brown, "The Distinctiveness of John's Gospel, " *Southwestern Journal of Theology* 8 No. 1 (October 1965), 25-34; D. Moody Smith, "The Presentation of Jesus in the Fourth Gospel," *Interpretation* 31 No. 4 (October 1977), 367, 378.
34. Eusebius, *Ecclesiastic History,* VI, XIV, 7.
35. Barrett notes, for example, a number of passages occurring in the same order in Mark and John, such as Mark 1:4-8/John 1:19-36; Mark 1:14ff./John 1:43; Mark 6:34-44/John 6:1-13; Mark 6:45-52/John 6:16-21; Mark 8:29/John 6:68ff.; Mark 9:30ff.; 10:1, 32, 46/John 7:10-14; Mark 11:1-10/John 12:12-15; Mark 14:3-9/John 12:1-8; Mark 14:17-26/John 13:1-17, 26; Mark 14:43-52/John 18:1-11; Mark 14:53—16:8/John 18:12—20:29. Additionally, there are close verbal parallels such as in Mark 1:7/John 1:27; Mark 1:8, 10, 11/John 1:26, 32-34; Mark 6:37, 38, 43, 44/John 6:7, 9, 10, 13; Mark 6:50/John 6:20; Mark 8:29/ John 6:69; Mark 11:9ff./John 12:13; Mark 14:3/John 12:3; Mark 14:5/John 12:5; Mark 14:7ff./John 12:7ff.; Mark 14:18/John 13:21; Mark 14:30/John 13:38; Mark 14:47/John 18:10; Mark 15:26/John 19:19. See C. K. Barrett, *The Gospel According to St. John: An Introduction with Commentary and Notes on the Greek Text* (London, 1956), pp. 34-45. On the general question see D. Moody Smith, "John and the Synoptics: Some Dimensions of the Problem," *New Testament Studies* XXVII No. 4 (July 1980), 425-444.
36. Harold Riesenfeld, *The Gospel Tradition and Its Beginnings: Limits to Form Criticism* (Philadelphia, 1970), pp. 1-30; B. Gerhardsson, *Memory and Manuscript* (Uppsala, 1961). Riesenfeld and Gerhardsson have not been without their critics, however. See Morton Smith, "A Comparison of Early Christian and Early Rabbinic Tradition," *Journal of Biblical Literature* 82 (1963), 169-176; J. J. Vincent, "Did Jesus Teach his Disciples to Learn by Heart," *Studia Evangelica,* Vol. III, F. L. Cross, ed. (Berlin, 1964), pp. 105-118.
37. C. H. Dodd, *The Interpretation of the Fourth Gospel* (Cambridge: Cambridge University Press, 1953), pp. 292-422.
38. Jesus clearly performed more than seven miracles (cf. Jn. 20:30), but it is these seven which appear to have provided a structure for John's Gospel. That these "signs" might have constituted a single and independent source has been proposed, among others, by Robert T. Fortna, *The Gospel of Signs: A Reconstruction of the Narrative Source Underlying the Gospel* (Cambridge, 1970), and is well reviewed by Robert Kysar, *The Fourth Evangelist and his Gospel: An Examination of Contemporary Scholarship* (Minneapolis: Augsburg, 1975), pp. 9-37.
39. Stephen Smalley, *John: Evangelist and Interpreter* (Exeter, 1978), p. 91. Smalley's correlation of signs and discourses, however, is different from what is presented here.
40. John Painter, *John: Witness and Theologian* (London, 1975), p. 45.
41. Leon Morris, *Commentary on the Gospel of John: The English Text with Introduction, Exposition and Notes* (Grand Rapids, 1971), p. 125.
42. R. H. Lightfoot, *St. John's Gospel: A Commentary* (Oxford, 1956), p. 150.
43. Writing of the significance of Jesus' preexistence in John, Fred B. Craddock says:

"Quite evidently the category is used to mean precreational, with both temporal and spatial connotations: temporal in that the Word was previous to creation, and spatial in that he came from outside, apart from the cosmos . . . pre-existence provides the category for addressing the world in judgment and in grace. The world is judged because the Word which came as Revealer-Redeemer is the selfsame Word by which the world was created . . . the world is addressed by grace because the same Word which created it has now come to it, speaking to the world from within it in Jesus Christ." *The Pre-existence of Christ in the New Testament* (Nashville, 1968), pp. 127, 128.

44. See W. F. Howard, *Christianity According to St. John* (Philadelphia, 1946), pp. 69, 70.
45. The assumption John is making should be noted. He is assuming that human nature has the capacity to contain within it the glory of Christ's divinity without negating or emasculating that glory. The mechanism of his union would appear through that "image" or "likeness" in which we are created, which is not incompatible with the divinity of the one Paul describes as the εἰκὼν τοῦ Θεοῦ (Col. 1:15). Cf. Anthony Tyrrell Hanson, *Grace and Truth: A Study in the Doctrine of the Incarnation* (London, 1975), pp. 37, 38.
46. Taylor, *The Person of Christ*, p. 103.
47. Cf. J. A. T. Robinson, "Use of the Fourth Gospel for Christology," *Christ and Spirit in the New Testament*, Barnabas Lindars and Stephen Smalley, eds. (Cambridge: Cambridge University Press, 1973), p. 65.
48. C. K. Barrett, "The Eschatology of the Epistle to the Hebrews," *The Background of the New Testament and Its Eschatology*, W. D. Davies and D. Daube, eds. (Cambridge: Cambridge University Press, 1956) p. 391.
49. E. F. Scott, *The Epistle to the Hebrews* (New York, 1922), p. 103.
50. The opening of Hebrews has caused difficulties because, unlike most of the other epistles, it is devoid of salutations and greetings. Futhermore, the literary form of the prologue has much in common with other hymnal fragments embedded in the New Testament writings. This supposition is strengthened by the fact that the epistle, both in its alternation between Christological substance and ethical exhortation and in its overall content, exhibits close similarities to the form of early Christian proclamation identified by C. H. Dodd. Cf. R. V. G. Tasker, *The Gospel in the Epistle to the Hebrews* (London, 1950).
51. The imagery for the heavenly existence is borrowed largely from Psalm 110 upon which, some feel, the epistle as a whole represents a kind of midrash. See David M. Hay, *Glory at the Right Hand: Psalm 110 in Early Christianity* (New York, 1973). There are, however, also lesser misdrashim such as 2:5-9 on Psalm 8:4-6; 3:7—4:11 on Psalm 95:7-11; 8:8-13 and 10:15-18 on Jeremiah 31:31-34; 10:5-10 on Psalm 40:6-8; 10:37, 38 on Habakkuk 2:3, 4; and 12:5-11 on Proverbs 3:11, 12. Cf. F. C. Synge, *Hebrews and the Scriptures* (London, 1959); Graham Hughes, *Hebrews and Hermeneutics: The Epistle to the Hebrews as a New Testament Example of Biblical Interpretation* (Cambridge: Cambridge University Press, 1979); and Richard Longenecker, *Biblical Exegesis in the Apostolic Period* (Grand Rapids: Eerdmans, 1975), pp. 158-185.
52. Writing on Hebrews 10:1, Bruce observes that " 'shadow' is used not so much in the Platonic sense of a copy of the heavenly and eternal 'idea' as in the sense of foreshadowing . . . both writers [i.e., Paul and the author of Hebrews] think of Christ and His new order as the perfect reality to which the earlier ordinances pointed forward." F. F. Bruce, *The Epistle to the Hebrews* (Grand Rapids: Eerdmans, 1964), p. 226.
53. Richard N. Longenecker, *The Christology of Early Jewish Christianity* (Grand Rapids, Mich.: Baker), p. 31.
54. See Jean Danielou, *The Development of Christian Doctrine Before the Council of Nicea, Vol. I: The Theology of Jewish Christianity*, John A. Baker, trans. (London, 1964), pp. 117-146.

55. Hebrews uses the word χαρακτήρ (1:3) to express the representing quality of the Incarnation. It is a word used to describe the shape left by a seal or those distinguishing characteristics that set one person apart from another; it has the idea, therefore, of conveying the exact reality of God. The author perhaps chose this word over εἰκων because it was more vivid, but the idea is similar. Thus in 2 Corinthians 4:4 and Colossians 1:15 Christ is described by Paul as the "image" of God. In these contexts, the word does not have the connotation of a pale representation, but such a precise replica that it conveyed the essential nature of the thing.

In 1:3 the Son is also described as the "effulgence" of God's glory (ὃ ὤναπαυγαθμα γαθμα τῆς δοξης) The identification between Christ and Wisdom is intended by this phrase if the Alexandrian Book of Wisdom is its background. There, Wisdom is described as "a clear effulgence of the glory of the Almight . . . an effulgence from everlasting light." But if this is the linguistic form, the content would appear to be more biblical, the term expressing "the idea that Christ is the radiance or outflowing of the divine glory, the living embodiment of the *Shekinah,* a conception illustrated in the story of the Transfiguration." Vincent Taylor, *The Names of Jesus* (London, 1953), p. 129.

56. C. H. Dodd has shown that the quotations from the Old Testament in the New Testament are not isolated texts which are picked randomly, but are parts of much larger portions of Scripture around which an early Christian consensus emerged which provided "the starting point for the theological constructions of Paul, the author to the Hebrews, and the fourth Evangelist. It is the substructure of all Christian theology and contains already its chief regulative ideas" (C. H. Dodd, *According to the Scriptures: The Substructure of New Testament Theology* [London, 1952], p. 127). Although it has been disputed that Θεος is ever used in conjunction with Jesus' name in the New Testament, there can be no question that Jesus was broadly interpreted as God incarnate and against that consensus, the use of Θεος in this text as a title for Jesus seems eminently probable.

57. Oscar Cullmann, *The Christology of the New Testament,* Shirley C. Guthrie and Charles M. Hall, trans. (Philadelphia: Westminster, 1963), p. 97.

58. Paul's relationship to Jesus as viewed by New Testament scholars is carefully surveyed by J. W. Fraser, *Jesus and Paul: Paul as Interpreter of Jesus from Harnack to Kümmel* (Nashville: Abingdon, 1974). A briefer survey can be found in Herman Ridderbos, *Paul and Jesus: Origin and General Character of Paul's Preaching of Christ,* David Freeman, trans. (Grand Rapids, 1958), pp. 3-20.

59. C. H. Dodd has carefully explored the New Testament for the presence of this common *testimonia* in his *According to the Scriptures: The Substructure of New Testament Theology* (London, 1952); see also the general treatment by F. F. Bruce, *This Is That: The New Testament Development of Some Old Testament Theses* (London, 1968).

60. Vincent Taylor has observed that many of the names of Jesus found in the Gospels and Acts are omitted by Paul, such as rabbi, rabboni, teacher, Master, prophet, son of David, son of Mary, son of Joseph, Son of Man, King of Israel, the pioneer, Holy One, Righteous One, and the Coming One. At the same time, the number of Pauline creations is "surprisingly small," and includes image of God, firstborn, beloved, wisdom of God, and Last Adam. Paul, in fact, is dependent upon and conserves the traditional names such as Christ, Lord, Son of God, Son, head of the corner, the stone, the rock, and the power of God. Taylor, *The Person of Christ,* pp. 34, 35.

61. J. Gresham Machen, *The Origin of Paul's Religion* (Grand Rapids, Mich.: Eerdmans, 1965), p. 129.

62. Archibald M. Hunter, *Paul and His Predecessors* (Philadelphia, 1961), p. 79.

63. C. K. Barrett, "New Testament Eschatology," *Scottish Journal of Theology* 6 No. 2 (June 1953), 144.

64. Geerhardus Vos, *Pauline Eschatology* (Grand Rapids, Mich.: Baker, 1979), p. 11.

65. H. E. W. Turner, "The Virgin Birth," *Expository Times* 68 (1956), 12-17; cf. Machen,

The Virgin Birth of Christ, p. 259. The chief argument for Paul's knowledge of the virginal conception here is the use of the aorist participle of γινομαι rather than the aorist passive participle, which is taken to mean that Jesus was the Son "become" of a woman rather than being "born" of one. It should be noted, however, that elsewhere the New Testament uses forms of the latter verb with respect to Jesus' birth (Luke 1:35; John 18:37); so the distinction of meaning between the participles is unnatural and forced.

66. Vos, *Paul and Jesus*, p. 74.
67. Cf. F. F. Bruce, *New Testament History* (New York: Doubleday, 1972), pp. 420, 421; F. F. Bruce, *Paul: Apostle of the Heart Set Free* (Grand Rapids: Eerdmans, 1977), pp. 97-99.
68. Bultmann, I, p. 135; cf. Karl Rahner, *Theological Investigations*, Cornelius Ernst, trans., 20 vols. (New York: Crossroad, 1961-), pp. 79-148, which is noteworthy for its broad treatment of the use of Θεος in the New Testament, but also because it is one of Rahner's rare excursions into the field of biblical study itself. See Cullmann's rebuttal of Bultmann in his *Christology of the New Testament* (Philadelphia: Westminster, 1980), pp. 306-314.
69. The derivation of Paul's notion of the Last Adam is debated. W. D. Davies proposes that it was his invention (see his *Paul and Rabbinic Judaism* [London, 1962], pp. 36-57), while Hunter argued that it was part of that tradition of thought received from his precursors (see *Paul and His Predecessors*, p. 129). More important is what it means. Prevailing opinions are canvassed and assessed in Robin Scroggs, *The Last Adam: A Study in Pauline Anthropology* (Philadelphia, 1966) and C. K. Barrett, *From First Adam to Last* (London, 1962). The theological aspects are dealt with incisively from a Reformed point of view in John Murray, *The Imputation of Adam's Sin* (Philadelphia, 1977).
70. Leon Morris, *The Apostolic Preaching of the Cross* (Grand Rapids: Eerdmans, 1956), pp. 144-213; Roger R. Nicole, "C. H. Dodd and the Doctrine of Propitiation," *Westminster Theological Journal* 17 (1955), 117-157; J. Clement Connell, "The Propitiation Element in the Atonement," *Vox Evangelica* IV (1965), 28-42. On the use of the term *blood* in this connection, see A. M. Stibbs, *The Meaning of the Word 'Blood' in Scripture* (London, 1947), who counters Vincent Taylor's unsatisfactory proposal that this term is used not of a life given in substitutionary sacrifice, but one that is merely released for other purposes.
71. H. R. Mackintosh, *The Doctrine of the Person of Jesus Christ* (Edinburgh, 1912), p. 53.
72. Reflecting a mood that is widely prevalent, G. W. H. Lampe argued in *God as Spirit* that since God is uni-personal, all the references to the Spirit are references to the one God, whether we call him Father, Son, or Spirit, and that Christ correspondingly was not the preexistent Son incarnate, but merely a man preminently indwelt by God. Lampe's argument is sharply and correctly rebutted in E. L. Mascall, *Whatever Happened to the Human Mind?* (London, 1980), pp. 97-117.
73. The peculiarity of Paul's expression ἐν Χριστῷ is evident when we note that in the Gospels, the relationship of Christ to people is always described by the preposition μετα (Matt. 12:30; Mark 3:14; Luke 23:43) and never ἐν. Adolf Deissmann's *Die neutestament Formel 'in Christo Jesu'* (1892) set the terms of the modern discussion. It was his contention that Christ was the sphere or element in which we live spiritually as air is that element in which we live physically. Deissmann's notion has not gone unchallenged. The biblical data are reviewed in John B. Nielson, *In Christ: The Significance of the Phrase "In Christ" in the Writings of St. Paul* (Kansas City, 1960) and developed with insight in a broader context in James S. Stewart, *A Man in Christ: The Vital Elements of St. Paul's Religion* (Grand Rapids, Mich.: Baker, 1975).
74. A useful review of literature relevant to this passage is to be found in Donald Guthrie, *New Testament Theology* (Downers Grove, Ill.: Intervarsity Press, 1981), pp. 352-357; and Paul Beasley-Murray, "Col. 1:15-20: An Early Christian Hymn Cele-

brating the Lordship of Christ," *Pauline Studies,* Donald A. Hagner and Murray J. Harris, eds. (Grand Rapids: Eerdmans, 1981), pp. 169-183.

75. The relevant literature is ably analyzed by Ralph P. Martin, *Carmen Christi: Philippians 2:5-11 in Recent Interpretation and in the Setting of Early Christian Worship* (Cambridge, 1967), but see the important correctives to Martin's own views in C. F. D. Moule, "Further Reflections on Philippians 2:5-11," *Apostolic History and the Gospel,* W. Ward Gasque and Ralph P. Martin, eds. (Grand Rapids, 1970). See also I. Howard Marshall, "The Christ-Hymn in Philippians 2:5-11," *Tyndale Bulletin* 19 (1968), 104-127; Paul D. Feinberg, "The Kenosis and Christology: An Exegetical-Theological Analysis of Phil. 2:6-11," *Trinity Journal* I No. 1, new series (1980), 21-46.

76. Cullmann, *Christology of the New Testament,* p. 176.

77. "μορθή here means that expression of being which is identified with the essential nature and character of God, and which reveals it." Marvin R. Vincent, *The International Critical Commentary: A Critical and Exegetical Commentary on the Epistles to the Philippians and to Philemon* (Edinburgh, 1897), pp. 57, 58. See also J. B. Lightfoot, *Saint Paul's Epistles to the Philippians* (London, 1888), pp. 110, 127-133.

78. To say that Christ had the essential characteristics of divinity is to say, among other things, that he preexisted. There have been numerous attempts to circumvent this notion, all of which R. H. Fuller declares to be failures. The only possible way around this assertion is to rearrange the passage into different strophes, as Jeremias has attempted to do (see his *"Zur Gedankenfuhrung in den paulinischen Briefen,"* *Studia Paulina,* J. N. Sevenster and W. C. van Unnik, eds. [Haarlem, 1956], pp. 152-154), but this approach invites serious objections. The tail of a surmised poetic form is clearly wagging the dog of exegetical meaning.

79. ". . . the text does not say that Christ emptied himself of *anything.* The self-emptying is qualified by the following participle . . . by taking the form of a slave." George Eldon Ladd, *A Theology of the New Testament* (Grand Rapids: Eerdmans, 1974), p. 420. See also Karl Barth, *Church Dogmatics,* G. Bromiley, trans., 4 vols. (Edinburgh, 1956), IV/1, 180-183.

80. Walter Elwell, "The Deity of Christ in the Writings of Paul," *Current Issues in Biblical and Patristic Interpretation,* Gerald F. Hawthorne, ed. (Grand Rapids, 1975), pp. 297-308.

81. "The apostle has not presented in his epistles a systematically developed doctrine concerning the nature and person of the Redeemer. It is wholly improbable that he ever applied his mind to the problem of defining the relation to each other of the divine and human elements in his person. The needs of Paul's time did not demand such an effort." George B. Stevens, *The Pauline Theology: A Study of the Origin and Correlation of the Doctrinal Teachings of the Apostle Paul* (New York, 1894), p. 199.

Chapter 3: Titles of Our Lord

1. The titles which Cullmann examines constitute an exhaustive list if Jesus' "names" can be considered titular in any sense. These are described in Vincent Taylor, *The Names of Jesus* (London, 1953).

2. The literature on these and the other titles to be examined is considerable. Brief but judicious treatments are provided by I. Howard Marshall, *The Origins of New Testament Christology* (Downers Grove, 1976) and C. F. D. Moule, *The Origin of Christology* (Cambridge: Cambridge University Press, 1977). The studies by Cullmann, entitled *The Christology of the New Testament* (Philadelphia: Westminster, 1980) and his disciple Ferdinand Hahn, *The Titles of Jesus in Christology,* H. Knight, trans. (London, 1969) approach Christology from the avenue of the titles. Both tend to

absorb the ontological aspect in the functional, but both provide a wealth of detail. The study by W. Marxsen, *The Beginnings of Christology: A Study of Its Problems,* Paul Achtemeier, trans. (Philadelphia: Fortress, 1969) and that by R. H. Fuller, *The Foundations of New Testament Christology* (New York: Scribner, 1965) cover the same materials and titles, but from a far more radical, critical position than do Cullmann and Hahn.

3. Philo Judaeus, *The Works of Philo Judaeus, the Contemporary Josephus,* Vol. IV, C. D. Yonge, trans., 4 vols. (London, 1855), p. 391.

4. Mackintosh, *The Doctrine of the Person of Jesus Christ,* p. 116.

5. J. H. Bernard, *A Critical and Exegetical Commentary on the Gospel According to St. John,* Vol. I, 2 vols. (Edinburgh, 1926), p. 2.

6. Cullmann, *The Christology of the New Testament,* p. 260.

7. See Carl Holladay, *Theos-Anēr in Hellenistic Judaism: A Critique of the Use of the Category in New Testament Christology* (Missoula, 1977). This position is decisively rejected by Martin Hengel, *Son of God: the Origin of Christology and the History of Jewish-Hellenistic Religion,* John Bowden, trans. (Philadelphia: Fortress, 1976). See also W. Lane, "Theos Anēr Christology and the Gospel of Mark," *New Dimensions in New Testament Study,* R. M. Longenecker and M. C. Tenney, eds. (Grand Rapids, 1974), pp. 144-161.

8. Moule, *The Origin of Christology,* pp. 27-31.

9. J. G. G. Dunn, *Baptism in the Holy Spirit* (Philadelphia: Westminster, 1977).

10. Fuller, *The Foundations of New Testament Christology,* pp. 31-33.

11. Cf. G. N. Stanton, *Jesus of Nazareth in New Testament Preaching* (Cambridge, 1974), pp. 86-116.

12. Morna Hooker, *Jesus and the Servant: The Influence of the Servant Concept of Deutero-Isaiah in the New Testament* (London, 1959), p. 1.

13. F. C. Burkitt, *Christian Beginnings: Three Lectures* (London, 1924), p. 37. Burkitt acknowledges his debt to Foakes Jackson and Kirsopp Lake, whose book *The Beginnings of Christianity* had appeared in two volumes in 1920 and 1922.

14. See H. H. Rowley, *The Servant of the Lord and Other Essays on the Old Testament* (Oxford, 1965); Colin G. Kruse, "The Servant Songs: Interpretive Trends since C. R. North," *Studia Biblica et Theologica* 8 (1928), 3-27; C. Stuhlmueller, "Deutero-Isaiah: Major Transitions in the Prophet's Theology and in Contemporary Scholarship," *Catholic Biblical Quarterly* 42 (1980), 3-29.

15. See the works of Bernard Anderson.

16. Hooker, *Jesus and the Servant,* pp. 64, 65, 103, 116, 123, 124, 126.

17. Cullmann, *The Christology of the New Testament,* p. 69.

18. See W. Zimmerli and J. Jeremias, *The Servant of God,* Harold Knight, trans. (Chatham, 1957), pp. 88-98.

19. This theme is traced through the four songs by H. Wheeler Robinson in the following way:

From a theological standpoint, it is the vicarious character of the suffering of the Servant which possesses supreme interest, and it should be noted that this suffering is a natural sequel of the whole character and mission of the Servant. The patient teacher of true religion described in the first Song is given a larger setting in the second, for he becomes conscious of God behind him and a world-task before him. It is the thought of the God who has equipped him for his task that enables him to put aside the temptation to feel that his work is vain, and it is God who shows him a mission that extends beyond the borders of the nation. It is in the third Song that he declares the cost of the task in suffering. . . . Notwithstanding this suffering, his persistent purpose endures, for he is sure of God, and the fourth Song reaches the climax of the cycle, by showing that this very suffering will make possible the Servant's great achievement. The other nations had interpreted it as the penalty for Israel's sin; the vindication of Israel by its reinstatement in its own land against all expectation will bring them to a new interpretation. The suffering remains a penalty, but for the sins of the nations, not for those of Israel: "by the stripes he bore there was healing for us." H. Wheeler Robinson, *The Cross in the Old Testament* (London, 1955), pp. 81, 82. See also the fine study by H. L. Ellison, *The Servant of Jehovah* (London, 1953).

20. Marshall, *The Origins of New Testament Christology*, p. 99.
21. Moule, *The Origin of Christology*, p. 37.
22. Matthew Black, "The Maranatha Invocation and Jude 14, 15 (1 Enoch 1:9)" in *Christ and Spirit in the New Testament* (Cambridge: Cambridge University Press, 1974), pp. 189-198.
23. H. Bietenhard, "Lord," *Dictionary of New Testament Theology*, Vol. II, Colin Brown, ed., 3 vols. (Grand Rapids, 1976), p. 511. See also Dio Cassius, *Epitome* Li.XX; Tactius, *Ann*, IV, XXXVII, 4; XV, 1XXIV, 4, on cases of emperor worship or apotheosis.
24. W. Bousset, *Kyrios Christos*, John Seely, trans. (Nashville, 1970).
25. Cullmann, *The Christology of the New Testament*, p. 234.
26. Cf. J. G. Gibbs, "The Relation between Creation and Redemption According to Phil. II:5-11, " *Novum Testamentum* XII No. 3 (1970), 270-283.
27. See G. W. Macrae, "Whom Heaven Must Receive Until the Time: Reflections on the Christology of Acts," *Interpretation* 27 (April 1973), 151-165.
28. See Paul Beasley-Murray, "Colossians 1:15-20: An Early Christian Hymn Celebrating the Lordship of Christ," *Pauline Studies,* Donald H. Hagner and Murray J. Harris, eds. (Grand Rapids: Eerdmans, 1981), pp. 169-183.
29. See Oscar Cullmann, *The Early Church: Studies in Early Christian History and Theology,* A. J. B. Higgins, ed. (Philadelphia, 1956), pp. 104-140. In this essay, Cullmann ably explores the connections between Christ's Kingly rule implicit in the title *kurios* and the church's present life and experience.
30. A useful survey of Paul's use of this term can be found in Lucien Cerfaux, *Christ in the Theology of St. Paul,* Geoffrey Webb and Adrian Walker, trans. (New York, 1959), pp. 461-479.
31. Full reviews of the literature are given in A. J. B. Higgins' two books, *Jesus and the Son of Man* (London, 1964) and *The Son of Man in the Teaching of Jesus* (Cambridge: Cambridge University Press, 1981). A brief but capable analysis is provided in Marshall's *The Origins of New Testament Christology*, pp. 63-82.
32. Rudolf Bultmann, *The History of the Synoptic Tradition*, John Marsh, trans. (New York, 1968), p. 152.
33. E. g., Similitudes of Eth. Enoch, Chaps. 37-71; Apo. of Ezra 13:1-13.
34. Moule, *The Origin of Christology*, pp. 11-21. In a footnote, however, Moule states that "I have told this story dozens of times now, and the fact that I am still in a small minority makes me wonder what is wrong with it. But I can, so far, not find the flaw . . ." (p. 11). I, too, believe Moule's argument needs to be given greater attention.
35. Taylor, *The Names of Jesus*, pp. 32-35.
36. Morna D. Hooker, *The Son of Man in Mark: A Study of the Background of the Term "Son of Man" and Its Use in St. Mark's Gospel* (London, 1967).

Chapter 4: Transition

1. In the New Testament, *paradosis* has reference to the substance of Christian teaching which has been transmitted rather than the organ or means of its transmission. Tradition may be of purely human origin, in which case it is to be rejected (Mark 7:3;

Matt. 15:3, 6; Gal. 1:14; Col. 2:8). But apostolic teaching is not in this category, for its origin is divine (1 Cor. 11:23; 2 Thess. 2:15; 3:6). Salvation depends on believing this tradition (1 Cor. 15:2). In this sense, tradition is the basis of theology. See F. F. Bruce, *Tradition: Old and New* (Exeter: Paternoster Press, 1970). For a contemporary Roman Catholic perspective, see Yves Congar, *Tradition and Traditions: An Historical and Theological Essay* (New York: Macmillan, 1967).

2. In the early years of the patristic period, biblical doctrine *(didaskalia)* and theology *(theologia)* were usually distinguished (see Ammon., *Jo.*, 1, 8; Dion., *Ar.d.n.*, 3.3; Max., *Prol. Dion.*). It is true that *didachē* and *kērygma* were often associated with *didaskalia*, and even creedal formulae, such as that which came from Chalcedon, were sometimes included under the rubric of "doctrine." But Origen typified the approach of most in asserting that *theologia* was the *interpretation* of the biblical doctrine. As such, it was more tentative than "doctrine" and certainly open to correction.

3. In Roman law a *praescriptio,* or judicial objection, could, in certain carefully defined circumstances, be entered which would disallow the case from being heard in court. Tertullian, who was well versed in these technicalities, applied this procedure to the problem of heresy in his *De Praescriptio ne Haereticorum.*

4. Owen Chadwick, *From Bossuet to Newman: The Idea of Doctrinal Development* (Cambridge: Cambridge University Press, 1957), p. 1.

5. The Protestant Reformation reasserted the primacy of Scripture and its exclusively authoritative role in the formulation of Christian belief. In a typical complaint, Martin Luther asserted that "our opponents skipped faith altogether and taught human traditions and works not commanded by God but invented by them without and against the Word of God; these they have not only put on a par with the Word of God but have raised far above it." Martin Luther, *Works*, Vol. XXVI, Jaroslav Pelikan, ed. (St. Louis: Concordia Press, 1963), p. 52. John Calvin likewise complained of the "tyranny of human tradition which is haughtily thrust upon it under the title of the Church." John Calvin, *Institutes of the Christian Religion*, Vol. XXI and XXII, *Library of Christian Classics*, John T. McNeil, ed. (Philadelphia: Westminster Press, 1960), pp. 5, 6; see also IV, pp. 18, 19, 20, 23. "All the fathers have abhorred and with one voice have detested the fact," he said, "that God's Holy Word has been contaminated by the subtleties of sophists and involved in the squabbles of dialecticians." *Ibid.*, pp. 3, 4. See also William Tyndale, *Expositions and Notes on Sunday Portions of the Holy Scriptures, Together with the Practice of Prelates*, Vol. II, H. Walter, ed. 2 vols. (Cambridge: Cambridge University Press, 1849), p. 142. In reasserting this position, however, the Protestant Reformers appeared to Catholics to have succumbed to "private judgment." In 1521 Luther had been condemned in this way: "a single monk, led astray by private judgment, has set himself against the faith held by all Christians for a thousand years and more, and impudently concludes that Christians up till now have erred." B. J. Kidd, ed., *Documents Illustrative of the Continental Reformation* (Oxford: Oxford University Press, 1911), p. 86.

6. James Orr, *The Progress of Dogma* (London: Hodder and Stoughton, 1901), p. 6.

7. In the contemporary period, Hans Küng, himself a Roman Catholic, argued this point in his book, *Infallible? An Inquiry* (New York: Doubleday, 1971). It provoked a major storm and a fierce debate with fellow-Catholic Karl Rahner. The debate was carried on in the December (1970) and February and March (1971) editions of *Stimmen der Zeit.* An account is given by L. Bruce van Voorst, "Küng and Rahner: Duelling over Infallibility," *The Christian Century* (May 19, 1971), 617-622; "Follow-up on the Küng-Rahner Feud," *The Christian Century* (August 25, 1971), 991-1000. John J. Kirvan edited some of the responses to Küng's attack in *The Infallible Debate*, but see also Stanley Obitts, "Religious Certainty and Infallibility: A Discussion with Hans Küng," *Toward a Theology for the Future*, David F. Wells and Clark H. Pinnock, eds. (Carol Stream, 1971), pp. 275-292.

8. John Henry Newman, *An Essay on the Development of Christian Doctrine* (Philadel-

phia: Westminster, Christian Classics, 1967). Peter Toon has discussed the responses to Newman's work in his *The Development of Doctrine in the Church* (Grand Rapids: Eerdmans, 1979), as well as subsequent reflection from both a Catholic and Protestant perspective. See also Jaroslav Pelikan, *Development of Christian Doctrine; Some Historical Prolegomena* (New Haven: Yale University Press, 1969). On the question of tradition as this relates to development, see Gabriel Moran, *Scripture and Tradition: A Survey of the Controversy* (New York: Herder and Herder, 1963); J. P. Mackey, *The Modern Theology of Tradition* (London: Logos Press, 1967).

9. *Con. DV.,* 8.

10. The assumption of Mary is clearly a case where the biblical warrant is lacking. In fact, as Jaroslav Pelikan notes, "Pope Pius did not attempt to prove that the doctrine of the assumption was taught as such in the Sacred Scriptures or confessed in the earliest documentary witnesses to the Christian and Catholic faith." Jaroslav Pelikan, "An Essay on the Development of Christian Doctrine," *Church History* XXXV No. 1 (March 1966), 3.

11. Newman, *An Essay,* pp. 169-206.

12. *Ibid.,* pp. 75-92.

13. Friedrich Schleiermacher, *The Christian Faith,* H. R. Mackintosh and J. S. Stewart, eds. (Edinburgh: T. and T. Clark, 1948), pp. 377-424. Also, Adolf Harnack, *What Is Christianity?,* Thomas Saunders, trans. (London: Williams & Norgate, 1901), pp. 19-77. At the root of this conception is the assumption that an identity exists between the divinity in Christ and that which is in human beings, even as there is between his humanity and ours. It is this identity that secures the continuity of Christian faith across the ages. Cf. H. Maurice Relton, *Studies in Christian Doctrine* (New York: Macmillan, 1960), pp. 145-153; Emil Brunner, *The Mediator; A Study in the Central Doctrine of the Christian Faith,* Olive Wyon, trans. (Philadelphia: Westminster, 1947), pp. 42-101.

14. Hans Werner Bartsch, ed., *Kerygma and Myth,* Reginald Fuller, trans. (London: S.P.C.K., 1954), p. 3; Rudolf Bultmann, *Jesus Christ and Mythology* (New York: Charles Scribner's Sons, 1958), pp. 11-21.

15. See H. Richard Niebuhr, *Christ and Culture* (New York: Harper and Bros., 1951), pp. 91-101.

16. Walter Bauer, *Orthodoxy and Heresy in Earliest Christianity,* Robert Kraft and Gerhard Krodel, eds. (Philadelphia: Fortress, 1971). Substantially the same position is set forth by Samuel Laeuchli, *The Serpent and the Dove* (Nashville: Abingdon, 1966).

17. H. E. W. Turner, *The Pattern of Christian Truth: A Study in the Relations between Orthodoxy and Heresy in the Early Church* (London: A. R. Mowbray, 1954), pp. 95-148.

18. "In most cases," observes Maurice Wiles, "the heretic's affirmations were on subjects about which the majority had no clearly formulated convictions." *The Making of Christian Doctrine: A Study in the Principles of Early Doctrinal Development* (Cambridge: Cambridge University Press, 1967), p. 32.

19. Ar. *Ap,* I, 4. Cf. Bas. *Const.,* II, 1.

20. Just. *Dialog.,* IV, 1. Cf. Athenag. *Leg.,* IV, 1.

21. Clem. *Strom.,* I, 5, 28.

22. A challenge to this development was mounted only occasionally in the East. See Chrys., *De inc. nat. Dei Hom.,* I-V.

23. Tert., *De praes. haer.,* 7.

24. See Harry A. Wolfson, *The Philosophy of the Church Fathers* (Cambridge: Harvard University Press, 1956), pp. 97-105.

25. On the history and meaning of the technical terms in debate, see G. L. Prestige, *God in Patristic Thought* (London: S.P.C.K., 1964), pp. 157-196.

26. The correlation between the views of the emperor in power and the party ascendant in the church during the Arian dispute is made clear in H. M. Gatkin, *The Arian Controversy* (London: Longmans, Green and Co., 1896).

27. Soz., *Hist. Eccl.*, I, XV, 3; J. N. D. Kelly, *Early Christian Doctrines* (New York: Harper and Row, 1960), pp. 226-237; *Early Christian Creeds* (London: Longmans, Green and Co., 1960), pp. 189, 190, 205-216.

Chapter 5: Classical Christology: The Patristic Age

1. Georg Wehrung, "Christology," *Twentieth Century Theology in the Making*, Javoslav Pelikan, ed., Vol. II: *The Theological Dialogue: Issues and Resources*, 3 vols. (New York: Harper and Row, 1970), p. 131.
2. Eus., *E. H.*, VI, 12.6.
3. *Ibid.*, VII, 30.1-22.
4. Paul, *Frag.*, VII, IX.
5. *Ibid.*, XI.
6. Cf. Robert Sample, "The Christology of the Council of Antioch (268 CE) Reconsidered," *Church History* 48 (March 1979), 18-26. See Eus., *E. H.*, XXX. 18, 19.
7. A careful exposition of both schools is provided by Aloys Grillmeier, *Christ in Christian Tradition: From the Apostolic Age to Chalcedon (451)*, John Bowden, trans. (Atlanta: John Knox Press, 1974), pp. 167-442.
8. *Ibid.*, p. 242.
9. See Jerry McCoy, "Philosophical Influences on the Doctrines of the Incarnation in Athanasius and Cyril of Alexandria," *Encounter* 38 (Autumn 1977), 362-391; C. Kannengiesser, "Athanasius of Alexandria and the Foundation of Traditional Christology," *Theological Studies* 34 (March 1973), 103-113.
10. R. V. Sellers, *Two Ancient Christologies: A Study in the Christological Thought of the Schools of Alexandria and Antioch in the Early History of Christian Doctrine* (London: S.P.C.K., 1954), p. 202. The same basic thesis is developed by Charles E. Raven, *Apollinariansim: An Essay on the Christology of the Early Church* (Cambridge: Cambridge Univeristy Press, 1923), and J. F. Bethune-Baker, *Nestorius and his Teaching: A Fresh Examination of the Evidence with Special Reference to the Newly Recovered Apology of Nestorius (Bazaar of Heraclides)* (Cambridge: Cambridge University Press, 1908).
11. Frances M. Young, "Reconsideration of Alexandrian Christology," *Journal of Ecclesiastical History* 22 (April 1971), 104. More recently, she has produced a full-scale treatment of patristic developments in *From Nicea to Chalcedon* (London, 1983).
12. See, for example, the severe criticisms of modern restatements of this type of Christology in W. Norman Pittenger, *The Word Incarnate: A Study of the Doctrine of the Person of Christ* (Digswell Place: James Nisbet, 1959), pp. 99-131.
13. Athanasius was not alone among Eastern or Greek thinkers in stating that Christ had a "rational soul." Cf. Victorinus, *Adv Ar.*, III, 3; Hilary, *De Trin.*, X, 19.
14. Ap. *Frag.*, 10. Unfortunately, some of Apollinarius' writings were destroyed; much of what remains is given in Greek with German translation by Hans Lietzmann, *Apollinaris von Laodicea und seine Schule* (New York, 1970). It is in this work that these "Fragments" may be found.
15. Ap., *Frag.*, 36.
16. *Ibid.*, 38.
17. *Ibid.*, 10; Ap., *Ep. ad Dion.*, I, 6.
18. Ap., *Frag.*, 45.
19. *Ibid.*, 74, 75.
20. *Ibid.*, 25.
21. The words are actually those of Gregory Nazianzen, *Ib.*, Cl. II.
22. G. L. Prestige, *Fathers and Heretics* (London: S.P.C.K., 1940), p. 249.
23. According to Socrates, Nestorius said, "I could not give the name of God to one who

was two or three months old" (*HE*, VII, 34). Bethune-Baker, after reviewing Nestorius' defense, concluded that he had been misunderstood. "He did not say that he could not bring himself to call a babe God, but he said that he could not bring himself to call God a babe" (Bethune-Baker, *Nestorius and His Teaching*, p. 77).

24. *Ibid.*, pp. 148-170.

25. *Ibid.*, pp. 171-188.

26. Sellers, *Two Ancient Christologies*, p. 156.

27. For a history and analysis of the council, see R. V. Sellers, *The Council of Chalcedon;* it should be borne in mind, of course, that Sellers continues in this book the thesis formulated in his *Two Ancient Christologies*.

28. Wolfhart Pannenberg, *Jesus—God and Man*, Lewis L. Wilkins and Duane A. Priebe, trans. (Philadelphia: Westminster, 1968), p. 287.

29. William Temple, "The Divinity of Christ," *Foundations: A Statement of Christian Belief in Terms of Modern Thought* (London: Macmillan, 1912), p. 230.

30. See Robert L. Ottley, *The Doctrine of the Incarnation*, Vol. II, 2 Vols. (London: Methuen, 1896), pp. 113-161. Javoslav Pelikan, *The Christian Tradition*, Vol I: *The Emergence of the Catholic Tradition* (Chicago: University of Chicago Press, 1971), pp. 266-277. On some typical Christological formulations, see Robert C. Chesnut, *Three Monophysite Christologies: Severus of Antioch, Philoxenus of Mabbug, and Jacob of Sarug* (Oxford: Oxford University Press, 1976). For contemporary discussion see N. Chitescu, "Position of Some Orthodox and Roman Catholic Theologians on the Wills of the Person of Jesus Christ and the Problem of Relations with the Non-Chalcedonians," *Greek Orthodox Theological Review* 13 No. 2 (1968), 288-308; G. I. Konidares, "Christological Decisions of Chalcedon, Their History Down to the 6th Ecumenical Synod (451-680-1)," *Greek Orthodox Theological Review* I No. 2 (1971), 63-78; V. C. Samuel, "Brief History of Efforts to Reunite the Chalcedonian and Non-Chalcedonian Sides," *Greek Orthodox Theological Review* 16 No. 1-2 (1971), 44-62; P. Verghese, "Monothelite Controversy: A Historical Survey (with Discussion)," *Greek Orthodox Theological Review* 13 No. 2 (1968), 196-211.

Chapter 6: Classical Christology: From the Dark Ages to the Reformation

1. John Calvin declared that "if the contest were to be determined by patristic authority, the tide of victory—to put it very modestly—would turn to our side." *Institutes of the Christian Religion* Vol. XXI and XXII, *Library of Christian Classics*, John T. McNeill, ed. (Philadelphia, 1960), p. 4. Cf. John Jewel, *An Apology for the Church of England*, Stephen Isaacson, trans. (London, 1829), p. 279.

2. Georg Hegel, *Hegel's Lectures on the History of Philosophy*, Vol. III, E. S. Haldane and Frances Simson, trans., 3 vols. (London, 1955), p. 37.

3. See, for example, R. W. Southern, *The Making of the Middle Ages* (New Haven: Yale University Press, 1953); C. Dawson, *The Making of Europe* (New York: New American Library, 1932); W. C. Bark, *Origins of the Medieval World* (Stanford: Stanford University Press, 1958).

4. On monophysitism see W. H. C. Frend, *The Rise of the Monophysite Movement* (Cambridge: Cambridge University Press, 1972); Robert L. Ottley, *The Doctrine of the Incarnation* (London, 1919), pp. 433-458.

5. B. J. Kidd, *The Churches of Eastern Christendom: From A.D. 451 to the Present Time* (London, 1927), p. 104.

6. John Leith, ed., *Creeds of the Churches* (Richmond, 1973), pp. 46-49.

7. *Ibid.*, p. 52.

8. John of Damascus, *De Orth. Fid.*, III, 3.

9. *Ibid.*, III, 4.

10. *Ibid.*, III, 8. Cf. Ottley, *Doctrine of the Incarnation*, pp. 458-471.
11. On the subsequent development in thought, see George A. Maloney, *A History of Orthodox Theology Since 1453* (Houston: Nordland, 1976). This volume deals with orthodoxy in Greek-speaking churches as well as the Bulgarian, Serbian, and Romanian churches. On North American developments, see Arthur C. Piepkorn, *Profiles in Belief*, Vol. I: *Roman Catholic, Old Catholic and Eastern Orthodoxy* (New York: Harper and Row, 1977), pp. 31-116.
12. See Joseph Pieper, *Scholasticism: Personalities and Problems of Medieval Philosophy* (New York: McGraw, 1964), pp. 100-108.
13. On the complexity of what scholastics understood by universals and, in particular, what Anselm thought, see *Anselm of Canterbury: Hermeneutical and Textual Problems in the Complete Treatises of St. Anselm*, Vol. IV, Jasper Hopkins, trans., 4 vols. (New York: E. Mellen, 1976), pp. 57-96.
14. Boethius, *The Theological Tractates*, H. F. Steward, E. K. Rand, and S. J. Tester, trans. (Harvard: Harvard University Press, 1973), p. 117.
15. Boethius' definition of *person* became standard in medieval thought and was accepted by Thomas Aquinas. But this acceptance did not occur without considerable debate. See Henry Chadwick, *Boethius: The Consolations of Music, Logic, Theology and Philosophy* (Oxford, 1981), pp. 193-195; R. G. Evans, *Anselm and a New Generation* (Oxford: Oxford University Press, 1980), pp. 154-161.
16. Hugh S. Victor, *Didascalicon*, I, 9.
17. *Ibid.*, I, 1.
18. Anselm, *De Incarnatione Verbi*, 10.
19. R. W. Southern, *Saint Anselm: A Study of his Monastic Life and Thought 1059-c. 1130* (Oxford, 1963), p. 81. On Anselm's view of the atonement, see G. C. Foley, *Anselm's Theory of the Atonement* (London, 1909).
20. Peter Lombard, *Sentences*, d. 6 Cap. 2.
21. Heiko Oberman, *The Harvest of Medieval Theology: Gabriel Biel and Late Medieval Nominalism* (Grand Rapids, 1967), p. 253.
22. S. Thomas Aquinas, *Summa Theologiae*, III, Q. 1, Art. 2.
23. *Ibid.*, III, Q. 1, Art. 3.
24. *Ibid.*, III, Q. 51, Art. 6.
25. *Ibid.*, III, Q. 48, Arts. 1-6.
26. See H. M. Monteau-Bonamy, *The Historical and Mystical Christ*, A. H. Henry, ed. (Chicago, 1958), pp. 41-53.
27. St. Thoma Aquinas, *Summa*, III, Q. 2, Art. 1.
28. *Ibid.*, III, Q. 2, Art, 4.
29. *Ibid.*, III, 4, Art. 2.
30. *Ibid.*, IV, 9, Art. 2.
31. *Ibid.*, III, 7, Art. 12.
32. A helpful commentary through the appropriate sections of the *Summa* is provided by Reginald Garrigou-Lagrange, *Christ the Savior: A Commentary on the Third Part of St. Thomas' Theological Summa*, Bede Rose, trans. (St. Louis, 1950).
33. Ottley, *Doctrine of the Incarnation*, p. 494.
34. Cf. Steven Ozment, *Mysticism and Dissent: Religious Ideology and Social Protest in the Sixteenth Century* (New Haven: Yale University Press, 1973).
35. Karl Holl, *What Did Luther Understand by Religion?*, James Luther Adams and Walter F. Bense, eds. (Philadelphia: Fortress, 1977).
36. See Gordon Rupp, *Luther's Progress to the Diet of Worms* (New York, 1964), pp. 17-19, 45-47.
37. Luther, XXI, p. 12
38. Luther's penchant for paradox has sometimes been interpreted as an appetite for irrationality. He has, on this account, been classified as a mystic. On these issues see B. A. Gerrish, *Grace and Reason: A Study in the Theology of Luther* (Chicago: University of Chicago Press, 1979), and Bengt R. Hoffman, *Luther and the Mystics: A*

Re-examination of Luther's Spiritual Experience and His Relationship to the Mystics (Minneapolis, 1967).

39. There is a large literature on the subject of authority in the Reformers. With respect to Luther, the subject is well covered by A. Skevington-Wood, *Captive to the Word: Martin Luther, Doctor of Sacred Scripture* (Grand Rapids, 1969).

40. See the two essays by Basil Hall entitled "The Calvin Legend" and "Calvin Against the Calvinists" in *John Calvin*, G. E. Duffield, ed. (Grand Rapids, 1966), pp. 1-37. The relationship between Calvin's thought and his immediate heirs is more difficult to elucidate with clarity. The reply to R. T. Kendall's *Calvin and English Calvinism to 1649* by Paul Helm needs careful consideration. It is entitled *Calvin and the Calvinists* (Edinburgh, 1982).

41. Calvin, *Institutes*, I, 9, 2.

42. Kenneth Kantzer, "Calvin and the Holy Scriptures," *Inspiration and Interpretation*, John F. Walvoord, ed. (Grand Rapids, 1957), pp. 115-155.

43. Calvin, *Institutes*, I, 6, 3; I, 5, 1; John Calvin, *Commentaries on the Epistle of Paul the Apostle to the Romans*, John Owen, trans. (Grand Rapids, 1948), pp. 353, 354, 369, 370; T. H. L. Parker, "Calvin's Concept of Revelation," *Scottish Journal of Theology* II (March 1949), 29-47.

44. See, for example, from his comments on John, Luther's *Works*, XXII, pp. 321-332, 335; XXIII, pp. 77, 83, 104, 105, 184, 367, 376, 377.

45. Ian D. Kingston Siggins, *Martin Luther's Doctrine of Christ* (New Haven, 1970), pp. 205, 206.

46. See Philip S. Watson, *Let God be God! The Interpretation of the Theology of Martin Luther* (Philadelphia, 1947), pp. 102-105.

47. Gustav Aulén, *Christus Victor: An Historical Study of the Three Main Types of the Idea of the Atonement*, A. G. Hebert, trans. (New York: Macmillan, 1964), pp. 1-15, 101-122. Cf. Siggins, *Martin Luther's Doctrine of Christ*, pp. 108-143.

48. See, for example, Luther, XXVII, pp. 259-263. On Luther's view of Christ's work, see the magisterial study by Gordon Rupp, *The Righteousness of God* (London, 1953).

49. See Herman Sasse, *This Is My Body: Luther's Contention for the Real Presence in the Sacrament of the Altar* (Adelaide, 1977).

50. Paul Althaus, *The Theology of Martin Luther*, Robert C. Schultz, trans. (Philadelphia: Fortress, 1966), pp. 181, 182.

51. Cf. Wilhelm Niesel, *The Theology of Calvin*, Harold Knight, trans. (London, 1956), pp. 246-250.

52. Calvin summed up his view in the statement that "the efficient cause of our salvation is placed in the love of God the Father; the material cause in the obedience of the Son; the instrumental cause in the illumination of the Spirit, that is, in faith . . . " Calvin, *Institutes*, III, pp. 14, 21.

53. Calvin's treatment of the "limited atonement" is curious. Actual affirmations of it are extremely scant. (For the few explicit references, see William Cunningham, *The Reformers and the Theology of the Reformation* [Edinburgh, 1866], p. 396). And, on the other hand, Calvin's remarks upon Romans 5:18 led John Owen to observe in a footnote that it "appears from this sentence that Calvin held general redemption" (John Calvin, *Commentaries . . . Romans*, p. 212). This ambiguity was to cause considerable strife at times in later Calvinism when both opponents and proponents of the limited atonement looked back to Calvin in justification of their views. The view taken here is that Calvin maintained particular redemption, but that he affirmed this in as chaste a way as he believed the biblical writers had.

54. Calvin, *Institutes*, II, 15, 1-2; IV, 19, 30; II, 15, 3-5.

55. *Ibid.*, II, 12, 1; II, 6, 4.

56. *Ibid.*, I, 13, 3; II, 14, 1-8.

57. *Ibid.*, II, 13, 4.

Chapter 7: The Enlightenment and Its Aftermath

1. The relationship between Christian faith and Western culture is difficult to depict precisely because, in fact, it is not a single relationship but is constituted by many, differing parts. Nevertheless, Christopher Dawson is correct in declaring that it is Christian values, rather than science or humanism, "which was the spiritual bond that transcended the divisions and antagonisms of race and class and nationality and created that society of peoples which was the community of Western Christendom" (Christopher Dawson, *The Historic Reality of Christian Culture: A Way to the Renewal of Human Life* [New York: Greenwood, 1960], p. 109). The Protestant Reformers, "a cadre of intellectuals," as Jaroslav Pelikan calls them, launched their proposals from the forefront of the culture. Christian thinkers today speak from outside the current assumptions and as intruders into and aliens within the culture. See Pelikan's *The Christian Intellectual* (London, 1966). Cf. Kenneth Cragg, *Christianity in World Perspective* (Oxford, 1968), pp. 169-192.

2. This problem is examined provocatively in Austin Van Harvey, *The Historian and the Believer* (London, 1967). See also Colin Brown, "History and the Believer," *History, Criticism and Faith,* Colin Brown, ed. (Downers Grove: InterVarsity Press, 1976), pp. 147-216.

3. The terms *discontinuity* and *continuity* are here used with an ontological reference. Where the reference is widened to include other factors, different arrangements follow. Conservative Protestant thought, for example, clearly affirms an ontological discontinuity. However, unlike Barthian theology, it believes in a revelational continuity inasmuch as in "general revelation" God discloses himself to all people through created reality and in particular through the moral structure of human nature. Unlike liberalism, conservative theology argues that this revelatory continuity is not soteriological in intent or result. The addition of other referents, such as revelation, obviously produces complications in the classification.

4. In terms of H. Richard Niebuhr's delineation of the problem, *discontinuity* is being equated with "Christ and Culture in paradox" and *continuity* with "The Christ of Culture," which are the two most viable options in our Western world. The proponents of "Christ the Transformer of Culture" have often, but not always, allied themselves with *continuity,* as have the advocates of "Christ above Culture," and those who propose "Christ against Culture" have usually stressed *discontinuity.* See Niebuhr's *Christ and Culture* (New York: Harper & Row, 1951).

5. See H. D. McDonald, "What Is Meant by Religious Experience?" *Vox Evangelica* II (1963), 58-70.

6. See David F. Wells, *The Search for Salvation* (Downers Grove: InterVarsity Press, 1978), pp. 142-146.

7. A. B. Bruce, *The Humiliation of Christ: In Its Physical, Ethical and Official Aspects* (New York, 1892), p. 85.

8. Cf. Ottley, *Doctrine of the Incarnation,* pp. 545-553; Bruce, *The Humiliation of Christ,* pp. 107, 115.

9. The reactions to the *Formula* are well traced out in several essays in Lewis W. Spitz and Wenzel Lohff, eds., *Discord, Dialogue, and Concord: Studies in the Lutheran Reformation's Formula of Concord* (Philadelphia: Fortress, 1977), pp. 119-207.

10. *Formula of Concord,* Art. VIII, 5.

11. This judgment is, of course, controverted by advocates of the *Formula's* position who may recognize defects but see its merits as sufficiently large to offset these defects. See, for example, Bjarne W. Teigen, "Article VIII, The Formula of Concord: The Person of Christ," *A Contemporary Look at the Formula of Concord* (St. Louis, 1978), pp. 232-252. Cf. Edmund Schlink, *Theology of the Lutheran Confessions,* Paul Koehneke and Herbert Bouman, trans. (Philadelphia, 1961), pp. 188-193.

12. *Formula,* Art. VIII, 8, 11, 12.

13. For the period of thought between the Reformation and the nineteenth century in Lutheranism, see Heinrich Schmid, *The Doctrinal Theology of the Evangelical Lutheran Church,* Charles A. Hay and Henry E. Jacos, trans. (Minneapolis: Augsburg, 1961), pp. 188-193. On the Reformed side, see Heinrich Heppe, *Reformed Dogmatics: Set Out and Illustrated from the Sources,* Ernst Bizer, ed., G. T. Thomson, trans. (Grand Rapids: Baker, 1978), pp. 488-509.

14. John Stewart Lawton, *Conflict in Christology: A Study of British and American Christology from 1889-1914* (New York, 1947), p. 119.

15. F. J. Hall, *The Kenotic Theory Considered with Particular Reference to Its Anglican Forms and Arguments* (New York, 1898), p. 1.

16. Bruce, *The Humiliation of Christ,* p. 138.

17. For a fuller exposition of the various theories see Lawton, *Conflict in Christology,* pp. 133-164, and Ronald G. Dawe, *Form of a Servant: A Historical Analysis of the Kenotic Motif* (Philadelphia, 1963), pp. 104-155.

18. Claude Welch, ed., *God and Incarnation in Mid-Nineteenth Century German Theology: Thomasius, Dorner, Biedermann* (Oxford, 1965), pp. 46-49.

19. *Ibid.,* p. 41.

20. *Ibid.,* p. 45.

21. *Ibid.,* p. 57.

22. See Charles Gore's *The Incarnation of the Son of God* (New York, 1891), and *Dissertations on Subjects Connected with the Incarnation* (London, 1907).

23. H. R. Mackintosh, *The Doctrine of the Person of Jesus Christ* (Edinburgh, 1912).

24. A. M. Fairbain, *The Place of Christ in Modern Theology* (New York, 1903). See also his *Christ in the Centuries* (London, 1893).

25. P. T. Forsyth, *The Person and Place of Jesus Christ* (London, 1909). One also needs to keep in mind Forsyth's discussion of Christ's work when considering Forsyth's view of Christ's person. These are principally *The Cruciality of the Cross* (London, 1910) and *The Work of Christ* (London, 1910).

26. Forsyth, *The Person and Place of Christ,* p. 229.

27. *Ibid.,* p. 307.

28. *Ibid.,* pp. 329, 330.

29. *Ibid.,* p. 333.

30. *Ibid.,* pp. 293, 294. On Forsyth's theology see John H. Rodgers, *The Theology of P. T. Forsyth* (London, 1965).

31. Bruce, *The Humiliation of Christ,* p. 176.

32. Daniel L. Pals, *The Victorian "Lives" of Jesus* (San Antonio, 1982), p. 3.

33. Albert Schweitzer, *The Quest of the Historical Jesus: A Critical Study of Its Progress from Reimarus to Wrede,* W. Montgomery, trans. (New York, 1948), p. 398. A briefer analysis of approximately the same territory is to be found in Charles C. Anderson, *Critical Quests of Jesus* (Grand Rapids, 1969).

34. See, for example, Hans-Werner Bartsch, "The Historical Problem in the Life of Christ," *The Historical Jesus and the Kerygmatic Christ: Essays on the New Quest of the Historical Jesus,* Carl Braaten and Roy A. Harrisville, eds. (New York, 1964), pp. 106-141.

35. See K. Adam, *The Christ of Faith: The Christology of the Church,* Joyce Crick, trans. (London, 1957), pp. 189-204.

36. For a development and justification of this view, see David F. Wells, *American Academy of Religion Studies in Religion,* Vol. XXII: *The Prophetic Theology of George Tyrrell* (Chico, 1981).

37. Friedrich Schleiermacher, *On Religion: Speeches to Its Cultured Despisers,* John Oman, trans. (New York: Harper & Row, 1958) pp. 41-101. Schleiermacher, Karl Barth has said, participated in "modern cultural awareness," not merely for apologetic reasons but for theological. He "proclaimed and demanded" this participation. It was a participation, however, in which Schleiermacher was consistently led to affirm

the opinion of culture and deny the opinion of traditional Christianity. Karl Barth, *Protestant Theology in the Nineteenth Century: Its Background and History*, Brian Cozens, trans. (Valley Forge, Penn.: Judson, 1973; London, 1972), pp. 435-473. The same judgments are rendered on Ritschl in Niebuhr's *Christ and Culture*, pp. 91-115.

38. George Tyrrell, "Medievalism and Modernism," *Harvard Theological Review* I No. 2 (July 1980), 308-324.

39. Immanuel Kant, *Critique of Pure Reason*, Norman Kemp Smith, trans. (London, 1929; New York: Doubleday).

40. Immanuel Kant, *Critique of Practical Reason and Other Writings in Moral Philosophy*, Lewis Beck, trans. (New York: Garland, 1977).

41. Jerry Gill, *On Knowing God* (Philadelphia: Westminster, 1981), pp. 19-21.

42. For more recent scholarship on Schleiermacher, see Terrence N. Tice, *Schleiermacher Bibliography: With Brief Introduction, Annotation, and Index* (Princeton: Princeton University Press, 1966).

43. Richard R. Niebuhr, *Schleiermacher on Christ and Religion* (New York, 1964), pp. 210-214.

44. Friedrich Schleiermacher, *The Christian Faith*, H. R. Mackintosh and J. S. Stewart, eds. and trans. (London, 1948), p. 385.

45. *Ibid.*, p. 387.

46. *Ibid.*, p. 402.

47. *Ibid.*

48. *Ibid.*, p. 411.

49. On the Ritschlian side of liberalism, a similar kind of Christology emerged. It led James Orr to assert that Christians were being asked "to value as God one who was not God." James Orr, *The Ritschlian Theology and the Evangelical Faith* (London, 1898), p. 263. James Denney made a comparable judgment in several of his works. The most sympathetic of the early treatments of Ritschl's thought and the one which created considerable acceptance of it was Alfred Garvie, *The Ritschlian Theology: Critical and Constructive* (Edinburgh, 1899), the section on Christology being pages 264-296, in which Denney is answered.

50. Emil Brunner has charged that Schleiermacher, building on Enlightenment ideas, ended up with a Jesus whom he regarded "merely as one of the representatives of piety, of religious humanity, even if one of the foremost, who thus in principle stands on our side, who is therefore not a new category but simply the highest point attainable by humanity." *The Mediator: A Study of the Central Doctrine of the Christian Faith*, Olive Wyon, trans. (New York, 1934), p. 90. In order to invest this figure with uniqueness, Schleiermacher invented the word *archetype*, but as it turned out the "archetype" does not imply the slightest break in the continuity of the history of humanity (*ibid.*, p. 91). Because as a person Christ was not unique, in his work he could achieve no more than what other "mediators" can do, which is to stimulate existing piety, "men who awaken religious feeling in the hearts of others" (*ibid.*, p. 92). At the root of Schleiermacher's errors were a doctrine of sin which was "quite extraordinarily superficial" (*ibid.*, p. 132) and his acceptance of the romantic notion of universal religion.

Chapter 8: Twentieth-century Turmoil

1. Hans Frei, *The Eclipse of Biblical Narrative: A Study in Eighteenth and Nineteenth Century Hermeneutics* (New Haven: Yale University Press, 1974), p. 323.

2. See David Kelsey, *The Uses of Scripture in Recent Theology* (Philadelphia: Fortress, 1975). Some useful descriptive material is also to be found in Robert K. Johnston, *Evangelicals at an Impasse: Biblical Authority in Practice* (Atlanta: John Knox, 1978).

3. G. Ernest Wright, *God Who Acts: Biblical Theology as Recital* (London, 1964).
4. Oscar Cullmann's approach to and use of Scripture is less spoken of and more acted upon in works such as his *The Christology of the New Testament*, Shirley C. Guthrie and Charles A. M. Hall, trans. (Philadelphia: Westminster, 1959), and *Salvation in History*, Sidney G. Sowers, trans. (London, 1967).
5. Carl Braaten, *History and Hermeneutics*, Vol. II: *New Directions in Theology Today* (Philadelphia, 1966), pp. 58, 59.
6. The issues are well reviewed in Hugh Anderson, *Jesus and Christian Origins: A Commentary on Modern Viewpoints* (Oxford, 1964); William Baird, *The Quest of the Christ of Faith: Reflections on the Bultmannian Era* (Waco: Word, 1971); I. Howard Marshall, *I Believe in the Historical Jesus* (Grand Rapids: Eerdmans, 1977).
7. See Colin Brown, "History and the Believer," *History, Criticism and Faith*, Colin Brown, ed. (Downers Grove: InterVarsity, 1976), pp. 147-224.
8. Cf. Raimundo Panikkar, *The Unknown Christ of Hinduism* (New York: Orbis, 1981).
9. Cyril C. Richardson, *The Doctrine of the Trinity* (Nashville, 1958), p. 48. The issues involved are also reviewed in A. E. J. Rawlinson, ed., *Essays on the Trinity and the Incarnation* (London, 1933), although the essays, written by Anglican theologians at Oxford, have their own distinctive perspective as a result. On the modern period, an unusually fine study is that by Claude Welch, *In This Name: The Doctrine of the Trinity in Contemporary Theology* (New York, 1952); on the biblical questions, see Peter Toon and James D. Spiceland, eds., *One God in Trinity: An Analysis of the Primary Dogma of Christianity* (Westchester: Crossway, 1980).
10. C. E. M. Joad, *Guide to Modern Thought* (New York, 1933), pp. 33-36.
11. See Hywel D. Lewis, *The Self and Immortality* (London, 1973), pp. 11-70. On the issues raised by Ryle, see R. R. Cook, "The Nature of Man—Has the Ghost in the Machine Finally been Exorcised?" *Vox Evangelica* XIII (1983), 66-77.
12. A fine analysis of this matter is provided by Leslie Stevenson, *Seven Theories of Human Nature* (Oxford: Oxford University Press, 1977).
13. G. C. Berkouwer, *The Person of Christ*, John Vriend, trans. (Grand Rapids: Eerdmans, 1954), p. 21. Cf. the statement of H. R. Mackintosh that "the doctrine of the two natures, in its traditional form, imparts into the life of Christ an incredible and thoroughgoing dualism. . . . Divine and human alternately vitiates the truth of incarnation. The simplicity and coherence of all that Christ was and did vanishes, for God is not after all living a human life. . . . Christ executed this as God, it is said, and suffered that as man. It could not be otherwise, since in the last resort deity is impassible. Now this leaves a profoundly disappointing impression of unethical mystery and even, in a sense, duplicity" *(The Doctrine of the Person of Christ* [Edinburgh, 1912], p. 294). Mackintosh's attitude was, even at the turn of the century, symptomatic of a growing disaffection with Chalcedon. It needs to be observed, however, that what he really took issue with was not Chalcedon itself, but a Nestorian interpretation of Chalcedon which he mistook for the orthodox doctrine!
14. G. C. Berkouwer, *The Triumph of Grace in the Theology of Karl Barth*, Harry Boer, trans. (Grand Rapids, 1956), p. 12. Cf. Karl Barth, *Church Dogmatics*, G. T. Thomson and G. W. Bromiley, trans., vol. IV, 5 vols. (Greenwood, S.C.: Attic Press; Edinburgh, 1936-1977), 4, 19, 207-210.
15. Barth, *Church Dogmatics*, Vol. III, 2, 485.
16. *Ibid.*, Vol. I, 1, 289.
17. *Ibid.*, Vol. I, 2, 137-171.
18. *Ibid.*, Vol. I, 2, 16-18.
19. *Ibid.*, Vol. I, 2, 152.
20. *Ibid.*, Vol. I, 2, 173-202.
21. *Ibid.*, Vol. I, 2, 157. The relationship of Adam and Christ is, of course, also developed in his book *Christ and Adam: Man and Humanity in Romans 5*, T. A. Smail, trans. (New York, 1957). Some interpreters maintain that a view is advanced in this book which is at odds with that in the *Church Dogmatics*. Perhaps more important is the

undoubted change in tone in Barth's *The Humanity of God* (Atlanta: John Knox, 1960), which he explained as change, not in his own outlook, but in the general theological climate.

22. Barth, *Church Dogmatics,* Vol. I, 2, 150.
23. *Ibid.,* Vol. III, 2, 56.
24. *Ibid.,* Vol. III, 2, 69.
25. *Ibid.*
26. *Ibid.,* Vol. III, 2, 70.
27. *Ibid.,* Vol. II, 1, 487.
28. *Ibid.,* Vol. II, 1, 490.
29. *Ibid.*
30. This aspect of Barth's formulation is clearly and accurately developed in Donald G. Bloesch, *Jesus is Victor! Karl Barth's Doctrine of Salvation* (Nashville: Abingdon, 1976), pp. 32-59.
31. See S. W. Sykes, "Barth on the Centre of Theology," *Kark Barth: Studies of His Theological Method* (Oxford: Oxford University Press, 1979), pp. 17-54. More critical—oftentimes scathingly so—is Gordon H. Clark, *Kark Barth's Theological Method* (Philadelphia, 1963).
32. *Karl Barth—Rudolf Bultmann: Letters 1922-66* (Grand Rapids, 1981), p. 49. Cf. Karl Barth, *How I Changed My Mind* (Richmond, 1960), p. 37.
33. Barth's views on natural theology and revelation are more fully developed in his *The Knowledge of God and the Service of God According to the Teaching of the Reformation: Recalling the Scottish Confession of 1560* (London, 1938). A sympathic and helpful analysis of the *imago Dei* in Barth's theology is given in David Cairns, *The Image of God in Man* (London, 1953), pp. 164-179.
34. A brief but good summary of this aspect of Barth's thought is found in Colin Brown, *Karl Barth and the Christian Message* (Chicago, 1967), pp. 99-319; also helpful as a brief synopsis is Klaas Runia, "Karl Barth's Christology," *Christ the Lord: Studies in Christology Presented to Donald Guthrie,* Harold H. Rowdon, ed. (Downers Grove, 1982), pp. 299-310.
35. Barth, *Church Dogmatics,* Vol. II, 2, 6-140. See the additional analysis made of this by Fred H. Klooster, *The Significance of Barth's Theology: An Appraisal With Special Reference to Election and Reconciliation* (Grand Rapids, 1961).
36. Barth, *Church Dogmatics,* Vol. II, 2, 12, 13.
37. Karl Barth, *The Epistle to the Romans,* Edwyn Hoskyns, trans. (Oxford: Oxford University Press, 1968), p. 285. On this general theme, see Henri Bouillard, *Karl Barth,* Vol. II, 3 vols. (Aubier, 1957), pp. 10-62.
38. John Godsey, *Karl Barth's Table Talk* (Richmond, 1963), pp. 15, 87.
39. See Norman Pittenger, *Process Thought and Christian Faith* (New York, 1968); Norman Pittenger, *The Lure of Divine Love: Human Experience and Christian Faith in a Process Perspective* (New York: Pilgrim, 1979); Norman Pittenger, "The Attributes of God in the Light of Process Theology," *Expository Times* 81 (October 1967), 21-23; "A Contemporary Trend in North American Theology: Process Thought and Christian Faith," *Expository Times* 76 (June 1965), 268-272; "The Reconception of Christian Faith in the Light of Process Thought," *Princeton Seminary Bulletin* 61 (Winter 1963), 29-37. I am indebted to Douglas McCready for gathering the basic materials on Pittenger in a guided research course he did with me.
40. Norman Pittenger, *Christology Reconsidered* (London, 1970), p. ix.
41. Norman Pittenger, *The Divine Triunity* (New York: Pilgrim, 1970); "God 'The One in Three, but Three in One,' " *Religion in Life* 40 (Spring 1970), 93-100. Cf. Bruce A. Demarest, "Process Trinitarianism," *Perspectives in Evangelical Theology,* Kenneth S. Kantzer and Stanley N. Gundry, eds. (Grand Rapids, 1979), pp. 15-36.
42. Norman Pittenger, *Cosmic Love and Human Wrong: The Reconception of the Meaning of Sin in the Light of Process Thinking* (New York, 1978).
43. See Victor Lowe, "Whitehead's Metaphysical System," *Process Philosophy and Chris-*

tian Thought, Delwin Brown, Ralph E. James, and Gene Reeves, eds. (New York: Irvington, 1971), pp. 3-20. Cf. H. D. McDonald, "Monopolar Theism and the Ontological Argument," *The Harvard Theological Review* LVIII No. 4 (October 1965), 387-416.

44. Norman Pittenger, *The Word Incarnate: A Study of the Doctrine of the Person of Christ* (Welwyn, 1959), p. 43. Cf. Norman Pittenger, "The Two Types of Christology: A Neoclassical Analysis," *Journal of Religion* 49 (January 1969), 18-40.

45. *Ibid., The Word Incarnate,* pp. 150-153.

46. *Ibid.,* pp. 255-268.

47. This is the argument developed by Lewis S. Ford, "The Possibilities of Process Christology," *Encounter* 35 (Autumn 1974), 282.

48. Pittenger, *Catholic Faith, in a Process Perspective* (New York: Orbis, 1981), p. 27.

49. Pittenger developed his view early on in his career that what is " 'diffused' elsewhere . . . is 'focussed' in our Lord Jesus Christ. But the difference between diffusion and focussing appears to me to be, *par excellence,* a difference of degree. There is always union between God and man . . . in Jesus Christ, that union is *the* union towards which all others point . . ." ("Degree or Kind? A Christological Essay," *Canadian Journal of Theology* II No. 4 [October 1956], 193).

50. Cf. Pittenger's essay " 'A Thing Is What It Does,' A Discussion of 'God,' " *Modern Churchman* XV (July 1972), 239-246.

51. Pittenger, *Christology Reconsidered,* p. 87.

52. Pittenger, *The Word Incarnate,* p. 93.

53. *Ibid.,* p. 95.

54. Schleiermacher, *The Christian Faith* (Philadelphia: Fortress, 1977), p. 387.

55. Pittenger, *Christology Reconsidered,* p. 38.

56. Pittenger, *The Word Incarnate,* p. 119.

57. On the distinction between "deity" and "divinity," see Pittenger's *The Lure of Divine Love,* p. 103.

58. Pittenger, *The Word Incarnate,* p. 242.

59. Colin Gunton has also charged that this theism, with its highly metaphysical and complex argumentation, is accessible only to an intellectual, gnostic elite. Referring to the process thought of Charles Hartshorne and Schubert Ogden, he declares that "revelation" has become a function merely of the human mind and therefore "the enlightened ones are those with the intellectual power to think themselves into the circle of belief" (Colin Gunton, "The Knowledge of God According to Two Process Theologians: A Twentieth-Century Gnosticism," *Religions Studies* II No. 1 [March 1975], 95). This opening for the "elite" is, in fact, gained at the price of divine reality. The biblical understanding of God is diminished so that the estimation of human powers and importance can be inflated. Indeed, R. W. Jensen charges that process thought leads to human deification, and Nels Ferré, among others, has delineated the cost that has been paid for such a gain: "The point is that there is in process philosophy no self-sufficient being. There is no being as such or in itself, no eternal being, no permanently real, as opposed to deficient, being. Nor is there eternal ground or goal of cosmic process, since reality itself is process in one of its basic aspects. The reality of satisfaction is momentary. God is almost entirely the reality of the total process in becoming. . . . God, on this scheme, is supposed to serve the purposes of the eternal being in classical western thought, although he is constantly created as well as creative . . . he has no eternal purpose either for history or for men" (Nels F. S. Ferré. "God Without Theism," *Theology Today* XXII No. 3 [October 1965], 376).

60. This term, which can be offensive to Catholics, is borrowed from the title of G. C. Berkouwer's book, *The Second Vatican Council and the New Catholicism,* Lewis Smedes, trans. (Grand Rapids, 1965). It is his contention, cautiously stated as it is, that Roman Catholic thought is in danger of breaking its continuity with the past. The danger Berkouwer sensed twenty years ago has come to pass, and not least in the thought of theologians like Schillebeeckx.

61. The history of and issues raised by "the Schillebeeckx case" are reviewed in Herwi Rikhor, "Of Shadows and Substance: Analysis and Evaluation of the Documents in the Schillebeeckx Case," *Authority in the Church and the Schillebeeckx Case,* Leonard Swidler and Piet F. Fransen, eds. (New York, 1982), pp. 244-267; Peter Hebblethwaite, *The New Inquisition? The Case of Edward Schillebeeckx and Hans Kung* (San Francisco: Harper and Row, 1980).

62. Edward Schillebeeckx, *Jesus: An Experiment in Christology,* Hubert Hoskins, trans. (New York: Crossroad, 1979); *Christ: The Experience of Jesus as Lord,* John Bowden, trans. (New York: Crossroad, 1980). My understanding of Schillebeeckx's Christology was greatly enhanced by Gabriel Fackre's paper, "Bones Strong and Weak in the Skeletal Structure of Schillebeeckx's Christology," read at the Boston Theological Society.

63. Edward Schillebeeckx, *Interim Report on the Books Jesus and Christ* (New York: Crossroad, 1980).

64. *Ibid.,* p. 3.

65. Edward Schillebeeckx, *Good and Man,* Edward Fitzgerald and Peter Tomlinson, trans. (New York, 1969), pp. 164-165.

66. Schillebeeckx, *Christ,* pp. 71-84.

67. Edward Schillebeeckx, *God the Future of Man,* M. D. Smith, trans. (New York, 1968), pp. 167-201. The epistemology assumed in this volume is also presupposed in his *Revelation and Theology,* M. D. Smith, trans. (New York, 1967). Especially important is his chapter "Revelation-in-Reality and Revelation-in-Word" (pp. 33-56).

68. Edward Schillebeeckx, *The Mission of the Church* (New York: Crossroad, 1973), p. 61.

69. Cf. Schillebeeckx, *Christ,* pp. 672-744.

70. Schillebeeckx, *Jesus,* pp. 320, 329-331.

71. *Ibid.,* p. 69.

72. Schillebeeckx, *Interim Report,* pp. 127, 128.

73. Schillebeeckx, *Jesus,* p. 65.